MORE
READING POWER

Reading for Pleasure • Comprehension Skills

Skills • Reading Faster

SECOND EDITION

Beatrice S. Mikulecky
Linda Jeffries

Longman
longman.com

Acknowledgments

We thank teachers and students for their feedback regarding *More Reading Power*. We have made every effort to respond to their concerns in this second edition.

BSM and LJ

More Reading Power reviewers:

Linda Adler, University of California at Riverside, Riverside, CA; **Jennifer Altman**, University of Washington, Seattle, WA; **Mary Bagot**, Southeastern Missouri State University, Cape Girardeau, MO; **Carol Call**, Miami-Dade Community College, Miami, FL; **Frank Devlin**, Beaver College, Glenside, PA; **Thomas Dougherty**, Dominican University, River Forest, IL; **Peggy Fallon**, Northern Essex Community College, Haverhill, MA; **Tom Fisher**, Felix Varela Senior High School, Miami, FL; **Jane Gill**, Fashion Institute of Technology, New York, NY; **John Peter Graziano**, California State University at Northridge; **Mary Hill**, North Shore Community College, Danvers, MA; **Helen Kallenbach**, Sonoma State University, Rohnert Park, CA; **B.E. Lafaye**, Tokaigakuen University, Nagoya, Japan; **Michele McMenamin**, Rutgers University–Livingston Campus, Piscataway, NJ; **Arlene Osano**, University of California at Riverside, Riverside, CA; **Gloria Rhodes**, University of California at Riverside, Riverside, CA; **Charlotte Seeley**, Newton North High School, Newton, MA; **Priscilla Taylor**, California State University at Los Angeles, Los Angeles, CA

More Reading Power:
Reading for Pleasure, Comprehension Skills, Thinking Skills, Reading Faster
Second Edition

Pearson Education, 10 Bank Street, White Plains, NY 10606

Senior acquisitions editor: Laura Le Dréan
Development director: Penny Laporte
Development editors: Mykan White, Dena Daniel
Vice president, director of design and production: Rhea Banker
Executive managing editor: Linda Moser
Production manager: Ray Keating
Production editor: Michael Mone
Director of manufacturing: Patrice Fraccio
Senior manufacturing buyer: Nancy Flaggman
Photo research: Dana Klinek
Cover design: Ann France
Text design: Wendy Wolf
Text composition: Carlisle Communications, Ltd.

Library of Congress Cataloging-in-Publication Data

Mikulecky, Beatrice S.
    More reading power: reading for pleasure, comprehension skills, thinking skills,
reading faster / Beatrice S. Mikulecky, Linda Jeffries.
        p. cm.
    ISBN 0-13-061199-9 (pbk. : alk. paper)
    1. English language—Textbooks for foreign speakers. 2. Reading
comprehension—Problems, exercises, etc. I. Jeffries, Linda. II. Title.

PE1128 .M555 2003
428.6'4—dc21
                                                        2002030160
ISBN: 0-13-061199-9

Printed in the United States of America
1 2 3 4 5 6 7 8 9 10–VHG–08 07 06 05 04

Contents

Introduction

To the Teacher

More Reading Power is unlike most other reading textbooks. First, the focus is different. This book directs the students' attention to their own reading processes, while most other books focus primarily on the content. Second, *More Reading Power* is organized to be used in a unique way. It contains *four separate sections* that correspond to four important aspects of proficient reading, and therefore it is like four books in one. *Teachers should assign work on all four parts of the book concurrently.*

In this, the second edition of *More Reading Power,* the approach remains the same. New features have been added and original exercises updated in response to feedback from teachers. Changes in this new edition:

- Part 1: Pleasure Reading—a new introduction and an expanded list of suggested books.
- Part 2: Comprehension Skills—updated exercises and an additional Pattern of Organization.
- Part 3: Thinking Skills—updated and divided into three sections for manageability.
- Part 4: Faster Reading—new Africa Today topic; new Global Issues readings.
- a format that is more user friendly.
- Teacher's Guide—sample syllabus included
- Separate Answer Key (not at the back of the student text)

The purpose of *More Reading Power* is to develop your students' awareness of the reading process so that they will be able to read in ways that are expected in school, college, or business. In order to allow the students to focus on the process of reading, the lexical and syntactic content of the materials have been controlled.

Many students have a conceptualization of reading that can interfere with their ability to read well in English. *More Reading Power* aims to help students acquire an accurate understanding of what it means to read in English. To accomplish this, the book addresses the reading process in a direct manner, and the various reading skills involved are presented as part of that process.

Student awareness of reading and thinking processes is further encouraged in many parts of the book by exercises that require them to work in pairs or small groups. In discussions with others, students formulate and articulate their ideas more precisely, and so they also acquire new ways of talking and thinking about a text. Students are asked to write and then to read each other's work so they can experience the connections between reading and writing.

The teacher is the most important element in a successful reading class. In your class, you can boost the value of *More Reading Power* by providing

- an anxiety-free environment in which students feel comfortable taking risks and trying new ways of reading.
- enough practice so the students can master new strategies.
- friendly pressure in the form of persuasion and timing.
- positive examples of how to approach a text.

- a model for the kind of thinking that good reading requires.
- an inspiring example of an enthusiastic reader.

Specific suggestions for using *More Reading Power,* as well as a sample syllabus, are located in the Teacher's Guide (pages 255–275). (For a more complete explanation of the theory and methodology found in *More Reading Power,* see *A Short Course in Teaching Reading Skills* by Beatrice S. Mikulecky (Addison-Wesley, 1990).)

A note about the Answer Key: In this second edition of *More Reading Power,* the Answer Key is supplied as a separate booklet. It is <u>not</u> included at the back of the student text.

To the Student

This book is different from other reading books, so you should use it in a different way. *More Reading Power* is divided into **four parts.** You should not finish one part at a time. Instead, you should **work on all four parts of the book every week.** This gives you practice in four different kinds of reading skills.

Part 1: Reading for Pleasure. The more you read, the better you will read. In Part One, you will choose books to read and you will learn how to keep a record of your reading. You will also talk about your books with your classmates and your teacher.

Part 2: Comprehension Skills. Reading is a very complex task involving many different skills. In this part, you will learn to use some essential reading skills.

Part 3: Thinking Skills. Reading is not just understanding the words or the grammar. It is not just translating. Reading is thinking. In order to read well in English, you must think in English. The exercises in Part Three will give you practice with following ideas in English.

Part 4: Reading Faster. There are many advantages to reading faster. Your comprehension will improve, you will save time on reading assignments, and your reading will become more enjoyable. In this part of the book, you will develop the skill of reading faster with good comprehension.

Why is reading important?

Reading is one important way to improve your general language skills in English. How can it help you?
- Reading helps you learn to think in English.
- Reading can enlarge your English vocabulary.
- Reading can help you improve your writing.
- Reading may be a good way to practice your English if you live in a non-English-speaking country.
- Reading can help you prepare for study in an English-speaking country.
- Reading is a good way to find out about new ideas, facts, and experiences.

Thinking about your reading habits

Your reading habits can make a big difference in your reading. Find out about your reading habits by answering these two questionnaires according to your own experience.

Fill in Questionnaire 1 about your reading habits in your first language (your native language). Then go on to Questionnaire 2 about your reading habits in English. (If your native language is English, skip Questionnaire 1. Go directly to Questionnaire 2.)

Questionnaire 1

Reading in Your Native Language

Native language: _____

For each statement, circle Y (Yes) or N (No).

1. I always read every word of a passage. **Y N**

2. Reading aloud helps me improve my reading. **Y N**

3. I say the words aloud when I read. **Y N**

4. I use different reading methods in my native language and in English. **Y N**

5. When I read in my native language, I understand more when I read slowly. **Y N**

6. If I don't know the meaning of a word, I always look it up in the dictionary. **Y N**

7. The best way to improve my reading in my native language is by learning as much grammar as possible. **Y N**

8. The best way to improve my reading in my native language is by learning as much new vocabulary as possible. **Y N**

9. When I am reading in my native language, I need to know every word in order to understand. **Y N**

10. To read well in my native language, I must be able to pronounce every word. **Y N**

11. I can't understand a paragraph if it has several new words in it. **Y N**

12. I use the same reading methods for all kinds of texts (books, newspapers, etc.). **Y N**

Questionnaire 2

Reading in English

For each statement, circle Y (Yes) or N (No).

1. I always read every word of a passage.   **Y N**

2. Reading aloud helps me improve my reading.   **Y N**

3. I say the words aloud when I read.   **Y N**

4. I use different reading methods in my native language and in English.   **Y N**

5. When I read in English, I understand more when I read slowly.   **Y N**

6. If I don't know the meaning of a word in English, I always look it up in the dictionary.   **Y N**

7. The best way to improve my reading in English is by learning as much grammar as possible.   **Y N**

8. The best way to improve my reading in English is by learning as much new vocabulary as possible.   **Y N**

9. When I am reading material in English, I need to know every word in order to understand.   **Y N**

10. To read well in English, I must be able to pronounce every word.   **Y N**

11. I can't understand a paragraph if it has several new words in it.   **Y N**

12. I use the same reading methods for all kinds of texts (books, newspapers, etc.).   **Y N**

Compare your answers in the two questionnaires. Are your answers the same for both?

Compare your answers with another student. Do you agree? Look at questions that you answered similarly and questions you answered differently.

Ideally, you circled **N** for every question in both questionnaires! If you marked some answers **Y,** then you may need to learn more about reading. *More Reading Power* will help you change your reading habits and become a better reader.

PART 1

Reading for Pleasure

Introduction to Reading for Pleasure

Reading, like sports or music, requires lots of practice. The best way to become a better reader is by reading a lot. The best readers are people who *love to read* and who *read often*. If you don't already love reading, you can learn to love it by reading for pleasure. Think about your pleasure reading habits as you fill out this questionnaire.

Pleasure Reading Questionnaire

1. For the following statements, give a number from 1 to 10.

   (1 = totally disagree; 10 = totally agree)

   _____ a. I enjoy reading for pleasure.

   _____ b. My parents enjoy reading for pleasure.

   _____ c. Most of my friends read for pleasure.

   _____ d. I read only books assigned by a teacher.

   _____ e. I have no time to read for pleasure.

2. Do you have a favorite book? Write the book's title and author here:

   _____

   What did you like about this book? _____

   _____

   Would you recommend it to a friend? Why or why not? _____

   _____

3. Circle the types of books you generally enjoy reading for pleasure:

   a. novels   e. mysteries

   b. romances   f. biographies

   c. spy thrillers   g. factual books (nonfiction)

   d. adventures   h. other (give examples) _____

   _____

4. In what language do you usually read for pleasure? _____

5. Do you read for pleasure in English? If so, what book(s) have you read?

   _____

   _____

Discuss your answers with some classmates. Have you read any of the books they recommend?

The Advantages of Reading for Pleasure

Some students may prefer to skip pleasure reading and spend their time studying grammar and vocabulary lessons. Others may think that pleasure reading is too easy. However, according to many experts, pleasure reading is the key to improving your English. Dr. Stephen Krashen, a leading expert on language learning, has studied the effects of regular reading for pleasure on language ability. In his research, he has found that students who read a lot improve their grammar and vocabulary, and they learn more about good writing.

Regular reading for pleasure can help you to

- improve your vocabulary.
- increase your reading speed.
- improve your comprehension.
- improve your writing.
- gain more knowledge.
- find examples of the many different ways people speak and write.

There are two main reasons why pleasure reading is such an effective way of improving your English. First, pleasure reading gives you an opportunity to have lots of contact with the language. This is especially true because pleasure reading is enjoyable, so you are likely to spend time doing it. You are also more likely to remember and learn from what you read.

Second, reading for pleasure allows you to build on your personal knowledge of English. No two students have the same knowledge of a language or the same language learning needs. Some students may need to learn more vocabulary, for example. Others may need to develop their ability to write good sentences in English. When students read for pleasure at their own pace in their own books, they can each learn what they need to learn.

Reading for pleasure is different from the reading that you do for study. When you read for pleasure, you don't have to read the same book that everyone else in the class is reading. You can choose any kind of book you want—a romance novel, a thriller, a mystery, a science fiction novel, a biography, or a history book. It is not *what* you read, but your *enjoyment,* that matters.

Pleasure reading is also different from study reading in another way. You do not have to remember the details of your pleasure reading book because you will not be tested about what you have read. All you have to do is *enjoy the book!*

Discussing Your Pleasure Reading

Talking about your pleasure reading is another way that you can improve your English language skills. When you tell your teacher, your classmates, or a friend about what you have read, you review the story in your mind, and you make more connections between the ideas in the book and what you already know. In fact, sometimes you find that your understanding of the story increases after you have talked about it. This happens because you automatically organize your ideas as you explain them to someone.

English speakers talk about their reading in ways that may be new to you. You will read "Good Morning," a short story by Mark Hager, in order to practice talking about reading.

Follow these steps as you read the story:

1. Read the title. As you read the story, try to imagine why the author decided to call it "Good Morning."

2. Read the story all the way to the end. Do not stop for new words. Just mark with a pencil any new words that you need to know in order to understand the story. You will have a chance to read the story a second time.

3. Talk about the story with another student. Discuss these questions:

   a. Where does the story take place?

   b. Who are the characters in the story?

   c. What happens in the story? In other words, what is the plot of the story?

   d. Were there any confusing parts to the story? Help each other to figure them out.

4. Read the story again. This time, when you come to vocabulary items that you still haven't figured out, write the word or words on the lines below.

   _____ _____ _____ _____

   _____ _____ _____ _____

   _____ _____ _____ _____

   _____ _____ _____ _____

5. Working with a group of three or four students, briefly retell the plot of the story. Then ask each other these questions:

   a. Did you like the story? Why?

   b. Which character did you like most? Why?

   c. Did you like the ending? Why?

   d. Is this story similar to other stories you have read? Explain.

   e. Do you know the meanings of my vocabulary items?

   f. Why did the author decide to title the story "Good Morning"?

Good Morning
by Mark Hager

When I was a boy, I walked through two miles of woods to get to our schoolhouse, and I would take my father's twenty-two rifle with me and hide it in a hollow tree before I got to the schoolhouse, and get it as I came home in the evening.

One evening, coming from school, I ran into a community uprising at Mr. Epperly's house. Mr. Epperly's cow had gone mad and was bawling lonesome bawls and twisting the young apple trees out of the ground with her horns, and the whole community was demanding that Mr. Epperly's dog, Old Ranger, be shot, as Old Ranger had fought and killed the mad dog that bit the cow.

Mr. Epperly wanted to know if it wouldn't be safe to put Old Ranger in the stable or someplace and keep *him* penned up until the danger period was over, but the neighbors said no; that Mr. Epperly's children might slip and feed him through the cracks and get bit.

Mr. Epperly said he could not do it himself, and wanted to know who would volunteer to do it, but none of the men would.

Mr. Epperly came to me, and said, "Joe, why can't you take him with you through the woods on your way home and do it?"

I told Mr. Epperly I did not want to shoot Old Ranger. I saw Mr. Epperly's three kids were already keeping close to the old dog.

Mr. Epperly then pulled a one-dollar bill from his pocket.

"I will give you this dollar bill if you'll do it," he said.

I considered. I had never yet had a one-dollar bill all my own and while the idea of shooting Old Ranger did not appeal to me, it did seem like a thing that was demanded by the whole community, and they all put at me to do it, trying to make me feel like a kind of hero, and pointed to the danger to Mr. Epperly's children. Then Mr. Epperly put a piece of clothesline around Old Ranger's neck and I started with him. The Epperly kids began to cry.

As I walked through the woods by the little path, I started looking for a place suitable to shoot a dog and leave him lay. I saw a heavy clump of wild grapevines, and I led him down under there and then got back up in the path. Old Ranger looked at me and whined and wagged his tail. He wanted to come to me. I recollected always seeing him wherever there was a splash of sunshine in Mr. Epperly's yard when I would pass there and Mr. Epperly's kids would join me for school.

I went down and untied Old Ranger and walked on. I came to a place where there was a hickory grove in a little flat where the underbrush was thin. I recollected how Old Ranger liked to go to the hickory groves and tree squirrels. I led Old Ranger down and tied him close to the trunk of a big hickory tree.

I started to take aim, but Old Ranger started prancing and looking up the tree. I remembered then hearing Mr. Epperly tell how Old Ranger would do that when he'd tree a squirrel and Mr. Epperly would raise the gun to shoot, and I could not fool Old Ranger like that.

Besides, there was too much light and Old Ranger could see me take aim. I decided to wait for the gloom. Soon as the sun dropped a few more feet behind the Wilson Ridge, there would be gloom, and maybe Old Ranger would not see so plainly how I pointed the gun.

While I waited for the gloom, the burning started in my pocket. I took the one-dollar bill out. I had a feeling there was something nasty about it.

While I thought of that, Old Ranger reared and barked and surged at the cord leash, and when I looked back out the path I saw Mr. Epperly's three kids, but they were running away. They had turned to run when Old Ranger barked. I guessed they had slipped off from their house and followed just to see where I left Old Ranger.

The thought struck me that they would run back to their house and tell I had not shot Old Ranger yet, and that would set the folks to worrying again, and I took aim. I thought I had better fire in their hearing. I took aim at Old Ranger, but I could not touch the trigger the way he looked at me and tried to speak, so I fired in the air so the Epperly kids could say they heard the shot.

I stuck the dollar back in my pocket, went down and hugged Old Ranger around the neck. I knew I would never shoot Old Ranger. I took him and walked on. I got to the edge of our field. I climbed on the gate and sat a long time and considered. I tried to think up how I could explain to my mother why I had brought Old Ranger home with me so that she would not be scared. I could not decide how I could ever explain with a good face that I had a one-dollar bill in my pocket I had been given to shoot Old Ranger.

I remembered where I had seen an empty castor-oil bottle at the edge of the path. It was still there, and I got it, and stuck the one-dollar bill in it, and buried the bottle in some soft dirt under the corner of the fence.

My mother decided that since I had fired the shot, she would let me keep Old Ranger for a month, with the community thinking he was dead, but it was the hardest month I ever spent.

The Epperly kids would not walk with me to school. They would pucker up to cry when they saw me, and the other kids down at the schoolhouse, they would say with a sneer, "What did you buy with your dollar bill?"

I could not answer. I could not tell them about the castor-oil bottle under the fence corner or Old Ranger in our stable; the Epperly kids searched the woods on both sides of the path to our house, hunting for the body of Old Ranger, but they would not ask me where I had left him, and other neighbors spoke of how Old Ranger's great booming voice was missed.

Mrs. Epperly was kind to me. I met her in the road one day, and she told me how she had scolded the kids for treating me like that. "But," she added, "if it was to do over, I would not allow it done. The children . . . Mr. Epperly, too, they're half crazy."

Then came the happy morning. "You can take Old Ranger home now, Joe," my mother said. "Been over a month. No danger now."

I went to the stable, got Old Ranger, and he reared and licked my face. I shouldered my book strap, and led Old Ranger down the path. I stopped at the fence corner and got the castor-oil bottle with the one-dollar bill in it. I had a time trying to hold Old Ranger's mouth shut so I could get in sight of the Epperly house before he barked.

At the right place where they could see us when they came running to the front porch, I let Old Ranger have his voice. Old Ranger let go with a great howl that rolled and rocked across the ridges, and the Epperlys came bounding. Mr. and Mrs. Epperly and the three kids. They alternated between my neck and Old Ranger's, and I don't know to this day which of us got the most hugging.

I handed Mr. Epperly the castor-oil bottle.

"Why did you do that?" he said.

"It felt nasty in my pocket," I said.

He tried to make me keep it and when I wouldn't, he just pitched it toward me and his three kids, and we started for the schoolhouse, feeling rich, with a whole dollar to spend.

Hints for Success in Reading for Pleasure

- Set a specific goal in your pleasure reading. Decide how many books you would like to finish reading during the semester.

- Make pleasure reading a part of your daily routine. Plan to read a certain number of pages or for a certain amount of time every day.

- Read for at least thirty minutes at one time so that you can become involved in your book. This is especially important when you start a new book. It may take a little time before you begin to enjoy it.

- Choose a paperback book (paperbacks are small and lightweight), and carry it with you wherever you go. Read it whenever you have some free time. This is a good way to escape boredom when you are waiting in line or riding a bus or subway.

- Keep a journal. When you finish several chapters, write your thoughts about the book in your journal and write about what you expect to happen next.

- Talk to your friends about your book.

- Keep a record of the books you read in the chart on page 251.

- Make an appointment with your teacher for a book conference when you have finished a book. This is not a test about the book. In fact, your teacher may not have read your book and may not know anything about it. This is your chance to talk and to share your feelings about the book.

- After you finish reading your book, fill in a copy of the Book Response Sheet on page 252 and give it to your teacher.

Guidelines for Choosing a Pleasure Reading Book

1. Choose a book that interests you. Ask your teacher, your friends, your family, and your classmates for suggestions. But choose the book that is best for you, not for them!

2. Preview the book to help you decide if you want to read it. Paperback book covers provide plenty of information for that. Pictures on the front cover can give some idea of what the book is about. On the back cover there is usually some information about the book's contents.

3. Choose a book that is not too easy or too difficult. If your book is too easy to read, you may become bored. If it is too difficult, you are likely to become discouraged. By reading the first few pages, you can tell if a book is too easy or too difficult for you. A book is easy if there are no unknown key words on a single page. It is too difficult if there are more than five unknown key words on a single page. (A key word is a word you must know in order to follow the author's general meaning.)

4. Choose a book that is printed clearly. Make sure the print is not too small. The size and clarity of the print will make a difference. You can read longer if the print does not make your eyes tired.

5. Remember, you are reading for pleasure. You don't need to memorize what you read when you read for pleasure! The important thing is to follow the story or the ideas presented by the author.

6. Some popular books have been made into movies. Avoid reading a book if you have already seen the movie. You may get bored if you already know what happens in the story. But *do* see a film version *after* you have read a book. It's often interesting to see how a film director has brought a book to life. You may enjoy comparing the director's ideas with your own.

7. Do not choose a book that you have already read in a different language. The fact that you are already familiar with it may make it less interesting. Also, do not choose a book that has been translated from another language. A translation is not always natural English, so it might be more difficult to read.

Suggested Books

Finding a good book is the first step in reading for pleasure. The books listed here have been read and enjoyed by many people around the world. They are usually available in most libraries and bookstores.

The authors of *More Reading Power* recommend these books, but remember, they are only suggested books. You may choose a title that is not on the list, of course. What matters most is reading a book that interests *you*.

The book list is divided into two parts, fiction and nonfiction. Both parts of the book list have books at three levels of difficulty:

Level One: These books are not difficult to read. If you have not read many books in English, you may want to begin with a selection from this level.

Level Two: The books in this section are a little more difficult.

Level Three: These books are for advanced readers.

Book list

An asterisk (*) after an author's name indicates that this author has written other books that you might enjoy. The number of pages in the books may be slightly different in different editions. The numbers given here are meant to give you a sense of how long the book is.

Fiction

Fiction books are not true stories. Reading fiction is helpful in learning English because in fiction you will find many examples of how people use the language in everyday life.

Level One

Sometimes I Think I Hear My Name, by Avi. The humorous story of a thirteen-year-old boy who tries to understand his parents. (139 pages)

Forever, by Judy Blume.* The famous story of teenage love. The question is, Can you love two people at the same time? A best-seller. (220 pages)

Sacajawea (a novel), by Joseph Bruchac. Based on the story of Sacajawea, a sixteen-year-old Shoshone Indian mother who helped Lewis and Clark explore North America's west. They found a safe way to travel from the Mississippi River to the Pacific Ocean. (199 pages)

My Brother Sam Is Dead, by James L. Collier and Christopher Collier. The story of the tragedy that strikes the Meeker family during America's Civil War, when one son joins the rebels. (216 pages)

Killing Mr. Griffin, by Lois Duncan.* A teenager casually suggests playing a cruel trick on the English teacher, but he does not intend to have the teacher die as a result. (243 pages)

The Friends, by Rosa Guy. A family moves to the United States from the West Indies. This story tells about the love and friendship they find. (185 pages)

Letters from Rifka, by Karen Hesse. In 1919, a Jewish girl and her family leave Russia and start the long journey to America. But Rifka is not allowed to board the ship with her family. Will she ever get to America and see her family again? (146 pages)

That Was Then, This Is Now, by S. E. Hinton.* Sixteen-year-olds Mark and Bryon have been like brothers since childhood, but now they begin to grow apart. (159 pages)

I Want to Keep My Baby, by Joanna Lee. A fifteen-year-old girl is going to have a baby and she must make some difficult decisions. (166 pages)

The Daydreamer, by Ian McEwan. Peter is a boy who lives somewhere between dreams and real life. In these stories, he finds out what it is like to be a cat, a baby, and an adult. (143 pages)

145th Street (short stories), by Walter Dean Myers. One street, ten stories of young people who live in New York's Harlem. There is danger, hopelessness, joy, and excitement. (151 pages)

The Glory Field, by Walter Dean Myers. The story of one family, from the time their ancestors were taken as slaves from Africa to the United States. Their farm in the South unites them in this story of pride, determination, struggle, and love. (196 pages)

Chain of Fire, by Beverley Naidoo.* The story of Nalida and Taolo, who struggled against apartheid in South Africa. (242 pages)

Harry Potter and the Sorcerer's Stone (or *Harry Potter and the Philosopher's Stone*), by J. K. Rowling.* This book tells of the adventures of a young boy who goes to a school for wizards. (312 pages)

My Name is Davy—I'm an Alcoholic, by Anne Snyder. A lonely high school student drinks too much. Can he end this behavior and find a better life? (128 pages)

The Pearl, by John Steinbeck.* A poor fisherman finds a big pearl and hopes to get rich by selling it. Can a pearl bring happiness to his family? (118 pages)

Charlotte's Web, by E. B. White. Written for children, this famous book is popular with all ages. It tells a story of love and loyalty that everyone can enjoy. (184 pages)

The Pigman, by Paul Zindel. Lorraine's crank telephone call to a man called "the Pigman" sets off a terrible chain of events, and she learns valuable life lessons. (158 pages)

Level Two

Little Women, by Louisa May Alcott.* This famous book tells of the joys and sorrows of the four March sisters and their mother in New England in the 1800s. (561 pages)

The Clan of the Cave Bear, by Jean Auel.* A story of prehistoric peoples told through the experiences of a heroic woman. (468 pages)

The Incredible Journey, by Sheila Burnford. Two dogs and a cat travel many miles to return to their home. (160 pages)

Diving In, by Kate Cann. A novel of summer love and all the difficulties and uncertainties of a relationship. (238 pages)

The White Mountains, by John Christopher. One hundred years in the future, Switzerland is the only free country left on earth. This is a science fiction thriller. (192 pages)

The Chocolate War, by Robert Cormier.* A high school student fights against a secret society of other students and becomes a hero in the school. (191 pages)

I Know What You Did Last Summer, by Lois Duncan. A group of friends have a terrible secret. Then they find out that someone knows their secret and wants revenge. (199 pages)

Johnny Tremaine, by Esther Forbes. The American Revolution as seen through the experiences of a youth in Boston. (269 pages)

My Side of the Mountain, by Jean George. A young boy tells about his adventures as he spends a year alone in the Catskill Mountains. (177 pages)

The Summer of My German Soldier, by Bette Greene. During World War II, German prisoners are sent to a camp near Patty's home town in Arkansas. A twelve-year-old Jewish girl, Patty, befriends an escaped German prisoner. (Language may be disturbing to some readers.) (230 pages)

Jazz Country, by Nat Hentoff.* A white youth in New York plays his trumpet in a jazz club in Harlem. (146 pages)

Flowers for Algernon, by Daniel Keyes. A sad tale of a mentally retarded man who is given an experimental drug. For a short time, he becomes normal. (216 pages)

Carrie, by Stephen King. A high school girl was always laughed at by her classmates. Then she discovers that she has special powers. A suspenseful horror story. (220 pages)

The Call of the Wild, by Jack London.* Buck, a St. Bernard/Scotch shepherd dog, lives a comfortable life as a wealthy family's pet. When he is kidnapped and taken to the Arctic to work as a sled dog, his life is changed forever. (143 pages)

Anne of Green Gables, by Lucy Maud Montgomery. How an orphan girl is accepted into a loving family and small community on Prince Edward Island, Canada. (309 pages)

Animal Farm, by George Orwell.* The story of what happens when overworked, mistreated animals take over a farm. A story that reflects any place where freedom is attacked. (139 pages)

The Road to Nowhere, by Christopher Pike. Teresa runs away from home and meets two mysterious hitchhikers. Together, they face a long night of terror. (212 pages)

The Witch of Blackbird Pond, by Elizabeth G. Speare. The story of Kit Tyler and her fight against prejudice. (249 pages)

Level Three

If Beale Street Could Talk, by James Baldwin. A talented New York musician is falsely accused of a crime and is put in prison. His girlfriend is determined to free him. (213 pages)

My Antonia, by Willa Cather.* A famous portrait of a pioneer woman, Antonia, the daughter of a Bohemian immigrant. She faces loneliness and other challenges of life on America's prairies. (175 pages)

And Then There Were None, by Agatha Christie.* Ten weekend guests who don't know one another meet on a private island. All they have in common is a secret, evil past. One by one, they die. (275 pages)

A Lesson Before Dying, by Ernest J. Gaines. The moving story of an unusual friendship between a young teacher and a man in prison for murder, waiting to be executed. (256 pages)

Father Melancholy's Daughter, by Gail Godwin.* When Margaret was six years old, her mother left the family and died soon after that. Now as an adult, Margaret searches for answers about her past. (404 pages)

The Firm, by John Grisham.* A young lawyer's first job seems to be perfect until he discovers that partners die mysteriously. A thriller. (501 pages)

For Whom the Bell Tolls, by Ernest Hemingway.* The story of Robert and Maria, who fall in love during the Spanish Civil War. Many people think this is one of the best war novels of all time. (471 pages)

The Bean Trees, by Barbara Kingsolver.* Driving west to start a new life, Taylor stops for gas. A woman gives her a little girl. The touching story of how they grow to love each other. (323 pages)

Being There, by Jerzy Kosinski. A man named Chance becomes an heir to a rich Wall Street businessman, an adviser to the U.S. president, and a popular TV personality. An ironic story of how an uneducated man can seem to be brilliant. (140 pages)

The Left Hand of Darkness, by Ursula LeGuin.* On a strange planet called Gethen, people do not see each other as men or women. This poses a challenge to an explorer from planet Earth. (304 pages)

The Sky Is Falling, by Sidney Sheldon.* Sheldon is a master storyteller. This thriller is about the mysterious death of Gary Winthrop, the last of five people in his family to die in a single year. (398 pages)

The Kitchen God's Wife, by Amy Tan.* An immigrant from China tells her daughter Winnie Lou about her past. Through her stories, we learn the details of Chinese life and tradition. (530 pages)

Dinner at the Homesick Restaurant, by Anne Tyler.* Three children were raised by a strong single mother. Now adults, they return home as their mother is dying, and they try to make sense of their past. (303 pages)

Nonfiction

Nonfiction books are factual. Books about history, biography, and science are examples of nonfiction. Reading nonfiction can help develop your vocabulary in a specialized area.

Level One

China's Son, by Da Chen. Da Chen was born in 1962, the grandson of a landlord in China. This is the story of how he survived the Cultural Revolution and achieved his goal of studying at Beijing University. (213 pages)

J. R. R. Tolkien: The Man Who Created the Lord of the Rings, by Michael Coren. Tolkien's life experiences as an orphan, a scholar, a soldier, and a professor helped him to write *The Lord of the Rings,* which is considered by many to be one of the best books ever written. (125 pages)

Boy, by Roald Dahl. A famous writer of children's books tells the story of his own childhood. This book also gives a sometimes funny and sometimes shocking picture of schools in England. (160 pages)

Rosa Parks: My Story, by Rosa Parks with Jim Haskins. On December 1, 1953, Mrs. Parks refused to give up her seat to a white man on a racially segregated bus in the U.S. South. As a result, the struggle for civil rights began. (188 pages)

Red Scarf Girl, by Ji Li Jiang. The memoir of a girl who was a teenager at the beginning of the Cultural Revolution in China. She tells of her family's struggle to survive. (272 pages)

Malcolm X: By Any Means Necessary, by Walter Dean Myers. The story of Malcolm Little, later known as the civil rights activist Malcolm X. How he went from a top student in Boston to imprisonment at age twenty and how these events led to his philosophy for political change. (200 pages)

Level Two

Go Ask Alice, by Anonymous (no name). In this true story in diary form, a fifteen-year-old girl tells how she became a drug addict and how she felt about herself and her life. (188 pages)

New Burlington: The Life and Death of an American Village, by John Baskin. A village is moved to make way for a new lake. The people from the village tell their own stories. (272 pages)

Hiroshima, by John Hersey.* After the United States dropped an atomic bomb on Hiroshima, Japan, John Hersey went there and interviewed six survivors. This book tells what he learned. (117 pages)

Farewell to Manzanar, by Jean and James Houston. A true story of Japanese Americans. They were forced to move to camps in the U.S. desert during World War II. (177 pages)

The Upstairs Room, by Johanna Reiss. The tale of two Jewish sisters in Holland who were saved by living in the attic of a Christian family during World War II. (196 pages)

Almost Lost, by Beatrice Sparks.* The true story of an anonymous teenager's life on the streets of a big city. (239 pages)

Stephen Hawking: A Life in Science, by M. White and G. Gribbin. A biography of Stephen Hawking, an English scientist with a very serious illness. Most other scientists think that he is the smartest man alive. (304 pages)

Level Three

I Know Why the Caged Bird Sings, by Maya Angelou.* One of the best-loved poets in the United States writes about her childhood experiences. She tells how she survived violence and racism, thanks to the strength and love of her family. (Language may be disturbing to some readers.) (246 pages)

An American Childhood, by Annie Dillard.* This story of the author's childhood gives a complete snapshot of growing up in the 1950s in Pittsburgh. (255 pages)

The Autobiography of Malcolm X, by Malcolm X with Alex Haley. The dramatic life story of an important figure in African-American history, as told by Malcolm X himself. (350 pages)

Half the Way Home: A Memoir of Father and Son, by Adam Hochschild. This book tells of the relationship between Adam and his powerful businessman father and how his father disapproved of him in so many ways. (198 pages)

Into the Wild, by Jon Krakauer. In 1992, a young man walked alone into the Alaskan wilderness. He had given away $25,000 and left his car. Four months later, his body was found. Why did he do it? (207 pages)

Long Walk to Freedom, by Nelson Mandela. This is the story of Mandela's life, written while he was in a South African prison. (544 pages)

Nisa: The Life and Words of a !Kung Woman, by Marjorie Shostak. The remarkable story of an African woman and her people, as told by an anthropologist. (402 pages)

PART 2

Comprehension
Skills

Introduction to Comprehension

Comprehension is part of life. Every waking minute, you are making sense of your world. In fact, your brain could be compared to a very complicated computer. Information is constantly coming in about what you see, hear, smell, touch, or taste. Your brain receives all the pieces of information, interprets them, sorts them, and saves them.

When your brain notices new information, it looks for a connection to information that you already have saved. If it finds a connection, the new information becomes part of a network and becomes a part of your long-term memory. If new information is not connected, it is usually forgotten.

The same process happens with reading comprehension. As you read, you make connections between what you are reading and what you already know. Sometimes the connection seems to happen by itself—especially when the information is important or interesting to you. But at other times, it is not so simple. The text may seem a mass of information with no meaning that will stick.

You can learn how to make sense of everything you read and how to remember it. In this part of the book, you will practice some important comprehension skills and learn to think in new ways about what your are reading.

UNIT 1 Previewing

Previewing for Better Comprehension

Previewing before you read can make a big difference in how well you understand what you read. The aim of previewing is to find out what you are going to be reading before you actually read. You preview to get an idea of what you will find in the text. Then your brain can begin making connections, and your comprehension will be faster and better.

Previewing is something you already do in your daily life. For example, when you receive a letter, you usually look first at the return address or the stamp to find out where it came from and who sent it. Then you make some guesses about what it will be about. When you read the newspaper or a magazine, you often look at the headlines and the pictures to get some idea of what the articles are about so you can decide which ones interest you.

By previewing for just a few seconds, you can pick up a great deal of information about the text you are going to read. You can preview any kind of text, including pleasure reading books, magazine articles, tests, and textbook assignments. The following exercises will give you practice previewing.

EXERCISE 1

You can tell a lot about a book from its cover! Borrow a paperback pleasure reading book from one of the other students in your class, or find a paperback book that you have not read. Looking only at the book cover, try to find the following information:

1. Title

2. Author

3. Fiction (not a true story) or nonfiction (factual information)?

4. What do you think this book is about?

5. List some of the adjectives that are found in the reviews or description on the back cover of the book.

6. Is there any information about the author on the book cover?

7. Would you like to read this book? Why?

8. Tell another student about the book.

Previewing a book's table of contents is another way to find out about it. Preview this table of contents. Then answer the questions on the next page. You should preview for no more than thirty seconds.

A Brief History of Time: From the Big Bang to Black Holes
by Stephen W. Hawking

CONTENTS

Working with another student, answer these questions. Do not look back at the table of contents.

1. Do you think this book is fiction (a story that is not true) or nonfiction (factual information)?

2. What do you think this book is about?

3. Did you notice any names? If so, write them here.

4. Would you be interested in reading this book? Why or why not?

Guidelines for Previewing Longer Passages

- Preview for only a few seconds. For example, for one page of text, you should spend no more than one minute previewing.

- Read the title. Does it tell you what the passage is about? Do you know anything about this subject?

- Decide what kind of text it is. Is it an essay, an argument, a story, an explanation? What can you expect from this kind of text?

- Look at the length and organization of the passage. Is it divided into parts? Do the parts have subtitles? What information do they give you?

- Notice if there are maps, pictures, charts, names, dates, or numbers in the passage.

- Look at the first line or sentence of each paragraph and the last sentence of the final paragraph. These sections often contain important information.

EXERCISE 3

Preview the following story. Read only the underlined parts. Then answer the questions on the following page. Time limit: Sixty seconds to preview.

Carmelita's Amazing Rescue
by Alissa Norman

<u>A</u>t the Santos <u>family's apartment</u> <u>in São Paulo, Brazil,</u> the doorbell is constantly ringing. All the friends and neighbors are there to hear <u>what happened to two-year-old Carmelita.</u> Her mother has tears in her eyes, but they are tears of relief, of thankfulness. Her Carmelita is smiling shyly, safe in her father's lap.

<u>The story could easily have ended very differently, not so happily.</u> It all started this morning just before noon. Mrs. Santos was returning from the supermarket with her daughter and a friend, their neighbor. They stopped on the stairway of their building at their <u>fifth-floor apartment</u>. The neighbor opened her door first, and little Carmelita ran past her. She knew the apartment well, since she had visited it many times. The friend put down her keys and shopping bags, and turned back a moment to Mrs. Santos.

At that moment, there was a sudden gust of wind and the door to the apartment slammed shut. <u>Carmelita was inside, alone.</u>

Then the friend remembered that she had left her <u>kitchen window open.</u> She and Mrs. Santos rushed to the Santos' apartment and telephoned the police. But there was no time to get help in opening the neighboring apartment. They could see that Carmelita was already leaning out of the kitchen window. She had climbed onto a chair, and soon she was climbing out onto the window sill. Mrs. Santos called to Carmelita to go back inside. But the little girl did not understand the danger and did not want to go back. She only waved to her mother.

<u>Then she lost her balance and her feet slipped off the window sill.</u> She managed to hold on for a while with her hands, but she began to be afraid. Her <u>mother screamed for help</u>, and now Carmelita was crying desperately.

And then she could hold on no longer. Several <u>people had run</u> out into the street on hearing all the screaming. They saw the child hanging onto the window sill and <u>got ready to catch her.</u> Down <u>she fell,</u> five long stories—and <u>landed safe and sound</u> in the <u>arms of three strong men.</u> They were Luis, Augusto, and Alfonso Nunes, father and sons. When they heard the screams, they ran from their auto repair shop across the street.

"I never thought we'd do it," said Alfonso afterwards. "But I kept thinking, if we don't catch her, she'll die and it'll be on my conscience all my life."

All the neighbors want to shake hands with the three heroes. Carmelita's parents cannot believe how close they came to losing their daughter. And <u>how lucky they are to have her still</u>.

Answer these questions. Do not look back at the story.

1. Where do you think this story originally appeared—in a textbook, a newspaper, or a magazine?

2. Where does this story take place?

3. Who is Carmelita?

4. What happened to her?

5. How was she saved?

Compare your answers with those of another student. Then go back and read the whole passage.

60 seconds

Preview the following passage. Follow the Guidelines for Previewing Longer Passages on page 19. Then answer the questions below. Time limit: Sixty seconds to preview.

Understanding and Overcoming Motion Sickness

by Judith Weaver

Kate will never forget that two-hour cruise on a small boat off the coast of Depoe Bay, Oregon. With about 25 other tourists, she was excited about sailing on the Pacific Ocean, but within half an hour, she felt dizzy, nauseous, and weak. Kate spent the next 90 minutes lying down in misery, counting the time until she could get back on solid ground. Motion sickness ruined the cruise and she has never ventured out on the ocean again.

Motion sickness comes in many forms, not just seasickness. Ninety percent of the human race is susceptible to motion sickness of one kind or another. Some people become sick when they sit in the backseat of a car; others cannot read or look at a map in any kind of moving vehicle. People get motion sickness on airplanes, motorcycles, amusement park rides, and even on camels!

Scientists have learned that motion sickness occurs when the brain is trying to make sense of a situation and there are too many conflicting messages. While the eyes are sending one message, the ears are trying to send a message about balance. The skin and bone joints, sensitive to air pressure, send still another message.

Many people who have experienced violent motion sickness try to avoid travel. But that is not always possible. So travelers should employ some well-known strategies to avoid getting sick. The most useful strategy concerns food: eat a light meal before traveling and bring along a packet of plain soda crackers to snack on regularly. Avoid alcoholic and carbonated beverages, high-fat foods, and spices. Care in choosing the location of your seat is another important strategy. In a car, sit in the front seat. On a plane, sit near the wings. On a boat, sit at the front and keep your eyes fixed on the horizon.

People who still get sick after trying these strategies can try medical help. Some rely on over-the-counter medications, although some of them can make you sleepy. Others use simple ginger capsules to settle their stomach. A large number of travelers use pressure bands on their wrists. It is not clear how these bands work, but they do prevent motion sickness.

Answer these questions. Do not look back at the passage.

1. Where do you think this story originally appeared?

2. Is this passage fiction or nonfiction?

3. What are some ways that people can get motion sickness?

4. What parts of the body are involved in motion sickness?

5. Is there any hope for people who suffer from motion sickness?

Compare your work with that of another student. Do you agree? Look back at the article to check your work.

Preview the following article. Then answer the questions on the following page. Time limit: Two minutes to preview.

Educating Girls Is a Real Lifesaver

by Victoria Brittain and Larry Elliott

Clare Short knows it. Every development economist knows it. The World Bank knows it: The education of girls is the surest way to reduce poverty. If there is to be a serious effort to improve the lot of the billions of people deprived of the basic ingredients of a decent life, schools in poor countries have to be full of girls as well as boys.

The reason is simple. All the evidence shows that taking girls out of the fields and homes, and putting them behind desks, raises economic productivity, lowers infant and maternal mortality, reduces fertility rates, and improves environmental management. Countries that have pursued gender equality over the past three to four decades have grown faster and become more equal.

Why, then, are 90 million primary school-age girls around the world not in school? For the same reason that when Charles Dickens was writing *David Copperfield* 150 years ago girls were absent from the British education system: Men in power mostly prefer it that way, or are not interested enough in changing the situation to commit energy and money to doing so. Or perhaps they do not quite believe the mountains of studies that have established beyond question the link between the eradication of poverty and those years in a schoolroom by ranks of girls.

The countries with the poorest record for having women in positions of power or influence have the worst figures for girls' education. High-profile intervention by organizations such as the World Bank has begun successfully with several countries, and more of the same will probably be needed to bring change in conservative, male-run states.

Even if there were no development payoff from gender equality in schools, the education of girls would still be a cause worth fighting for. Education is a human right, and the denial of it to girls, in the systematic way it is denied in some feudal societies, is a scar on the community in the twenty-first century.

To be born a girl in a rural area in Nepal, Pakistan, Indonesia, Morocco, Togo, or Sudan—half a dozen of the most shameful performers—means being doomed to a life without school, education, or clean water, marriage and babies coming too early, too many births, children who die of preventable diseases, backbreaking work in the fields, subordination to husband and his family, and an early death. Sexual exploitation is also a danger for a female deprived of education. The uneducated woman transmits to her children the same doomed life.

Every year, almost 12 million children under the age of five needlessly die of infectious diseases associated with poverty. But each additional year spent by their mothers in primary school lowers the risk of premature child deaths by about 8 percent. In Pakistan, an extra year of school for 1,000 girls could prevent sixty infant deaths.

There are places that show how different things can be. In the southern Indian state of Kerala—communist in politics, Christian in ideology—where literacy is almost universal, the infant mortality rate is the lowest in the developing world. Schooling is the route to lowering infant mortality.

Each extra year of school also reduces the birthrate and cuts maternal deaths. In Brazil, illiterate women have an average of 6.5 children, whereas those with secondary education have 2.5.

With women and girls being the main farmers in Africa and southern Asia, their education offers a chance to develop more efficient farming practices, improve output, and raise awareness of the ecological needs of the land with tree planting and crop rotation. With malnutrition at the level it is in these regions, and environmental degradation posing a threat that exacerbates the global warming affecting us all, the world community cannot afford to ignore this avenue of change.

1. Where do you think this story originally appeared?

2. Is this passage fiction or nonfiction?

3. What is the article about?

4. Did you notice the names of any countries mentioned in the article? If so, which ones?

5. Does the article contain any numbers or dates? If so, write them here.

Compare your work with that of another student. Do you agree? Look back at the passage to check your work.

Remember:
Whenever you have something new
to read, always preview!

UNIT 2　Scanning

What Is Scanning?

Scanning is very high-speed reading that you do when you are looking for a specific piece of information. When you scan, you have a question in mind. You do not read every word, only key words that will answer your question. Practice in scanning will help you learn to skip over unimportant words so that you can read faster.

In this unit, you'll practice scanning many different kinds of materials. You should do the work on each exercise as quickly as possible.

Example:

Look at the list of exhibits at the National Zoo in Washington, D.C.

Will you be able to see an exhibit that features the Amazon rain forest in March?

Key words: *Amazon, rain forest, March*

National Zoological Park　3001 Connecticut Ave, NW　(202) 673-4717
Open daily: 10:00 A.M.–4:30 P.M.

Exhibits to visit during March:

- "Panda House" features two Chinese pandas, Mei Xiang and Tian Tian.
- "American Prairie" features prairie dogs, bison, and other animals and plants from the grasslands of North America.

- "Great Cats" features live tigers and lions, graphic displays, and a walk-through trail.
- "Animales de Latinoamerica" features iguanas, condors, flamingos, blue frogs, and wildcats.

Exhibits to visit during April:

- "Pollinarium" illustrates the biological process of pollinating plants and features butterflies, bees, hummingbirds, and flowers.
- "Bat Cave" features 400 bats.

- "Cheetah Conservation House" features cheetahs, zebras, gazelles, and marabou storks.
- "Amazonia" replicates a tropical rain forest and features various fish and plants.

According to the list, you will be able to see an Amazon rain forest exhibit in April, but not in March. Did you read the whole list of exhibits to find this information? No! You knew the key words, so you knew what to look for. You scanned the list to find the information that you needed.

Scanning in Everyday Life

Scanning is a skill that you often use in daily life. For example, you might scan the list of names in a telephone directory in order to find a phone number. On the lines below, write other examples of things you can scan.

_____   _____

_____   _____

_____   _____

Scanning Advertisements

EXERCISE 1

Read each question and underline the key words. Then scan the following car advertisement to find the correct answers. Work quickly!

1. What is the cheapest car in this ad?

2. Which cars have power windows?

3. How many super cabs are available?

4. Does the Escape Wagon have power steering?

5. Can college graduates get a rebate for all the cars in this ad?

6. For which cars can you get a "Daniel Discount"?

7. Which car has "cash back"?

8. Which car has an original list price of $22,790?

9. How many cars have cassette players?

10. In what town is Daniel Ford located?

Compare your answers with those of another student.

Would you buy one of these cars or trucks? Why or why not?

Read each question and underline the key words. Then scan the following supermarket ads to find the correct answers. Work quickly!

A. Scan only ad I, from the Sunny Market supermarket, to answer these questions.

1. How many different beverages are advertised?

2. What is the price of a pie?

3. How many ounces (oz.) of vegetables can you buy for .79?

4. How many Eggo Waffles are in a package (pkg.)?

5. What are the names of the companies that sell frozen carrots?

6. Which juice is 100% natural?

7. How many slices of pizza can you buy for $2.39?

8. Which pizza is cheaper?

9. What is the weight of the frozen bread dough?

10. Is the pink lemonade cheaper than the apple juice?

FROZEN FOODS at Sunny Market

Minute Maid OJ
Calcium Fortified, Country Style or Regular. 12 oz. Can, or Reduced Acid 10 oz. Can. Frozen
.99

Seneca Juice
100% Natural Grape, Granny Smith Apple, or Apple. 12 oz. Can. Frozen
1.29

Lemonade
Sunny Market. Regular or Pink. 12 oz. Can. Frozen
2 for $1

Large Crispy Bagels
Sunny Market. Assorted Varieties. 15.6 oz. Pkg. of 5. Frozen
.69

Eggo Waffles
Homestyle or Buttermilk. 11 oz. Pkg. of 8. Frozen.
1.29

Cool Whip Lite
Extra Creamy or Regular. 8 oz. Container. Frozen.
.99

Homestyle Pie
37 oz. Pkg. Frozen.
1.99

White Bread Dough
Sunny Market. 5 lb. Pkg. of 5. Frozen
1.89

Birds' Eye Vegetables
Deluxe Baby Whole Carrots, Broccoli Florets, Sugar Snap Peas, Tendersweet Corn, Baby Broccoli Spears, Whole Green Beans, or Tiny Tender Peas. 8 oz. Pkg. Frozen
.79

Sunny Market Carrots
Whole Baby 16 oz. or Crinkle Cut 20 oz. Bag. Frozen
.89

Elio's Pizza
6 Slice Double Cheese 19 oz. Pkg. Frozen
2.39

Cheese Ravioli
Sunny Market. 16 oz. Pkg. of 36 Frozen
1.39

Weaver Chicken
Fried Crispy Dutch Frye 28 oz. Pkg. of Batter Dipped or Dutch Frye Breasts. 22 oz. Pkg. Frozen
3.49

Totino's Pizza
Party. Assorted Varieties. 9.8 oz. Pkg. Frozen
1.39

Fish Sticks
Van de Kamp's Value Pack. 26.4 oz. Pkg. of 44. Frozen
3.49

Ad 1

B. Scan both the Sunny Market ad and the Beacon Supermarket ad to answer these questions.

1. Which supermarket's ad has a lower price for orange juice (OJ)?

2. Do both ads include chicken?

3. Which ad has a lower price for Totino's Pizza?

4. Which brand of cheese ravioli is cheaper, Sunny Market or Ravioli Kitchen?

5. How many different kinds of Bagel Bites can you buy?

6. Do both ads include fish?

7. How many different brands of pizza are found in the Beacon Supermarket ad (ad 2)?

8. Is Cool Whip less expensive in ad 1 or ad 2?

9. What is the name of the company that makes garlic bread?

10. Which ad offers more different kinds of foods, ad 1 or ad 2?

TIMESAVING FROZEN FOODS
at Beacon Supermarket

Spinach Ravioli Beacon Super. 16 oz. Pkg. of 36. Frozen — **1.49**

Celeste Zesty Pizza Four Cheese Italian Bread 9.25 oz. Pkg. Frozen — **1.59**

Cheese Pizza Tree Tavern. 16 oz. Pkg. Frozen — **1.99**

Pizza Shells Calise. 27 oz. Pkg. of 3. Frozen — **1.99**

Garlic Bread Cole's. Butter Flavored. 16 oz. Pkg. Frozen — **1.59**

Tina's Burritos Assorted Varieties. 5 oz. Pkg. Frozen — **3 for $1**

Banquet Chicken Country Fried or Regular. 25 oz. Pkg. Frozen — **2.99**

Van de Kamp's Fish Value Pack. Bread Sticks. 26.4 oz. Pkg. or Battered Portions. 25 oz. Pkg. Frozen — **3.49**

Tropicana OJ 100% Pure. Regular or Homestyle. 12 oz. Can. Frozen — **.99**

Cool Whip Extra Creamy or Regular. 12 oz. Container. Frozen — **1.29**

Tony's Pizza Italian Pastry, Pepperoni, Extra Cheese, or Supreme. 15.3 oz. Pkg. Frozen — **2 for $4**

Totino's Party Pizza Assorted Varieties. 9.8 oz. Pkg. Frozen — **1.29**

Jeno's Pizza Rolls Assorted Varieties. 6 oz. Pkg. Frozen — **1.39**

Cheese Pizza Beacon Super. 9 Slices. 24 oz. Pkg. Frozen — **2.19**

Bagel Bites Double Cheese or Cheese & Pepperoni. 7 oz. Pkg. of 9. Frozen — **1.99**

Ravioli Kitchen Cheese Ravioli. 22 oz. Pkg. of 48. Frozen — **2 for $3**

Ad 2

Compare your answers with those of another student.

If you were shopping and you had only $7.50 to spend, which items would you buy? Where would you shop, at the Sunny Market or at the Beacon Supermarket?

Scanning a Table

Read each question and underline the key words. Then scan the Table of Atomic Weights to find the correct answers. Work quickly!

1. What are the four kinds of information given in this table?

2. What is the symbol for iron?

3. What is the atomic number for tin?

4. Which has a higher atomic weight, zinc or lead?

5. What is the atomic weight of hydrogen?

6. Which has a higher atomic number, phosphorus or chlorine?

7. What is the symbol for silicon?

8. Which has a higher atomic weight, gold or platinum?

9. Which element has the highest atomic weight?

10. Find an element that was probably named for a scientist.

Check your answers with those of another student.

Write three more questions about this table. Ask your partner to scan for the answers. Work as fast as you can.

1.

2.

3.

Table of Atomic Weights*

Element	Symbol	Atomic number	Atomic weight	Element	Symbol	Atomic number	Atomic weight
Actinium	Ac	89	(277)	Mercury	Hg	80	200.59
Aluminum	Al	13	26.9815	Molybdenum	Mo	42	95.94
Americium	Am	95	(243)	Neodymium	Nd	60	144.24
Antimony	Sb	51	121.75	Neon	Ne	10	20.179
Argon	Ar	18	39.948	Neptunium	Np	93	237.0482
Arsenic	As	33	74.9216	Nickel	Ni	28	58.71
Astatine	At	85	(210)	Niobium	Nb	41	92.9064
Barium	Ba	56	137.34	Nitrogen	N	7	14.0067
Berkelium	Bk	97	(249)	Nobelium	No	102	(254)
Beryllium	Be	4	9.01218	Osmium	Os	76	190.2
Bismuth	Bi	83	208.9806	Oxygen	O	8	15.9994
Boron	B	5	10.81	Palladium	Pd	46	106.4
Bromine	Br	35	79.904	Phosphorus	P	15	30.9738
Cadmium	Cd	48	112.40	Platinum	Pt	78	195.09
Calcium	Ca	20	40.08	Plutonium	Pu	94	(242)
Californium	Cf	98	(251)	Polonium	Po	84	(210)
Carbon	C	6	12.011	Potassium	K	19	39.102
Cerium	Ce	58	140.12	Praseodymium	Pr	59	140.9077
Cesium	Cs	55	132.9055	Promethium	Pm	61	(145)
Chlorine	Cl	17	35.453	Protactinium	Pa	91	231.0359
Chromium	Cr	24	51.996	Radium	Ra	88	226.0254
Cobalt	Co	27	58.9332	Radon	Rn	86	(222)
Copper	Cu	29	63.546	Rhenium	Re	75	186.2
Curium	Cm	96	(247)	Rhodium	Rh	45	102.9055
Dysprosium	Dy	66	162.50	Rubidium	Rb	37	85.4678
Einsteinium	Es	99	(254)	Ruthenium	Ru	44	101.07
Erbium	Er	68	167.26	Samarium	Sm	62	150.4
Europium	Eu	63	151.96	Scandium	Sc	21	44.9559
Fermium	Fm	100	(253)	Selenium	Se	34	78.96
Fluorine	F	9	8.9984	Silicon	Si	14	28.086
Francium	Fr	87	(223)	Silver	Ag	47	107.868
Gadolinium	Gd	64	157.25	Sodium	Na	11	22.9898
Gallium	Ga	31	69.72	Strontium	Sr	38	87.62
Germanium	Ge	32	72.59	Sulfur	S	16	32.06
Gold	Au	79	196.9665	Tantalum	Ta	73	180.9479
Hafnium	Hf	72	178.49	Technetium	Tc	43	98.9062
Helium	He	2	4.00260	Tellurium	Te	52	127.60
Holmium	Ho	67	164.9303	Terbium	Tb	65	158.9254
Hydrogen	H	1	1.0080	Thallium	Tl	81	204.37
Indium	In	49	114.82	Thorium	Th	90	232.0381
Iodine	I	53	126.9045	Thulium	Tm	69	168.9342
Iridium	Ir	77	192.22	Tin	Sn	50	118.69
Iron	Fe	26	55.847	Titanium	Ti	22	47.90
Krypton	Kr	36	83.80	Tungsten	W	74	183.85
Lanthanum	La	57	128.9055	Uranium	U	92	238.029
Lawrencium	Lr	103	(257)	Vanadium	V	23	50.9414
Lead	Pb	82	207.2	Xenon	Xe	54	131.30
Lithium	Li	3	6.941	Ytterbium	Yb	70	173.04
Lutetium	Lu	71	174.97	Yttrium	Y	39	88.9059
Magnesium	Mg	12	24.305	Zinc	Zn	30	65.37
Manganese	Mn	25	54.9380	Zirconium	Zr	40	91.22
Mendelevium	Md	101	(256)				

*Based on atomic weight of carbon-12 = 12.0000. Numbers in parentheses are mass numbers of most stable isotopes.

Scanning Listings from Newspapers

Read each question and underline the key words. Then scan the TV listings to find the correct answers. Work quickly!

1. Which channel shows a movie starring Clint Eastwood?

2. What hours are included in the listing?

3. What movie listed is given four stars?

4. At what time can you watch a basketball game?

5. How many news programs are shown at 11:00 P.M.?

6. What is the title of the movie to be shown on Channel 56 at 8:00 P.M.?

7. In what year was the movie *Copacabana* produced?

8. At what time and on which channel can you watch a program about Columbus?

9. Which channels show more movies, the numbered or the named?

10. Which channel has Spanish language programs?

Compare your answers with those of another student.

Write three more questions about this TV listing. Ask another student to scan for the answers. Work as fast as you can.

1.

2.

3.

	6:00	6:30	7:00	7:30	8:00	8:30	9:00	9:30	10:00	10:30	11:00
2	The News Hour with Jim Lehrer		Greater Boston	Theater Talk	American Family		American Masters: Ralph Ellison				Charlie Rose
4	News		NBC News	Olympic Winter Games: Hockey, Alpine Skiing, Skating							News
5	News		ABC News	Chronicle	My Wife and Kids	According to Jim	Drew Carey	Seinfeld	20/20 Downtown		News
6	News	CBS News	A Current Affair	Inside Edition	To Be Announced	Friends	Drew Carey	Special Report	48 Hours (R)		News
7	News	CBS News	Wheel of Fortune	Jeopardy!	Extra	Will and Grace	Just Shoot Me	Frasier	48 Hours (R)		News
9	News	ABC News	Entertainment	Hard Copy	The Wonder Years	The Wonder Years	Doogie Howsier	Doogie Howsier	Civil Wars (R)		News
10	News	NBC News	Entertainment	Olympic Winter Games: Hockey, Alpine Skiing, Skating							News
11	The News Hour with Jim Lehrer		Business Report	New Hampshire	Evening at Pops		Keeping America No. 1: Business	Columbus & The Age of Discovery			News
12	News	ABC News	Wheel of Fortune	Jeopardy!	60 Minutes		Breakdown ★★★ (1997) Kurt Russell, J.T. Walsh				News
27	Ocurrio Asi	Noticiero	La Intrusa		Amigas y Rivales		Don Francisco Presenta				Carma
38	Wheel of Fortune	Jeopardy	Cheers	M*A*S*H	Inside the Third Reich (Part 2) (1982) Rutger Hauer, Derek Jacobi				Odd Couple	Hogan's Heroes	M*A*S*H
44	Religion & Ethics		BBC World News		Championship Ballroom Dancing				States of Mind (Part 7 of 7)		Nightly Business
50	Simon & Simon		Star Trek		Copacabana ★ (Color, 1947) Groucho Marx Carmen Miranda				All in the Family	All in the Family	Twilight Zone
56	Growing Pains	Friends	The Nanny	Everybody Loves Raymond	Running on Empty ★★★ (1988, Drama) Christine Lahti, River Phoenix				News		Arsenio Hall
58	Inner City Beat		Feature Story	Feature Story	Candid Camera		Childhood: A Journey		Rodina: "Russian Homeland"		50 Years Ago

	6:00	6:30	7:00	7:30	8:00	8:30	9:00	9:30	10:00	10:30	11:00
BRAVO	Off the Air				Circus of Tomorrow		La Gazza Ladra				
CNN	The World Today		Moneyline	Crossfire	Primenews		Larry King Live		World News		Sports Tonight
ESPN	Inside the PGA	Up Close	Sports Center	College Basketball: Xavier at Temple						Sports Tonight	Sports Center
FAMILY	The Wonder Years	Friends	The Waltons: "The Long Night"		Big Brother Jake	Maniac Mansion	As Time Goes By		The 700 Club		Batman
HBO	← (4:30) Stanley/Iris	Lisa ★★ (1990, Suspense) Cheryl Ladd, D.W. Moffett			Another 48 Hrs. ★★ (1990, Action) Eddie Murphy, Nick Nolte				Tales from Crypt	Dream On	One Night Stand
LIFE	Supermarket	Golden Girls	Intimate Portrait		Unsolved Mysteries		The Attic: The Hiding of Anne Frank ★★★ (1988) Mary Steenburgen				thirtysomething
MC	← (5:00) People Across the Lake		Pascali's Island ★★ (1988, Drama) Ben Kingsley, Charles Dance				Narrow Margin ★★★ (1990, Crime Drama) Gene Hackman, Anne Archer				Trust ★★ (1990)
NESN	Sportfishing	Tennis Now	College Basketball: Purdue at Northwestern							Baseball Action	High Five
NICK	What Would	Wild Kids	Looney Tunes	Rocky/ Bullwinkle	F Troop	Superman	Get Smart	Dick Van Dyke	Dragnet	Alfred Hitchcock	Lucy Show
SHOW	The Gods Must Be Crazy II ★★★ (1989) Nixau, Lena Farugia				Keep the Faith, Baby		Comedy Club		Raging Bull ★★★ (1980, Drama) Robert DiNiro, Cathy Moriarty		
SPORT	Horse Racing	Horse Racing	Forever Baseball	Talking Sports	NBA Basketball: Celtics Encore: New York Knicks at Boston Celtics				Team Tennis: Los Angeles Strings at Newport Beach Dukes		
TBS	Cosby	Andy Griffith	Beverly Hillbillies	Sanford & Son	A Fistful of Dollars ★★★ (1964) Clint Eastwood, Marianne Koch				Wild Wild West ★★ (1999) Will Smith		
TNT	Hollywood	This Old House	NYPD Blue		The Pretender				In Cold Blood (10:15) ★★★★ (1967) Robert Blake, Scott Wilson		
USA	Cartoon Express		MacGyver: "Second Chance"		Murder, She Wrote		Black Mask ★★ (1996) Jet Li				
WPIX	Charles in Charge	Happy Days	Star Trek: The Next Generation		Body Heat ★★★ (1981, Crime Drama) William Hurt, Kathleen Turner				News		Cheers
WWOR	Cosby	Real TV	Gimme a Break	Temperatures	Incredible Hulk		Quincy, M.E.		News		

Read each question and underline the key words. Then scan the list of paperback best-sellers to find the correct answers. Work quickly!

1. Which book has two authors? #8

2. What is the title of the book that is set in Nova Scotia? #5

3. Who wrote a book with a plot set in Arkansas? #2

4. For how many weeks has *Scarlet Feather* been on the list? 4 m

5. What is the title of the book by Anita Shreve?

6. Who wrote the book about the smallpox virus? #8

7. What is the price of *The Vendetta Defense*? $7.99

8. What is *Tell No One* about? disappearance

9. Who wrote a book about the New York Police Department? JD Robb

10. What company published *Heart of a Warrior*? Avon

Compare your answers with those of another student.

Write three more questions about the paperback best-sellers list. Ask your partner to scan for the answers. Work as fast as you can.

1.

2.

3.

Is there a book listed that interests you? Which one?

Why does this book interest you?

Paperback Fiction

This Week		Weeks on List

1   **REUNION IN DEATH,** by J. D. Robb. (Berkley, $7.99.) Lt. Eve Dallas of the New York Police Department must contend with an evil woman she helped send to prison years earlier.   3

2   **A PAINTED HOUSE,** by John Grisham. (Dell, $7.99.) The experiences of a seven-year-old boy whose parents live and work in the cotton fields of Arkansas.   13

3   **SCARLET FEATHER,** by Maeve Binchy. (Signet, $7.99.) Tom Feather and Cathy Scarlet, friends from cooking school, start a catering company in Dublin.   4

4   **1ST TO DIE,** by James Patterson. (Warner Vision, $7.99.) Four women search for a killer who is stalking newlyweds.   9

5   **FALL ON YOUR KNEES,** by Ann-Marie MacDonald. (Scribner Paperback Fiction, $14.) The story of a family on Cape Breton Island, off Nova Scotia.   9

6   **HEART OF A WARRIOR,** by Johanna Lindsey. (Avon, $7.99.) A California woman falls for a strikingly handsome Nordic man who is nearly seven feet tall.   3

7   **FINAL TARGET,** by Iris Johansen. (Bantam, $7.50.) After seeing her nanny and Secret Service agents killed, the president's daughter becomes catatonic.   4

8   **ROBERT LUDLUM'S THE CASSANDRA COMPACT,** by Robert Ludlum and Philip Shelby. (St. Martin's, $7.99.) An American operative tries to prevent the theft of Russia's store of the smallpox virus.   2

9   **TELL NO ONE,** by Harlan Coben. (Dell, $6.99.) Eight years after his wife's disappearance, a doctor comes to suspect that she is still alive.   4

10   **THE LAST TIME THEY MET,** by Anita Shreve. (Back Bay/Little, Brown, $13.95.) Two writers who once had a passionate affair meet years later.   9

11   **A DARKNESS MORE THAN NIGHT,** by Michael Connelly. (Warner Vision, $7.99.) While investigating the murder of a movie actress, Detective Harry Bosch becomes the chief suspect in another homicide case.   4

12   **THE VENDETTA DEFENSE,** by Lisa Scottoline. (HarperTorch, $7.99.) A Philadelphia lawyer finds herself defending Anthony (Pigeon Tony) Lucia, an old man accused of murdering his lifelong enemy.   1

Scanning a Newspaper Article

You are doing a report on ethnic diversity, and you find this newspaper article. Read each question and then scan the article on the next page to find the correct answers. Work quickly!

1. How did David Henry Hwang describe Hawaii?

2. What is the name of the former governor of Hawaii quoted in this article?

3. In what year were the population statistics calculated?

4. What is the source of the statistics given in the table?

5. What is the name of the professor who studies Hawaiian society?

6. How many people in Hawaii are fully or partially Hawaiian?

7. How many Chinese residents are listed?

8. What is the percentage of Samoans and Tongans?

9. How many ethnic groups live in Hawaii?

10. Does any ethnic group have a majority?

Check your answers with those of another student.

Write three more questions about the population of Hawaii. Ask another student to scan for the answers. Work as fast as you can.

1.

2.

3.

Hawaii's Ethnic Rainbow: Shining Colors, Side by Side

The United States is going through an identity crisis. Nationally, early in the twenty-first century, the white population is expected to go from a majority to less than 50 percent. Ethnic groups—especially Hispanic and Asian—are increasing due to immigration, and already there's more interracial marriage, especially in such trend-setting states as California and New York.

Sociologists and others ponder: How will all these people with different roots get along?

Time magazine celebrated the Fourth of July recently with a cover story about the nation's ethnic diversity and asked the questions "Who Are We?" and "What Do We Have in Common?"

To someone in Hawaii, all this concern about ethnic diversity seems like so much fuss. For most of this century, Hawaii has been a multicultural society, a community of different ethnic groups where no one group is the majority.

Back in 1961, sociologist Lawrence Fuchs came to Hawaii and wrote *Hawaii Pono,* a very good book about the islands' march toward statehood. In it, he concluded:

"This is the promise of Hawaii, a promise for the entire nation, and indeed, the world, that peoples of different races and creeds can live together, enriching each other, in harmony and democracy."

But not many people beyond Hawaii's shores have paid much attention to what's going on socially here.

So when New York-based playwright David Henry Hwang spoke at the University of Hawaii last summer about Hawaii being a model multicultural community for the rest of the country, it raised the obvious question: What could others learn from Hawaii?

The Hawaii model

Former Gov. John Waihee liked to call Hawaii "a marketplace bazaar." He made several speeches about the Hawaii model to Mainland audiences.

"In Hawaii, you have something a little different, in which people are encouraged to be proud of their heritage," said Waihee. "There's a pride in

Hawaii's Population

Here are the latest population statistics by ethnic group for Hawaii. Total population in 2000 was 1,156,014 excluding military and dependents.

	Population	Percent
Japanese	211,364	18.3%
Hawaiian/Part Hawaiian	254,910	22.1%
Caucasian	237,019	20.5%
Filipino	141,696	12.3%
Mixed (Non-Hawaiian)	230,410	19.9%
Chinese	47,108	4.1%
Korean	11,510	1.1%
Samoan/Tongan	11,173	1.1%
Black	10,829	1.1%

Source: State of Hawaii DataBook 2000. Because of rounding, percentages may not total 100.

that kind of a society that allows you to pick and choose and enjoy the cultural contributions and uniqueness of different groups.

"In a way, we've tried to call that culture which allows everybody to kind of exchange, go in and out of, enjoy various things . . . in its best sense, local culture," he said. "What glues it all together is the native Hawaiian culture."

UH professor and political analyst Dan Boylan is an even bigger cheerleader for Hawaii's multicultural model, pointing out multicultural societies in Southeast Asia and the Pacific where ethnic groups don't get along.

"We are the nation's experiment in multiculturalism. I don't think anybody's paid attention to that at all," Boylan says. "We get along because no one group has enough people to be in the majority and to dominate," Boylan adds, "and that extends into politics.

"Our political model is no one constitutes that 50.1 percent that's necessary to oppress anyone else," he explains. "Whoever has wanted to govern in this state has had to form a coalition across ethnic lines. [Unlike those on the Mainland] politicians in Hawaii have to appeal to different ethnic groups to win elections."

UNIT **3** Skimming

What Is Skimming?

Skimming is high-speed reading that can save you time and help you get through lots of material quickly. It is different from other kinds of high-speed reading, such as previewing and scanning. You skim to get the general sense of a passage or book, not specific details. When you skim, you have a general question about the whole text, such as "Will this passage be useful to me?" or "What is this writer's opinion?" or "What is the writer's purpose or general idea?"

When Do You Skim?

You skim whenever you want to get some general ideas about an article or a book. For example, when you

- want to find out about a recent election. There is a long magazine article on the subject, but you don't have time to read it all.

- need some information about the theories of Sigmund Freud. You have found many books about Freud, and now you need to know which one will be most useful.

- went to a movie and you thought it was terrible. You notice a review of that movie in today's newspaper. You want to find out quickly if the reviewer agrees with you.

- are reading a detective story and you are in a hurry to know who did the crime.

How Do You Skim?

When you skim, you should not read the whole text. Your eyes should move very quickly over the pages and you should read only the parts of the text that will help you answer your question or questions. The following passage about skimming shows the parts of a text that are usually most helpful. These parts often give the writer's ideas or opinions. However, every text is different. When you are skimming, you need to be flexible. What you read will depend on the question you are asking and the way the passage is written. The following passage gives you an example of how to skim.

Example:

Writers usually introduce their topic and their ideas about that topic right at the beginning. Read the first sentences or paragraph quite carefully. They will give you some idea of what the writer is going to say and how the passage will be organized. This will help you decide what else to skim for.

If the text is long, you might also read the second paragraph. Sometimes the first paragraph is only an introduction and the second paragraph contains more useful information about the whole text...
....

After that, you should look at the beginning of each paragraph...
.....................................maybe read a few words..
.....................................in the middle.................and note if there are lots of names or dates
....
Usually the topic sentence is at the beginning. But sometimes it may be at the end.....
....
....skip
some paragraphs...if they do not seem important. ....
....
....
....

However, you should read the last paragraph more carefully. The author may summarize the important points at the end or come to a conclusion. These are the general rules about skimming and this is all the text you need to read when you skim!

Guidelines for Effective Skimming

- Always work as fast as you can. Don't let details slow you down.

- Always keep in mind your reason for skimming. To help you concentrate, make a question for yourself and skim for the answer.

- Be flexible. The amount of material that you skim depends on your purpose and on the passage.

Skimming News Stories and Magazine Articles

A. Read these questions and then skim the following news story for the answers. Work as quickly as you can—no more than one minute for the skimming. Compare your answers with those of another student.

1. Who is Ted O'Brien?

2. What happened to him?

3. Why are people worried about him?

4. What do you think will happen to him?

THE BOSTON GLOBE • Tuesday, September 4, 2001

Broadcaster O'Brien Missing on N.H. Hike

by Thomas C. Palmer, Jr.
and Allen Lessels

CONWAY, N.H.—Rescue teams tramped through the White Mountains woods into this morning searching for longtime Boston radio and television broadcaster Ted O'Brien, who failed to return from a hike on Sunday.

The 60-year-old midday news anchor for WBUR went on a solo hike on some difficult and lightly traveled trails about 10 miles west of the Maine border, according to New Hampshire officials and studio managers.

When he did not return by evening, O'Brien's wife, Susan, called WBUR to say that he was missing. She notified the Carroll County, N.H., sheriff's office, which alerted the New Hampshire Fish and Game Department.

Rescue officials, who used six dogs to help in the operation, were expected to suspend their search early this morning and resume at daylight.

WBUR managers, who held a press briefing yesterday afternoon, said O'Brien had no health problems they knew of and that he stayed in good physical condition.

Jane Christo, general manager of the National Public Radio affiliate station at Boston University, said the staff was optimistic that he would be found. "The weather is good. Ted is in good shape. It's an easy place to get lost," she said.

But Lieutenant Rick Estes of the Fish and Game Department, who headed the search, said it is difficult territory.

"As far as terrain, it's desperate," he said. "It's a very, very nasty place. There's a lot of ice-damaged trees. The foot trails in that particular area are very, very little used and hard to stay on."

It was the second time in eight days that a visitor has disappeared in the White Mountains. A search for Abraham Hauer of Brooklyn, N.Y., ended tragically when well-organized groups of fellow Orthodox Jews found his body last Tuesday near Franconia. Hauer had died of natural causes while hiking.

Christo said O'Brien's wife told her that he had been dressed "appropriately" for a hike, though apparently not for staying out overnight in the mountains. "He was probably not as equipped as he should have been," said Estes, who estimated that the low temperature early yesterday would have been in the 40s.

B. Here is another news story on the same subject. Read these questions and then skim the news story for the answers. Work as quickly as you can—no more than one minute for the skimming. Compare your answers with those of another student.

1. In the end, what happened to Ted O'Brien?

2. How did he feel about his adventure?

3. How did his wife feel when he was found?

4. Why did he get lost?

THE BOSTON GLOBE • Wednesday, September 5, 2001

O'Brien Turns Up Safe, Sound, Thankful

Boston newsman was lost for 2 days in N.H. woods

by Mac Daniel and Allen Lessels

DIANA'S BATHS, N.H.—He wore a T-shirt on his head, hugged himself inside his fleece sweatshirt, inhaled the cool mountain air and breathed it deep into his chest to warm it while battling critters that sounded like elephants in the darkness, zig-zagging his way toward a host of unknowns.

But after rescuers spent two days canvassing a 50-square-mile, boulder-strewn section of the White Mountain National Forest, WBUR newscaster Ted O'Brien emerged from the Moat Mountain Trail yesterday with a half-eaten peanut butter sandwich and a warm mozzarella stick in his pocket, awed, terribly thankful, and embarrassed to the core about trying an arduous hike far beyond his skills.

A team of four volunteers and New Hampshire Fish and Game rescuers had just resumed their search around 9:30 A.M. when they met O'Brien about 1-1/2 miles from the trailhead, walking toward them wearing a Sail Boston baseball cap and holding a termite-eaten hiking stick.

"Hi," O'Brien said to the group. "You wouldn't by any chance be looking for Ted O'Brien, would you?"

Yesterday, O'Brien walked into the arms of his waiting wife, Susan, who hit him a few times on the arm for putting her through a series of wrenching emotions.

"Frankly, this is an embarrassing incident," said her 60-year-old husband, a veteran of the Boston news scene. "If I had been sensible, it'd have been a one-day story, not a two-day story."

Basically, O'Brien said, he was in way over his head.

"When something like this first happens, you think, OK, now what?" he said. "But you have to believe. I don't think anybody ever really thinks it's not going to work out well. Even if you never come out, you think it's going to work out well."

After hiking a short and smooth portion of the Moat Mountain Trail several weeks ago with his son Tim, O'Brien wanted to do it solo, estimating 6-1/2 hours to traverse the Class III hike—the most difficult grade—which climbs some 3,000 feet in elevation. He took along a bottle of water, two peanut butter sandwiches, and four cheese sticks.

He planned to follow it to the Attitash Trail all the way to Bear Notch Road, a distance veterans say would take even a seasoned hiker some 11 hours.

"I fought him with every rational and then irrational argument not to do this," said Susan O'Brien, who argued with her husband about his plans. "I think that people do not have enough respect for this kind of situation. And his idea was that thousands of people go up here every year, no trouble."

Read these questions and then skim the following magazine article for the answers. Work as quickly as you can—no more than two minutes for the skimming. Compare your answers with those of another student.

1. What does the writer mean by the title?

2. What does she think about the Internet? How can you tell?

3. Have you ever read or talked about this issue before?

4. According to the article, how do educators feel about this issue?

5. What do you think about this issue? Do you agree or disagree with the writer?

Will the Net Replace Thinking?

by Laura Sessions Stepp

It is 2 A.M. and Daniel Davis, a first-year University of Maryland student, has not even started his English paper on biological warfare, due that day.

No problem. He'll just do what he has done before a dozen times or more. He sits down at his computer in his dorm room, signs on to Yahoo's search engine, and begins his quest. Six hours and several bags of chips later, the paper pops out of his printer, complete.

He doesn't consider visiting the campus library or opening a book. "You can find whole pages of stuff you need to know on the Web, fast," he says.

So Davis is a procrastinator. So what? Professors are used to that. But six hours? That's a whole new kind of extreme.

Welcome to the world of Net thinking, a form of reasoning that characterizes many students who are growing up with the Internet as their primary, and in some cases, sole source of research. Ask teachers and they'll tell you: Among all the influences that shape young thinking skills, computer technology is the biggest one.

Net thinkers at school appear to value breadth over depth and other people's arguments over their own.

"Students' first recourse for any kind of information is the Web. It's absolutely automatic," says Kenneth Kotovsky, a psychology professor at Carnegie-Mellon University in Pittsburgh who has examined the study habits of young people.

Good? Bad? Who knows? The first popular Internet browser, Netscape, came out only about a decade ago. What we do know after millennia of training minds in scholarly disciplines is that something has changed and it's not apt to change back.

On the good side, Net thinkers are said to generate work quickly and make connections easily. "They are more in control of facts than we were 40 years ago," says Bernard Cooperman, a history professor at the University of Maryland. But they also value information-gathering over deliberation, breadth over depth, and other people's arguments over their own.

This has educators worried.

"Seven years ago, I was writing about the promise of digital resources," says Jamie McKenzie, a former school superintendent and library director who now publishes an e-zine on educational technology. "I have to say I've been disappointed. The quality of information on the Internet is below what you find in print, and the Internet has fostered a thinner, less substantial thinking."

The problem is no longer plagiarism of huge downloaded blocks of text—software can detect that now, when a teacher enters a few lines of a paper. The concern is the Internet itself.

Marylaine Block, a librarian and Internet trainer in Iowa, is blunt: "The Internet makes it ungodly easy now for people who wish to be lazy."

Jeffrey Meikle, chairman of the American studies department at the University of Texas, sees the new world every time he walks into the main library on the Austin campus. There, where the card catalogue used to be, sit banks of computer terminals.

"My students are as intelligent and hard-working as ever," he says, "but they wouldn't go to the library if there weren't all those terminals."

All Web resources are not equal, of course. What aficionados call "the deep Web," includ-ing subscription services such as Nexis and JSTOR, enables students to find information that is accurate, thorough and wide-ranging.

"I think the Internet encourages intellectual thinking," says Nora Flynn, a third-year student at Maryland. "You can go to so many sources, find things you never heard of. It forces me to think globally."

But many students don't have access to these costly, sophisticated resources or don't know how to use them. This leaves them relying on the free Web, a dangerous place to be without a guide.

Anyone can post anything on the free Web, and anyone frequently does. A student who typed "Thomas Jefferson" into the Google search engine would get 1.29 million hits; Eminem would bring up 1.37 million. Narrowing one's search to certain words may not help. The gamelike quality of screen and mouse encourages students to sample these sources rather than select an appropriate text and read deeply into it or follow an argument to its conclusion. The result is what Cooperman calls "cocktail-party knowledge."

He's the model of a man of books: short-sleeve shirts, glasses, slight stoop, a pensive air. "The Web is designed for the masses," he says. "It never presents students with classically constructed arguments, just facts and pictures."

Many students today will advance an argument, he continues, then find themselves unable to make it convincingly. "Is that a function of the Web, or being inundated with information, or the way we're educating them in general?"

The Net has a kind of magical quality that leads younger students to say to librarians such as Block, "It has to be true. If it weren't true, they wouldn't let it be there."

Says Block, "I have to tell them there is no 'they.'"

Skimming Book Reviews

Book reviews are published in newspapers and magazines. In a review, the writer usually tells something about the subject of the book and gives an opinion. By skimming a book review, you can quickly find out if the book would be interesting or useful for you.

EXERCISE 3

Here is a review of a book titled Go Ask Alice. *Read these questions and then skim the review for the answers. Work as quickly as you can—no more than one minute for the skimming. Compare your answers with those of another student.*

1. Is this book serious or funny?

2. Is it a good book to give to a fourteen-year-old girl? Why or why not?

3. Would you like to read this book? Why or why not?

GO ASK ALICE: A REAL DIARY

Author Anonymous—185 pp. New York: Simon & Schuster Inc.

In this diary, the reader enters a girl's life at about the time of her fifteenth birthday. It seems a very ordinary life in many ways. She argues with her parents and doesn't enjoy schoolwork. She worries about what others think of her, and at times she feels she is ugly, fat, and unappreciated. But on the other hand, she loves her family and they care a great deal about her. She is bright and can do well in school when she wants to, and she has friends whom she enjoys being with. And then her father's job changes, the family moves to another part of the country, and her life falls apart.

How her life falls apart and how she struggles to put it back together again is the story we follow in this anonymous diary. We never learn the name of the author ("Alice" refers to Alice in Wonderland), but after just a few pages we feel we know her well. Indeed, we probably all do know someone like her: an unhappy, insecure teenager who suffers tremendously for the real or imagined slights of her parents and her peers.

For this girl and for all too many like her, this adolescent lack of self-esteem is accompanied by a desperate need for approval and gratification. When she changes schools, she is faced with the ordeal of being the friendless new student in school. The humiliation she suffers at the hands of her uncaring and sometimes cruel fellow students further destroys her self-image.

Then, over the summer, new friends play a trick on her, adding LSD to her Coke. After that experience, she tries LSD again, and begins to experiment with other kinds of drugs. Before long, she is an addict and drugs have taken over her life, alienating her from family, friends, and school. Eventually, she runs away from home, lives for a time as a prostitute, and ends up on the streets, filthy, hungry, and ill. There are moments of hope when she manages, with the help of her family, to break out of the drug habit. Several times she attempts a new start, only to be betrayed by her own insecurity or by the terrible pressure of her drug-taking friends.

Through all this, she writes faithfully in her diary, and so we follow every twist and turn of events, every high and low of her emotions. Though the language is that of a teenager, it is so alive and vivid that we are drawn in to her life, participating in her anguish, her alternating lucidity and recklessness, her love for her family and their desperate love for her. As a diary, it does not offer any solutions or any general truths about the teenage drug problem, but it does help us understand one person's choices and the consequences for her.

Here is a review of a book titled Ice Bound. *Read these questions and then skim the review for the answers. Work as quickly as you can—no more than two minutes for the skimming. Compare your answers with those of another student.*

1. Is this a good book for someone interested in geography and adventure? Why or why not?

2. Why did Jerri Nielsen go to a South Pole research station?

PERSonal life ↓↓

3. What happened to her there?

After ERdoctor

4. Would you like to read this book? Why or why not?

ICE BOUND: A DOCTOR'S INCREDIBLE BATTLE FOR SURVIVAL AT THE SOUTH POLE

by Dr. Jerri Nielsen
Talk Miramax Books, 362 pp., $23.95

Jerri Nielsen was trying to escape monsters in her personal life when she volunteered to work at a South Pole research station in 1998. What she ended up with, in 11 Antarctic months, was a near-death experience, international celebrity status, and a new outlook on life.

Dramatic as it was, the experience didn't solve Nielsen's personal problems. (This is, after all, a true story. Fiction might have ended differently.) But it did give the former emergency-room doctor the perspective that comes to those who have taken a long, hard look into the abyss.

"Ice Bound" is a family story. Or rather, the story of one family being torn apart by emotional abuse and infidelity, while another pulls together to deal with a serious illness in its ranks. It's also a cancer survivor's story, with all the medical minutiae and soul-searching that suggests. Most of all, though, "Ice Bound" is the story of ordinary people doing extraordinary things under some of the most difficult conditions on the planet.

Nielsen first came to the world's attention in the summer of 1999, when she performed a biopsy on herself (using ice as her only anesthetic) and discovered that she was suffering from an aggressive form of breast cancer.

The situation was certainly dramatic. Nielsen was the only doctor within 600 miles, trapped on the ice in the middle of the polar winter with little in the way of advanced medical supplies. Her sole link with the outside world came through e-mail, and that worked only when a communication satellite passed over the Pole.

Despite Nielsen's request that publicity be avoided, her employer—a subcontractor to the

National Science Foundation—was overwhelmed by media interest in the "South Pole doctor." Although NSF didn't release her name, reporters quickly filled in the blanks from information that was released. Nielsen's family and friends were soon fielding a barrage of interview requests back in the United States. Her ex-husband, with whom she had gone through a bitter divorce, told reporters that Nielsen was a bad mother who had abandoned her children and was probably making up the whole thing to get attention.

Meanwhile, at the bottom of the world, Nielsen's odds didn't look particularly good. Under the best of circumstances, women with her type and stage of breast cancer have a 50/50 chance of survival. And the Amundsen-Scott South Pole Station hardly provided the best of circumstances.

In temperatures cold enough to coagulate jet fuel, 41 people were living and working in perpetual exterior darkness under a polar dome designed to house a staff of 17. As the medic, it was Nielsen's job to keep the scientists and on-site construction crew healthy until fresh personnel and supplies would arrive with the coming of the Antarctic spring.

As Nielsen's cancer progressed, though, the doctor increasingly became the patient. Because it was too cold at that point to land an airplane at the Pole, the NSF arranged to have cancer-fighting drugs and other medical supplies air-dropped.

To a large degree, Nielsen treated herself after that, while continuing to care for other "Polies" with injuries. She did, though, have plenty of help administering her weekly chemotherapy sessions.

Following directions from a stateside oncologist, a welder and a maintenance man on the base learned to administer the IVs. A heavy-equipment mechanic mixed the potentially deadly drugs and monitored the IV drips. Others at the station videotaped the sessions and worked to keep the communications lines open so doctors 9,000 miles away could give advice if something went wrong.

By the time an Air National Guard LC-130 made the coldest-ever landing at the Pole, with temperatures hovering around 60 degrees below zero, on October 16, Nielsen had to be carried to the plane. Once she was in America, the NSF slipped her past waiting reporters and she was taken directly to Indiana University Hospital. There she had a lumpectomy (later she was forced to have a full mastectomy) and more chemotherapy.

Behind her on the Pole, she left the closest friends she had ever made—a group she rightly calls modern-day heroes. Unfortunately, "Ice Bound," Nielsen's account of the ordeal, has a rushed and almost amateur quality to it. It reads in places like it's the product of a vanity publisher.

The good doctor isn't always a sympathetic character, either, leaving her old life in shambles and heading to the Pole while her father was seemingly on his death bed. Even now, more than 15 months after Nielsen's emergency evacuation from the Pole, she hasn't been able to arrange a reunion with her three teenage children.

But taken as a whole, "Ice Bound" is a worthwhile read. The details of life at the fringes of human development are fascinating, and the stages of anger, depression, and anguish Nielsen passes through ring true even to a reader who hasn't been faced with a terminal illness or been estranged from loved ones.

At one point, Nielsen writes that Antarctica is a "blank slate on which you could write your soul." In "Ice Bound," Nielsen bares her soul—warts, frostbite, and all.

Skimming for Research

Skimming is especially useful when you are doing research. You can skim materials to find information quickly or to get a general sense of the passage. In the following exercises you will skim passages from a web site and an encyclopedia to learn about Eleanor Roosevelt.

EXERCISE 5

Internet web page

This passage about Eleanor Roosevelt is from an Internet site (http://www.udhr.org). Read these questions and then skim the passage for the answers. Work as quickly as you can—not more than three minutes for the skimming. Compare your answers with those of another student. Then go back and read the passage again.

1. Does this passage give you information about Eleanor Roosevelt's childhood?

2. What is most of this passage about?

3. Does this passage give a positive or a negative impression of Mrs. Roosevelt? How can you tell?

4. What did Mrs. Roosevelt feel was her greatest accomplishment?

5. What can you tell about Mrs. Roosevelt as a person?

Eleanor Roosevelt

"Where, after all, do universal human rights begin? In small places, close to home—so close and so small that they cannot be seen on any maps of the world. Yet they are the world of the individual person; the neighborhood he lives in; the school or college he attends; the factory, farm, or office where he works. Such are the places where every man, woman, and child seeks equal justice, equal opportunity, equal dignity without discrimination. Unless these rights have meaning there, they have little meaning anywhere. Without concerted citizen action to uphold them close to home, we shall look in vain for progress in the larger world."

—Eleanor Roosevelt

Eleanor Roosevelt regarded the Universal Declaration as her greatest accomplishment.

Although she had already won international respect and admiration in her role as First Lady to President Franklin D. Roosevelt, Eleanor Roosevelt's work on the Universal Declaration of Human Rights would become her greatest legacy. She was, without doubt, the most influential member of the United Nation's Commission on Human Rights.

Unlike most other members of the Commission, Mrs. Roosevelt was neither a scholar nor an expert on international law. Her enthusiasm for her work at the United Nations was rooted in her humanitarian convictions and her steady faith in human dignity and worth. Although she often joked that she was out of place among so many academics and jurists, her intellect and compassion were great assets and proved to be of crucial importance in the composition of a direct and straightforward Universal Declaration of Human Rights.

With characteristic modesty, Eleanor Roosevelt considered her position on the Commission to be one of ambassador for the common man and woman: "I used to tell my husband that, if he could make me understand something, it would be clear to all other people in the country, and perhaps that will be my real value on this drafting commission!"

The delegates to the Commission on Human Rights elected Eleanor Roosevelt their Chairperson. Like so many individuals throughout the world, the delegates recognized Eleanor Roosevelt's unparalleled humanitarian convictions. During her tenure in the

White House she had assisted her physically disabled husband in political matters, serving as his "eyes and ears," traveling throughout the United States to gauge the mood of the people. Through this work, she became widely esteemed as a person who both understood and felt the plight of the common man and woman.

Even prior to her years in the White House, Eleanor Roosevelt was actively engaged in politics and advocacy on the local and national level. She was an astute, accomplished, and intelligent woman, thoroughly familiar with the world of political negotiation. Just as she had served as a liaison of sorts between the President and his constituency, so she acted as a liaison between the Commission and the hopes of humanity. She may have lacked certain factual knowledge, but she had a keen sense of what the average person expected out of life—what men, women, and children needed to flourish as individuals.

Her commonsense approach, constant optimism, and boundless energy were integral to the smooth facilitation of meetings. On any given issue, her colloquial style and good humor were engaged not only to win over the majority of delegates who generally supported a particular U.S. position, but to confound those who opposed it. A New York Times reporter who was present at the Commission meetings wrote of the power Mrs. Roosevelt's personality had over certain unreasonable diplomats:

> The Russians seem to have met their match in Mrs. Roosevelt. The proceedings sometimes turn into a long vitriolic attack on the U.S. when she is not present. These attacks, however, generally denigrate into flurries in the face of her calm and undisturbed but often pointed replies.

If Mrs. Roosevelt made one sort of impression with her familiar style, she made another with her commitment to produce a universally accepted, "living" declaration. She was recognized as a tireless worker, stating triumphantly at one point, "I drive hard and when I get home I will be tired! The men on the Commission will be also!" Many of the delegates found this aspect of her personality less agreeable than her charm. One went so far as to suggest that his own human rights were violated by the length of the meetings!

Envisioning a declaration with enduring principles that would be perpetually recognized by all nations, she was a strong advocate of true universality within the Declaration. She was adamant that different conceptions of human rights be deliberated during the UDHR's composition:

> We wanted as many nations as possible to accept the fact that men, for one reason or another, were born free and equal in dignity and rights, that they were endowed with reason and conscience, and should act toward one another in a spirit of brotherhood. The way to do that was to find words that everyone would accept.

Eleanor Roosevelt's personal sense of accomplishment with the finished Declaration was unparalleled in her life. Her speech before the General Assembly as she submitted the Declaration for review demonstrates the historical significance she placed upon its adoption:

> We stand today at the threshold of a great event both in the life of the United Nations and in the life of mankind. This declaration may well become the international Magna Carta for all men everywhere. We hope its proclamation by the General Assembly will be an event comparable to the proclamation in 1789 [of the French Declaration of the Rights of Man], the adoption of the Bill of Rights by the people of the U.S., and the adoption of comparable declarations at different times in other countries . . .

Eleanor Roosevelt's concern for humanity made her the driving force behind the Universal Declaration of Human Rights. Her leadership of the Commission on Human Rights led to the composition of a Declaration that has endured as a universally accepted standard of achievement for all nations. As our respect for and understanding of the Universal Declaration has grown, so too has our gratitude and admiration for this modest woman who passionately pursued what she imagined would become a cornerstone in the struggle for human rights and fundamental freedoms for everyone everywhere.

She lived her life in the center of what many would regard the twentieth century's most consequential events, the Great Depression, World War II, the establishment of the United Nations, and the adoption of the Universal Declaration of Human Rights. She confronted both opportunity and adversity with a sense of optimism and determination. A former Democratic presidential candidate, Adlai Stevenson, once said of Eleanor Roosevelt, "She would rather light a candle than curse the darkness."

Encyclopedia entry

The passage on page 52, about Eleanor Roosevelt, is from an encyclopedia. Skim to compare the information from the web site in Exercise 5 and the information in this encyclopedia entry. Read these questions and then skim for the answers. Work as quickly as you can—just three minutes for the skimming. Compare your answers with those of another student.

1. What information does the encyclopedia entry add to what you already know about Mrs. Roosevelt?

2. In which ways are the two passages similar? In which ways are they different?

3. If you were writing a report on Mrs. Roosevelt's life, which source would be more useful, the web page or the encyclopedia entry? Why?

4. If you were writing a report about the United Nations, which source would be more useful, the web page or the encyclopedia entry? Why?

5. Which is easier to skim, the web page or the encyclopedia entry? Why?

Eleanor Roosevelt

ROOSEVELT [ro′zə velt] **Eleanor** (1884–1962), one of America's great reforming leaders, who had a sustained impact on national policy toward youth, blacks, women, the poor, and the United Nations. As the wife of President Franklin D. Roosevelt, she was the country's most active First Lady. But she was also an important public personality in her own right.

Early Life. Anna Eleanor Roosevelt was born in New York City on Oct. 11, 1884. Her parents, Elliott and Anna Hall Roosevelt, were members of socially prominent families, and she was a niece of President Theodore Roosevelt. She had an intensely unhappy childhood. Her mother, widely known for her beauty, called Eleanor "granny," and her father, whom she adored, was banished from the family because of alcoholism. Her parents died when she was young, and she was raised strictly by her grandmother Hall. Her childhood and adolescent experiences left her with a deep sense of insecurity and inadequacy and a craving for praise and affection.

She first attended private classes and at the age of 15 was sent to Allenswood, a finishing school near London. With the encouragement of the headmistress, Marie Souvestre, the shy girl emerged as a school leader. She returned to New York in 1902 to make her debut in society, but soon sought to escape its rituals through work with the city's poor at a settlement house. On March 17, 1905, she married her distant cousin Franklin D. Roosevelt. She was given in marriage by President Theodore Roosevelt.

Wife and Mother. In the next 11 years Eleanor Roosevelt gave birth to six children, one of whom died in infancy. In the bringing up of her children, she submitted to the domination of her formidable mother-in-law. After her husband's election to the New York State Senate in 1910, she performed the social role expected of the wife of a public official. As the wife of the assistant secretary of the navy during World War I, she pitched into war work with the Red Cross.

Personal Independence. The end of the war coincided with a grave personal crisis, the discovery of her husband's love for another woman. Eleanor and Franklin Roosevelt were reconciled, but when they returned to New York in 1921 she determined to build a life of her own. She had become active in the League of Women Voters, the Women's Trade Union League, and the women's division of the Democratic party. Her personal emancipation was completed after Roosevelt was stricken with polio in 1921.

Eleanor Roosevelt was determined to keep alive her husband's interest in public affairs. Encouraged and tutored by Louis Howe, Roosevelt's close adviser, she became her husband's political stand-in. By 1928, when Roosevelt returned to the political wars as a candidate for governor of New York, she had become a public figure in her own right. In 1926 she helped found a furniture factory in Hyde Park to aid the unemployed. In 1927 she became part owner of the Todhunter School in New York City, serving as vice principal and teaching history and government.

First Lady. When her husband became president in 1933, she feared the move to the White House would make her a prisoner in a gilded cage. But as First Lady, she broke many precedents. She initiated weekly press conferences with women reporters, lectured throughout the country, and had her own radio program. Her syndicated newspaper column, *My Day,* was published daily for many years. Traveling widely, she served as her husband's eyes and ears and became a major voice in his administration for measures to aid the underprivileged and racial minorities.

In 1941 she made her one venture while her husband was president into holding public office herself, as codirector of the Office of Civilian Defense. But she resigned following criticism of some of her appointments. During World War II she visited troops in England, the South Pacific, the Caribbean, and on U.S. military bases.

Later Years. When her husband died on April 12, 1945, Eleanor Roosevelt assumed that the "story was over." However, she went on to 17 more years of notable public service, perhaps the most satisfactory of her career. She was appointed a member of the U.S. delegation to the United Nations by President Harry Truman in December 1945. As chairman of the Commission of Human Rights she was instrumental in the drafting of the UN Declaration of Human Rights. She resigned from the United Nations in 1952, but was reappointed by President John Kennedy in 1961. She remained active in Democratic party politics and was a strong supporter of Adlai Stevenson in the presidential campaigns of 1952 and 1956 and at the Democratic convention in 1960.

In her later years Eleanor Roosevelt presided over her large family at ValKill, her home at Hyde Park. She kept up a voluminous correspondence and a busy social life. "I suppose I should slow down," she said on her 77th birthday. She died the next year on Nov. 7, 1962, in New York City, and was buried in the rose garden at Hyde Park next to her husband. Her many books include *This Is My Story* (1937), *This I Remember* (1949), and *On My Own* (1958).

JOSEPH P. LASH

UNIT 4

Using Vocabulary Knowledge for Effective Reading

Guessing Unknown Vocabulary

What do you usually do when you come to a word you do not know in your reading? Do you

a. look it up in the dictionary?

b. ask your teacher?

c. ask another student or a friend?

d. first try to guess what it means?

The best strategy is *d, first try to guess what the word means.*

If you answered *a, b,* or *c,* then you are not reading as effectively and efficiently as you could be.

Guessing is the best strategy. Guessing

• is fast because you don't have to interrupt your reading.

• helps your comprehension because you stay focused on the general sense of what you are reading.

• helps build vocabulary because you are more likely to remember the words.

• allows you to enjoy your reading more because you don't have to stop often.

Guessing Word Meaning in Context

When you try to guess the meaning of an unknown word, you use the text surrounding the word—the context.

Example a:

Sometimes you can guess the meaning of a word from the other words in the sentence. Try to guess the meaning of *gargantuan* in this sentence:

Some of the trees in Redwood National Park are truly gargantuan, and in fact they are the tallest trees in the world.

You can guess from the last part of the sentence that *gargantuan* means "very large."

Example b:

Sometimes you need to read several sentences in order to guess the meaning of an unknown word.

Do you know the meaning of the word *misogynist?* If not, try to make a guess:

A misogynist is _____

Now read these sentences and then try again to guess what *misogynist* means.

a. Mary realized that Mr. Ashman was a misogynist soon after she started working as his assistant.

b. It is difficult for a woman to work for a misogynist. She is never sure if his criticism is based on her work or on the fact that she is a woman.

c. Mary knew that no woman would ever get a top-level job in a company run by a misogynist.

A misogynist is _____

We know from sentence *a* that a misogynist is a man (Mr. Ashman). From sentence *b* we learn that a misogynist may sometimes criticize a woman just because she is a woman. Then from *c* we understand that a misogynist may not be fair to women. From these sentences, we can conclude that a misogynist is someone who dislikes women.

Exercises 1–4 will help you develop the skill of guessing vocabulary from the context. While you are doing the exercises

- do not use a dictionary!

- do not talk about the vocabulary with other students until you have tried to make a guess on your own and everyone else has finished.

- do not try to translate the unknown words into your own language. Instead, you should try to describe them or give words with similar meanings in English.

EXERCISE 1

Guess the meaning of each word from the context of the sentences below it. Compare your answers with those of another student.

1. What does *porch* mean? _____

   On nice days, old Mrs. Willows always sat out on her front porch and watched the people pass by.

   After lunch in summer, we always moved out to the porch, since there was usually some wind there, but we were protected from the sun.

2. What does *soggy* mean? _____

   The window had been left open during the storm, and the papers on my desk were a soggy mess.

   We gathered up the soggy towels and bathing suits and hung them all in the sun to dry.

3. What does *sketch* mean? _____

   Many artists make a pencil sketch of their subject before they start to paint it.

   Mr. Johnson showed me a rough sketch of the house he is planning to build.

4. What does *shrink* mean? _____

I washed the T-shirt in cold water so it wouldn't shrink.

If you want to have enough spinach for dinner, you need to buy a lot. It shrinks to almost nothing when you cook it.

5. What does *peak* mean? _____

When he won the race at the Olympics, he was at the peak of his career.

It took us all day to climb to the peak of Mount Mansfield.

6. What does *swell up* mean? _____

Jill's skating accident made her foot swell up until she could no longer wear her shoe.

Poor Simon! After he had his tooth pulled out, the whole side of his face swelled up.

EXERCISE 2

Guess the meaning of each word from the context of the sentences below it. Compare your answers with those of another student.

1. What does *turn up* mean? _____

Don't worry about the book that you lost. I'm sure it will turn up.

Do you remember the umbrella I couldn't find last week? It turned up in the back of the car.

2. What does *lid* mean? _____

William took the lid off the pot to see what his mother was cooking for supper.

Sometimes the lid to the honey jar gets stuck, and it's hard to get it off.

3. What does *glance* mean? _____

I always glance at the headlines in the morning, but I rarely have time to read the whole newspaper.

As he ran up the stairs of the school, William glanced at his watch—late again!

4. What does *promptly* mean? _____

Gerald always came home promptly on Tuesdays so that he could watch his favorite TV show.

The firefighters arrived promptly and were able to stop the fire from spreading to other houses.

5. What does *foul* mean? _____

We were all shocked by the foul language the little boy was using.

With the windows closed for so long, there was a foul smell in the room.

6. What does *dew* mean? _____

In the early morning, you could see the dew on every leaf and every branch.

When we got up, the tent was wet with dew outside, but we were warm and dry inside.

Guess the meaning of each word from the context of the sentences below it. Compare your answers with those of another student.

1. What does *deserve* mean? _____

   Those women work very hard and deserve to be paid more.

   Since Peter won the spelling contest, he deserves a special reward.

2. What does *stain* mean? _____

   Polly was very angry when she saw the ugly stain on her new rug.

   When you spill fruit juice on a tablecloth, it can make a stain that does not wash away.

3. What does *strict* mean? _____

   Ellen's parents were very strict with her and did not allow her to go out in the evening.

   Mrs. Tilley was not popular with the children in her class. She was very strict and she punished anyone she thought had broken a rule.

4. What does *grab* mean? _____

   A witness saw a young man grab Mrs. Knox's purse and run away with it.

   As we were crossing the street, I heard a car coming, so I grabbed Selena's hand and pulled her back just in time.

5. What does *plug in* mean? _____

   There was only one place in the classroom to plug in the television monitor, and that was on the back wall of the room.

   No wonder the printer isn't working! It is not plugged in.

6. What does *bald* mean? _____

   Although he was only forty years old, Dr. Jerash was already almost entirely bald.

   Some bald men will try almost anything to make their hair grow back.

Guess the meaning of each word from the context of the sentences below it. Compare your answers with those of another student.

1. What does *shatter* mean? _____

   The picture has been framed with special glass. It won't shatter if you drop it.

   The bomb shattered the windows of all the buildings nearby.

2. What does *greenhouse* mean? _____

   Many of the vegetables you buy in the winter are grown in greenhouses.

   During the storm, a tree fell on the greenhouse and broke the glass on one side.

3. What does *patch* mean? _____

Rosa was able to patch the hole on Bruno's jacket so well that his mother never noticed.

No one was around to help me fix the flat tire on my bicycle, so I had to patch it myself.

4. What does *shallow* mean? _____

The water in the river was too shallow for swimming, but we got wet and cool anyway.

Jane told the children to stay in the shallow part of the swimming pool.

5. What does *gloomily* mean? _____

After hearing the war reports, Stefan walked gloomily home through the dark city.

After the soccer team lost the game, the girls talked gloomily about their bad luck.

6. What does *collapse* mean? _____

The earthquake caused many old buildings to collapse.

Just as Don started eating his meal, the chair collapsed under his weight and he fell to the floor.

EXERCISE 5

In the paragraphs below, one word has been replaced with a nonsense word. Working with another student, first read the whole paragraph. Then use the context to guess what that nonsense word means. If you do not know the exact meaning in English, try to describe it.

1. What is a "zip"? _____

Everyone who visits Russia should first get a zip. If you come by train, you must already have a zip. You will not be allowed to enter at all without one. Travelers without zips will be sent back where they came from. Zips are given on the spot if you arrive by plane or by car. However, you may have to wait a long time for one. This can be avoided by getting a zip before you leave home.

2. What is a "zap"? _____

Various kinds of zaps are available in Oslo. Some are for only an hour, some for a day, some for three days. The three-day zap is useful for the tourist who wants to visit different parts of the city. It allows you unlimited travel for three days on the local trains and buses. Zaps—and information about the buses and trains—are available at all tourist offices.

3. What is a "zep"? _____

In Paris it is wise to get yourself a zep as soon as possible. It is very easy to get lost if you leave the main streets. You can buy zeps in the train station, but they are not complete. Better zeps can be found in the bookstores. These have more details, and they show all the named streets.

4. What is a "zop"? _____

   Trains connect the larger cities in Tunisia, but there are not many smaller train lines. To travel between the smaller cities and towns, most people take buses or zops. These zops are often cheaper than the buses or trains. They leave as soon as they have five people who want to go to the same place. That might be a distant city or a town nearby. The destination of the zop is written on a sign on the roof of the vehicle.

5. What is a "zup"? _____

   The zups always run along the same routes in Istanbul. They usually stop only at the main bus stops. But if you ask the driver, you can get off anywhere. These zups are faster and more comfortable than the buses. At the same time, they are also much cheaper than normal taxis. The cost of a trip is divided among the passengers, usually four or five people. For these reasons, zups are a very popular way of getting around the city.

EXERCISE 6

In the paragraphs below, one word has been replaced with a nonsense word. Working with another student, first read the whole paragraph. Then use the context to guess what that nonsense word means. If you do not know the exact meaning in English, try to describe it.

1. What is a "zip"? _____

   Nobody wants a zip near his or her home. First of all, they usually do not smell very pleasant. If the wind is from their direction, you may get that smell at home. And zips often attract lots of insects, such as flies and mosquitoes, as well as animals such as rats and mice. A nearby zip may also mean you will have noisy trucks on your street all day. Finally, the most serious problem with zips is that they may pollute the drinking water. This does not always happen, but sometimes the garbage has dangerous chemicals in it. Then when it rains, the chemicals enter the water underground and make it unsafe to drink.

2. What is a "zap"? _____

   When people think about sources of water pollution, they do not usually think of zaps. However, as the demand grows for fish to eat, the number of zaps is increasing. In some areas, they are beginning to create environmental problems. In fact, when fish are in their natural environment, they do not pollute, but in zaps, the situation is not natural. There are usually lots of fish in very little water, which means that the water must be changed very often. Each time it is changed, the dirty water must be thrown away. It is usually poured directly from the zaps into a river or the ocean. The chemical balance of the river or coastline is changed by this dirty water, and the plants and animals living there may suffer.

3. What does "zep" mean? _____

   In the United States and in many European countries, there is a serious problem. What should be done with the garbage? There is no more room for garbage dumps. It is not possible to burn garbage, because that pollutes the air, so the governments are looking for ways to reduce the amount of garbage that is produced. One way to do this is to zep as much as possible. Not all kinds of garbage can be zepped, of course. The easiest things to zep are probably glass and paper. However, one can also zep many kinds of metal and plastic. Many cities now require people to zep these materials. The people must separate them from the regular garbage. Then special trucks take them away and bring them to private companies that will buy them and use them again.

EXERCISE 7

In the paragraphs below, one word has been replaced with a nonsense word. Working with another student, first read the whole paragraph. Then use the context to guess what that nonsense word means. If you do not know the exact meaning in English, try to describe it.

1. What is a "zip"? _____

   Experiments have shown that some animals have an extraordinary sense of direction. The zip is a good example of this. In 1957, some scientists took eighteen zips from their home on the island of Midway in the Pacific Ocean. These zips were sent by airplane to some distant places, such as Japan, the Philippines, and the Hawaiian Islands. Then they were set free. Scientists already knew that zips could fly for great distances because of their huge wings. But no one thought that the zips would be able to find their way home. After all, Midway is just a very little island in the middle of a very large ocean. However, fourteen of the zips did get to Midway. They got there very quickly, too. One flew from the Philippines—2,560 miles, or 4,120 km—in only 32 days!

2. What does "zap" mean? _____

   Another animal with a very good sense of direction is the Monarch butterfly. The Monarch is a beautiful orange-colored butterfly. It is one of the larger kinds of butterflies, but is still only an insect. All Monarchs spend the winter in a certain area of central Mexico. In the early spring, they begin to zap north. The butterflies that leave Mexico will die on their way. However, their children will zap all the way to the northern United States or Canada. Then, in the fall, these new butterflies start zapping south. They have never been to Mexico, but they manage to find the place their parents left. They will even go to live in the same trees. Scientists believe that genetic programming makes this possible, but they do not know how.

3. What is a "zep"? _____

   Genetic programming is also probably the answer to the mystery of the salmon. These fish are born in zeps far from the ocean. When they are big enough, they travel all the way down the zep. Then they swim out into the deep ocean water, sometimes for thousands of miles. One salmon from Washington State in the United States was caught halfway to Japan. But no matter how far away they are, the fish start home in the spring. Somehow they know where home is. Along all the many miles of coast, each salmon finds the mouth of its own zep. Then it swims all the way up to the very same spot where it was born.

Recognizing Words That Connect Ideas

Do you ever find that you understand the words you are reading, but you cannot understand what the writer is trying to say? Sometimes this happens when you do not pay attention to the connecting words. Connecting words are often short, but they are very important. They tie several words together to form the writer's ideas.

Two useful kinds of words to notice are pronouns and synonyms. They are often used to refer to a word or group of words. The word or group of words that they replace is called the referent.

Pronouns

Writers use pronouns instead of repeating the same word or name many times. Pronouns can be singular or plural. This means they can replace a single name/idea or a group of names/ideas. In order to understand what you read, it is important to be sure that you know the referent for each pronoun.

Example: Modern technology has dramatically changed the way we view the world. With air travel, satellite communications, and computers, <u>it</u> seems a much smaller place these days.

What does *it* refer to?
The world is the referent for *it*.

Here is a list of some commonly used pronouns:

he, she, it, we, you, they, who	myself, yourself, herself, himself
me, him, her, us, them	this, these, those, that, there, itself
my, your, her, his, our, their, its	

EXERCISE 8

In each paragraph, the pronouns are underlined. Write the referent for each pronoun on the lines below. Compare your work with that of another student.

The Problem of Old Computers

1.   When a computer stops working or is replaced, one of three things can happen to (1) <u>it</u>. (2) <u>It</u> might be fixed up and given to someone else who can use (3) <u>it</u>. Or perhaps (4) <u>it</u> could be taken apart and the various parts could be recycled. The greatest possibility is that (5) <u>it</u> might be sent to the dump. There (6) <u>it</u> would join countless other computers in filling up the limited dumping space.

1. it _____

2. It _____

3. it _____

4. it _____

5. it _____

6. it _____

2.   In the United States, about 10 million computers are thrown away every year! Because most unwanted computers are sent to a dump, (1) <u>they</u> have caused a problem. The computer industry and the government are working on ways to solve (2) <u>it</u>. (3) <u>They</u> have concluded that there must be changes in the way computers are built. (4) <u>They</u>

must be made in ways that will allow their parts to be recycled. (5) <u>These</u> include the electronic parts, the glass screen of the monitor, and pieces of the printer.

1. they _____   4. They _____

2. it _____   5. These _____

3. They _____

3.   A new company has started to recycle computer parts. When old computers and computer parts are received at the company, (1) <u>they</u> are carefully broken down into parts. (2) <u>These</u> include circuit boards, bits of aluminum, gold, and electronic chips. Sometimes it takes an hour to break an old personal computer down into its parts. Eventually, (3) <u>they</u> are all carefully sorted and stored. Then the company sells (4) <u>them</u> to the many customers it has found for used parts.

1. they _____   3. they _____

2. These _____   4. them _____

EXERCISE 9

In each paragraph, the pronouns are underlined. Write the referent for each pronoun on the lines below. Compare your work with that of another student.

Pedicabs

1.   A pedicab is a small cab that is pulled by a bicycle. This human-powered transportation has been popular in Asian countries for many years. Two years ago, a local businessman decided to introduce (1) <u>it</u> in Denver, Colorado. So far, (2) <u>he</u> has four of (3) <u>them</u> on the road. He explained that (4) <u>they</u> do not take the place of taxis, because people use (5) <u>them</u> for short rides. The passengers are often people who don't want to walk because (6) <u>they</u> are dressed in evening clothes.

1. it _____   4. they _____

2. he _____   5. them _____

3. them _____   6. they _____

2.   The drivers of pedicabs are usually students with strong legs and friendly personalities. (1) <u>They</u> pay the owner $15 to $25 to rent a pedicab for a night. (2) <u>He</u> expects (3) <u>them</u> to keep the cabs in good condition. A typical driver earns about as much as (4) <u>he</u> would by working as a waiter. (5) <u>He</u> can keep all the money that passengers pay (6) <u>him</u>. One pedicab driver said that (7) <u>he</u> feels like a businessman. (8) <u>He</u> can earn a good wage and be (9) <u>his</u> own boss.

1. They _____   6. him _____

2. He _____   7. he _____

3. them _____   8. He _____

4. he _____   9. his _____

5. He _____

3.   Pedicabs could be a good addition to the total transportation system in many cities. In Denver, the owner of a pedicab company plans to invest in a total of twenty of (1) <u>them</u>. (2) <u>He</u> believes that (3) <u>they</u> will be popular with baseball fans at the new baseball stadium. (4) <u>They</u> can use (5) <u>them</u> to ride to their parked cars or to nearby restaurants. Furthermore, (6) <u>he</u> thinks that pedicabs could help carry some of the crowds at special events like the Olympics. And (7) <u>he</u> thinks (8) <u>they</u> would be useful in port cities where cruise ships dock. Tourists could use (9) <u>them</u> to get from the port to the city center.

1. them _____   6. he _____

2. He _____   7. he _____

3. they _____   8. they _____

4. They _____   9. them _____

5. them _____

Synonyms

Writers make their writing interesting and enjoyable to read by using a variety of words. They may use several different words to name the same thing. It is important to remember that even though two different words are used, they refer to the same thing.

Example: An <u>orange</u> can be a delicious snack. This <u>citrus fruit</u> is also very healthful because it is a good source of vitamin C.

Both *orange* and *citrus fruit* name the same thing. *Orange* is the referent for *citrus fruit*.

EXERCISE 10

In the following sentences, circle the synonym or synonyms for the underlined word. Sometimes the synonym will be more than a single word. Compare your work with that of another student.

Estonia

1. During its history, <u>Estonia</u> was occupied and ruled by forces from Germany, Sweden, and other countries. Nevertheless, this small eastern European nation still boasts a rich cultural heritage.

2. The Estonians are especially proud of their historic <u>capital city</u>. The walls and gates of old Tallinn date back to the thirteenth century.

3. A favorite activity of Estonians is <u>singing in groups</u>. They are very fond of giving choral concerts.

4. Every year, an all-Estonian song <u>festival</u> is held. This event is a century-old tradition much loved by everyone.

5. On the square in the center of old Tallinn stands the <u>old city hall</u>. This beautiful medieval building is used now for concerts and special events.

6. Tartu, a smaller city to the southeast of Tallinn, is the home of Estonia's oldest and largest underline{educational institution}. Tartu University is the only university in the world where Estonian is the language of instruction.

7. Both Tallinn and Tartu were originally built to be underline{fortresses}. The two strongholds were built on hills with good views of the surrounding countryside.

8. Many Estonians have country underline{homes} on the nearby island of Saaremaa in the Baltic Sea. They visit their simple cottages often and plant large gardens there.

9. A controversial underline{organization} was recently recognized by the government. Now the Society of Estonian Nudists can meet legally in their clubs—without clothes.

10. Estonians love a good cup of underline{coffee}. In the center of Tallinn, there are many small shops where people can enjoy their favorite beverage.

Referents in a longer passage

EXERCISE 11

In this exercise, you will reread the news story in Unit 3, Exercise 1 (page 40). Read the story all the way to the end. Then go back and number the paragraphs in the story. (There are ten paragraphs in all.) Fill in the table below with the referent for each synonym or pronoun. Check your work with that of another student.

Paragraph	Synonym or Pronoun	Referent
1	who	*Ted O'Brien*
2	midday news anchor	
3	he	
3	she	
3	which	
4	who	
4	the operation	
4	their	
5	who	
5	they	
5	he	
6	it's	
7	who	
7	it	
8	he	
8	that particular area	
9	his	
10	her	
10	he	

Read this essay all the way to the end. Then fill in the table below with the referent for each synonym or pronoun. Check your work with that of another student.

The Effects of Dumping Hazardous Wastes
by Elizabeth A. Mikulecky

(1) In recent years, concern about the environment has been growing. (2) The public has become aware of many common, dangerous dumping practices. (3) These methods of disposal, some of which have been going on for years, have increased as the population has grown. (4) Recent publicity has drawn public attention to one form of environmental pollution—the dumping of hazardous chemical wastes.

(5) These dangerous materials include heavy metals (such as mercury) and other by-products of technology. (6) Such chemicals cause cancer, brain damage, and high infant mortality rates.

(7) Dumping of the wastes is difficult to supervise. (8) And, in fact, even careful dumping has resulted in the destruction of whole areas.

(9) When wastes are first put into a dump, they are usually sealed in large metal drums. (10) As time passes, the metal rusts, and the waste materials begin to leak out into the surrounding soil. (11) This has two effects on the environment. (12) First, the local soil is often permanently destroyed and it must be removed. (13) It becomes additional hazardous waste to be stored somewhere else. (14) Second, the chemical waste can sink lower and lower into the soil and reach the water tables deep in the earth's surface. (15) The latter effect produces pollution of the water sources for many miles around. (16) Sometimes the wastes spread into a river bed. (17) From there, they are likely to be carried to one of the oceans, spreading the pollution around the world.

Sentence	Synonym or Pronoun	Referent
3	these methods of disposal	
3	some of which	
5	these dangerous materials	
6	Such chemicals	
9	they	
11	This	
12	it	
13	It	
15	The latter effect	
17	there	
17	they	

UNIT 5 Making Inferences

Inferring Missing Information

Good readers constantly make inferences as they read. That means they think like a detective and look for clues in the text. Then they use these clues to guess about the text and about the writer's ideas. This is especially important when some ideas are not directly stated. Making inferences also helps a reader get around difficult vocabulary or sentence structure.

In the following exercises, you will practice inferring information. If you find words that you do not know, skip over them. Look for the clues that will help you answer the inference questions.

Example: Here is a postcard from a friend. The postcard got wet, so you can't read the postmark or the first line. Read the postcard and answer the questions that follow. Discuss your inferences with another student.

D——,

———————————————

a quiet, pleasant city. Not much of a nightlife for Sarah. She was hoping to meet some other people her age. But everyone here is very nice and they all speak excellent English. Now we're driving north, taking lots of ferries across the fjords. The scenery is just lovely. You should see Arnie with his camera! He's taken hundreds of pictures. The evenings are especially beautiful, this strange light until midnight. We never feel like going to bed. In a few days, we'll be in the land of the midnight sun. Arnie and Sarah send their love.

PM
14' Nov
1994

Carmen Garza
14 Palomino St.
Juarez, TX 78216
U.S.A.

1. To which country has the person gone on vacation? How can you tell?

2. How can you tell that the person is not visiting Alaska, sometimes known as "the land of the midnight sun"?

3. What can you tell about the person who sent the postcard and the people she is traveling with?

For question 1, the correct answer is *Norway*. You can infer this because Norway is a quiet country famous for its fjords, lakes, and natural beauty. It is also known as "the land of the midnight sun."

For question 2, you can tell that the postcard was not sent from Alaska because it says that the people speak English well. The person would not mention that fact if she were in Alaska.

For question 3, you can guess that the postcard was probably sent by a woman who is traveling with her husband (Arnie) and her daughter (Sarah). The daughter is probably a teenager or young adult who likes a busy nightlife. The husband likes taking pictures.

Making Inferences from Conversations

Have you ever overheard part of a conversation and tried to imagine what it was about? If so, you were making inferences.

Example: Practice making inferences from the following dialog. Read the conversation and infer the answers to the questions below.

A: Excuse me. Do you live around here? Is this Elm Street?

B: No, this is Maple Avenue.

A: Maple Avenue? . . . Oh, dear. I really don't understand this! I'm looking for Elm Street and I thought this was it.

B: No, no. Elm Street isn't anywhere near here.

A: But wasn't that the high school back there?

B: No, that was the town hall.

A: Oh. Then I really *am* confused. Can you take a look here and show me where I am?

B: Sure. Let's see . . . You're over here. See? This is Maple Avenue and here's the high school. Now, if you want to get to Elm Street, you'd better take the bus . . .

1. Who are these people? *A visitor from out of town and someone who lives there.*

2. What are they talking about? *Where they are—the visitor is lost and wants to know where she is on the map.*

3. Are they men or women? How can you tell? *It is impossible to tell.*

EXERCISE 1

Read the conversation. Infer answers to the questions below and discuss them with another student.

A: Why is he taking so long?

B: He has to get changed, you know. He's got all that makeup to take off.

A: Well, we've been here forty minutes now. It's cold out here. Are you sure we're at the right door?

B: Yes, I'm sure. Come on. Let's not give up now. I've just got to see him close up.

A: They say he's really quite ugly.

B: Oh, no, that's not true. I've seen him on TV a couple of times. He's got the cutest smile.

A: Well, I don't know. I'm just about frozen. If he doesn't come out in another two minutes, I'm going home.

B: Oh, look! Here he comes. Quick, where's your pen?!?

1. Where are these people?

2. What are they doing?

3. Who are they talking about?

4. Are they men or women? How can you tell?

EXERCISE 2

Read the conversation. Infer answers to the questions below and discuss them with another student.

A: Excuse me. Would you mind turning down the music, please?

B: What's that?

A: I said, could you please turn the music down! My whole apartment is rattling!

B: Oh. Is that better?

A: A little better. It *is* after midnight.

B: Oh, come on, man. It's still early. It's my birthday, you know, so I asked a few friends over. You want to come in?

A: No, no. I'm not the party type and I've got to get up early tomorrow.

B: But it's Sunday tomorrow. What do you have to get up for so early?

A: That's none of your business. The rules say no noise after 11:00 P.M. So if you're going to continue, I'll have to call the police.

B: Oh, all right. Don't get so uptight about it all.

1. Where are these people?

2. Who are they?

3. What is the problem?

4. Are they men or women? How can you tell?

Read the conversation. Infer answers to the questions below and discuss them with another student.

A: Is this the kind of thing you're looking for?

B: It's hard to tell. You see, she's got very definite ideas about what she likes.

A: How about a nice little item like this?

B: Hmmm. You'd think I'd know by now, but every year I have the same problem! Those do look nice, but they're a bit too old-fashioned. She doesn't think of herself that way.

A: Then what about these. They're more classic.

B: No, no. She's not the classic type. Something more modern . . . like those over there.

A: The ones with all the colors? We usually sell those to, well . . . to younger women.

B: She's fond of color. Always has been. Says I'm so dull in my business clothes. . . .

A: Shall I gift wrap them?

B: No, that's not necessary. I'll just put the box in my pocket.

1. Where are these people?

2. What are they talking about?

3. What did "B" put in his pocket?

4. How old is "B"?

Read the conversation. Infer answers to the questions below and discuss them with another student.

A: Welcome back! How was it?

B: Terrible.

A: Really? You were so excited about going.

B: I know, but I sure am glad to be back.

A: What happened?

B: First of all, there was the weather. It rained every day. Not just a little, but all day! There we were with these gorgeous beaches and no sun!

A: I guess you didn't get much of a tan.

B: Look at me! I'm as pale as I was before.

A: At least you must have gotten some rest.

B: Rest! The second day we were there, my husband got sick. He was sneezing and coughing for three days and nights. Then I caught his cold. I felt awful until the day we left.

A: Well, how was the food?

B: That was the only nice thing about the whole week. Except that we were too sick to enjoy it half the time. Anything new here in the office?

A: Not much. It's been a slow week.

1. Where are these people?

2. What is their relationship?

3. What are they talking about?

4. Are they men or women? How can you tell?

Making Inferences from Descriptions

In each of these paragraphs, someone is talking about his or her job without stating what the job is. Working with another student, infer what the job is and write it below. Then underline the words or phrases that helped you guess.

1.　"The minute you climb in, you start feeling excited. There's nothing so exciting for me, not even a jet plane. You get in and start up and off you go. And then you've got to pay attention every minute. There's always someone doing something crazy who's likely to end up under your wheels. I sometimes think it's a miracle if I can get all the way there with no accidents. You've always got to be thinking ahead. That's hard when you have to keep going for so many hours alone. There's a lot of people in this job who have stomach problems from the tension. They lose their hearing, too, because of the noise. You've got to be tough on this job, you know."

Job: _____

2.　"My day starts at four o'clock in the morning. That's when my feet hit the floor. I'm at work at five-thirty, and I finish at two in the afternoon. In between I do a lot of walking. I wear out a lot of shoes each year—maybe four or five pairs. And my poor feet, at the end of the day they're really hurting. The other problem is the dogs. Sometimes you can make friends with them and they'll follow you around. But other times, they can be mean. I've been bitten a couple of times. I can't say as I care much for dogs any more. But it's not all bad, my job. One thing I like is the way you meet a lot of people. You learn all about their private lives, too. It never gets boring."

Job: _____

3.　"The most important thing is to understand people. You've got to know what they're thinking. If you can figure that out, you can get them to do anything. They come in with an idea about what they want. You get them talking about themselves, about what they like. If it's a man, you talk about baseball, or something like that. If it's a woman, you ask her about fashions. That way they get comfortable with you. You ask them a lot of questions and get them saying yes. Then they just get into the habit of saying yes. In the end, you can put them into anything you want, if you're really good. They need a little car for the city; you send them home with a truck. Of course, I wouldn't really do that. It wouldn't be right. You've got to sell on this job, but you also have to be fair. It's not fair to take advantage of people too much. There are some people in this business who'd do anything. But I don't believe in that."

Job: _____

Making Inferences from Short Stories and Plays

The authors of novels, stories, or plays often do not explain everything about the characters or situations. In order to follow the writer's ideas, you need to "read between the lines." That means you need to infer the author's meaning from the descriptions or the dialogs. In the following exercises, you will practice making inferences about characters and situations.

Remember that you do not need to understand every word. If you find words you do not know, skip them and read on. Look for the clues that will help you infer the answers to the questions.

EXERCISE 6

Read this scene from Red Carnations, *a play by Glenn Hughes. Working with another student or a group of students, infer the answers to the questions below. Underline the words or phrases that helped you.*

Red Carnations

Boy: (*crossing to bench*) I think I will sit down, if you don't mind. It's a devil of a bore standing first on one foot and then on the other. (*He sits down on the opposite end of bench.*)

Man: Have a cigar?

Boy: No, thanks; I'll just finish this cigarette. (*He turns directly to the MAN, and as he does, his eye lights on the carnation in the other's lapel. He shows annoyance. He takes one from his own lapel, hesitates a moment, then replaces it. The MAN, noticing the action, smells his.*)

Man: Pretty flowers, carnations, aren't they? Wonderful fragrance they have, too. I am very fond of them, and I see your taste runs in the same direction.

Boy: (*disturbed*) Yes, indeed. Very fine flower. But I—well, I hope you won't think me silly, but as a matter of fact, if it doesn't make any difference to you, would you mind keeping your carnation out of sight for a while, until—well, just to be a good sport, if you would hide it for a few minutes, I'd be very grateful.

Man: (*good-naturedly*) Now, I'd like nothing better than to do you a favor, Mr.—Mr.—

Boy: Smith.

Man: Thank you, Mr. Smith. That's strange. Very strange.

Boy: What is strange? The name of Smith?

Man: Yes, strange that you should have it, when that is my name, too.

Boy: Oh, your name is Smith, too? Well, after all, there are lots of us in the world—lots of us Smiths, I mean—so there is no reason why such a coincidence—

MAN: Of course not, of course not—only, I was thinking about the red carnations.

BOY: Well, I don't see—

MAN: I may be mistaken, of course. But two Smiths, meeting in the same spot at the same hour, both wearing red carnations! You must confess it's a bit—

BOY: By Jove! So it is! (*He looks intently, suspiciously, at the MAN.*) I wish you could move to another spot, or take that flower out of your lapel, or—it isn't absolutely necessary for you to wear it, is it?

MAN: But it is! Absolutely! And you are going to cause me all sorts of trouble if you don't move, or change your name, or at least throw away your carnation.

BOY: I shall do nothing of the kind. I can't! My Lord, man, she doesn't know me! That is, she doesn't know what I look like. That is why she asked me to wear a red carnation.

MAN: But that is exactly *my* predicament. The woman *I* am to meet does not know *me* by sight. She asked *me* to wear a red carnation. So you see, I can't help you out. After all, a man must look to his own affairs first.

BOY: What a beastly coincidence! (*brightening*) Oh, well, it may not matter. One of them will arrive before the other does. If you recognize her as your—ah—friend, you can speak up at once, and get on out of the way. If mine should arrive first, I shall do the same.

1. What is the relationship between the two characters in this scene from the play?

2. Where are they?

3. What happened before this passage in the play?

4. Who are the women they are meeting?

5. What do you think will happen after this in the play?

Read this scene from **The Cactus Flower,** *a play by Abe Burrows. Working with another student or a group of students, infer the answers to the questions below. Underline the words or phrases that helped you.*

The Cactus Flower

TONI: *[From the ladder]* May I help you, Madam?

STEPHANIE: *[Every inch the upper middle class lady]* I'm really not looking for anything in particular. I just thought I'd browse a bit.

TONI: Fine. I'm here if you want me.

STEPHANIE: I've heard there's a marvelous recording of uh *[Trying to think of something]* of Horowitz's last concert. Do you have it?

TONI: Horowitz? We're all out, but I can send it to you.

STEPHANIE: That will be fine. I believe my husband has a charge account here. Send the record to . . . *[Laying it on]* Mrs. . . . Julian . . . Winston.

[TONI *has been putting records away as she talks. Now when she hears* JULIAN'S *name, she misses the shelf with a record and it drops.]*

TONI: *[Coming down ladder and crossing to* STEPHANIE] You?

STEPHANIE: *[Nodding]* Me.

TONI: You didn't come on account of Horowitz?

STEPHANIE: No. You see, Miss Simmons—

TONI: Call me Toni.

STEPHANIE: *[Graciously]* Thank you. Toni . . . Dr. Winston, my husband, said that you were most anxious to meet me. Well, here I am. *[She sits and crosses her legs.]*

TONI: *[After a moment, a bit impatiently]* Did he . . . did he tell you about his—our plans?

STEPHANIE: *[Same gracious smile]* The divorce? Naturally.

TONI: *[After another pause]* Well?

STEPHANIE: Well what?

TONI: You don't mind?

STEPHANIE: My husband and I are in complete agreement about the divorce.

TONI: *[Letting out a sharp breath of relief]* Whew! That makes me very happy!

STEPHANIE: *[As sweetly as possible]* I'm glad.

TONI: You see, Mrs. Winston—*[Sudden thought]* You know, I don't know your first name.

STEPHANIE: *[Thinks for a moment]* Mrs. Winston will do very nicely. Of course, I won't be Mrs. Winston very much longer. *[There is a slight touch of real and fake sadness in that last phrase.]*

TONI: *[Suddenly]* Then you *do* mind.

STEPHANIE: Of course I don't. Things between the doctor and me have become . . . impossible.

TONI: I can't tell you how good that makes me feel.

STEPHANIE: [Looking at her with a smile] I've really made your day.

TONI: It's just that I didn't want to be the cause of your divorce. I never pushed Julian into it. I am no home wrecker.

STEPHANIE: I'll remember that. [Rises, speaks gravely] Now, Toni, may I ask you a question?

TONI: Anything.

STEPHANIE: Are you absolutely sure you love Julian?

TONI: You *can't* ask *that!*

STEPHANIE: I just did. Do you love him?

TONI: Madly! Wildly! Desperately!

STEPHANIE: Just so long as you're fond of him. I don't want him to end up unhappy and bitter.

TONI: Oh, I understand, especially after he's just had such a terrible marriage.

STEPHANIE: [Stiffening] Not so terrible! Our marriage, after all, lasted ten years and we still have a very deep respect for each other.

TONI: Of course.

STEPHANIE: I've always had to look after Dr. Winston, my husband. You know, aside from his profession, at which he's a master, the doctor is a very vulnerable man. An idealist . . . a child . . . a silly child . . . damned silly child.

TONI: Also an adorable child.

STEPHANIE: I guess you *do* love him. Well, now that you've heard what you wanted to hear, I'll be running along. [Holds out her hand to TONI. TONI takes it.] I do hope you have better luck with Julian than I did.

TONI: Mrs. Winston. . . . What about you? What are you going to do?

STEPHANIE: Forget about me. I'll ride off into the sunset . . . or something.

TONI: It's just that . . . I want to be sure you're all right.

STEPHANIE: I'll write you every day. [She starts for street door.]

TONI: [flurrying after her and stopping her] Mrs. Winston, who's going to tell the children?

1. What is the relationship between the two characters in this scene of the play?

2. Where are they?

3. What happened before this passage in the play?

4. What do you think will happen after this in the play?

Read this passage from "Til Death Do Us Part," a story by Becky Hagenston. Working with another student or a group of students, infer the answers to the questions that follow. Underline the words or phrases that helped you.

Til Death Do Us Part

Joyce watched Adam and his father playing horseshoes with Jerry and the Reverend, under the gold-washed trees. Adam's parents had insisted on having the rehearsal dinner at their house, and there were cubed cheeses, baby quiches, and shrimp cocktail laid out on picnic tables on their wooden patio.

Adam hadn't swept Joyce off her feet or made her forget herself. She would not describe herself as "crazy, wacko in love." She loved him—not madly, not crazily, but sanely and contentedly. It didn't matter that certain young men made her feel woozy, like Cousin Charlie had, or that she sometimes fell in love in elevators. That, she decided, was a sickness similar to the flu. It passed soon enough, and then you recovered and went on with things. It was what got people like Kathy and her mother into trouble.

Joyce's mother was pleased because Adam came from a "healthy family environment." His parents had been married for thirty-four years, and he'd grown up in this farmhouse on a country road that was still unpaved, five miles from Nathan Hale's house. Joyce couldn't remember what Nathan Hale had done, but she liked that his house was still there, after so many years. There was something reassuring and permanent about it.

Adam had grown up climbing these same trees, playing with the horseshoes that were now thudding and clanging across the lawn. In this place, Joyce had the same feeling she sometimes got when she went back to Ebenezer Church—that it could be ten years ago, or sixty, or a hundred. That every moment was present and intact, swirling seamlessly into right now.

Sometimes it seemed to her that she had left pieces of her self under furniture that had never belonged to her, and in schoolyards with children who had never learned her name. It made her sad, as if there were small ghosts that looked like her, wandering lost in places they didn't recognize. She had tried to explain this to Adam once, when he was showing her the remains of a rocket he and his brothers had built in the barn when he was nine.

"I don't have any relics of my childhood to show you," she'd said. "I couldn't take you to any tree houses or point out any tire swings I used to play on. It was like, with every new father, everything just began again. My mother would give a lot of stuff away, so she wouldn't be reminded of whoever it was she had just divorced. And she threw away a lot of photo albums, so I'm not even sure what certain people looked like anymore."

"Well, you've turned out great," Adam had told her. "And maybe if your life hadn't gone that way, you wouldn't be the person you are now."

"Maybe," said Joyce, doubtfully. "Besides, we've got about sixty years ahead of us to collect relics." Joyce was always relieved when he said things like that, even if she herself was not entirely convinced. Now, pulling a cube of cheddar cheese from its red-frilled toothpick, she squinted toward the lawn and imagined her sons and daughters playing on this same grass. It was much easier to picture these people who didn't exist than to imagine the older version of herself who would be right here, watching them.

1. What is the relationship between Joyce and Adam? Does the title of the story help you to infer this? Why?

2. Where are they?

3. What can you tell about Joyce's past?

4. Which character do you think expresses the way the author feels?

5. What do you think will happen after this in the story?

Read the following passage from "A Domestic Dilemma," a story by Carson McCullers. (A dilemma is a problem with no easy solution.) Working with another student or a group of students, infer the answers to the questions that follow. Then underline the words or phrases that helped you.

A Domestic Dilemma

The children were in the living room, so intent on play that the opening of the front door was at first unnoticed. Martin stood looking at his safe, lovely children. They had opened the bottom drawer of the secretary and taken out the Christmas decorations. Andy had managed to plug in the Christmas tree lights and the green and red bulbs glowed with out-of-season festivity on the rug in the living room. At the moment he was trying to trail the bright cord over Marianne's rocking horse. Marianne sat on the floor pulling off an angel's wings. The children wailed a startling welcome. Martin swung the fat little baby girl up to his shoulder and Andy threw himself against his father's legs.

"Daddy, Daddy, Daddy!"

Martin set down the little girl carefully and swung Andy a few times like a pendulum. Then he picked up the Christmas tree cord.

"What is all this stuff doing out? Help me put it back in the drawer. You're not to fool with the light socket. Remember I told you that before. I mean it, Andy."

The six-year-old child nodded and shut the secretary drawer. Martin stroked his fair soft hair and his hand lingered tenderly on the nape of the child's frail neck.

"Had supper yet, Bumpkin?"

"It hurt. The toast was hot."

The baby girl stumbled on the rug and, after the first surprise of the fall, began to cry; Martin picked her up and carried her in his arms back to the kitchen.

"See, Daddy," said Andy. "The toast—"

Emily had laid the childrens' supper on the uncovered porcelain table. There were two plates with the remains of cream-of-wheat and eggs and silver mugs that had held milk. There was also a platter of cinnamon toast, untouched except for one tooth-marked bite. Martin sniffed the bitten piece and nibbled gingerly. Then he put the toast into the garbage pail.

"Hoo—phui—What on earth!"

Emily had mistaken the tin of cayenne for the cinnamon.

"I like to have burnt up," Andy said. "Drank water and ran outdoors and opened my mouth. Marianne didn't eat none."

"Any," corrected Martin. He stood helpless, looking around the walls of the kitchen. "Well, that's that, I guess," he said finally. "Where is your mother now?"

"She's up in you alls' room."

Martin left the children in the kitchen and went up to his wife. Outside the door he waited for a moment to still his anger. He did not knock and once inside the room he closed the door behind him.

Emily sat in the rocking chair by the window of the pleasant room. She had been drinking something from a tumbler and as he entered she put the glass hurriedly on the floor behind the chair. In her attitude there was confusion and guilt which she tried to hide by a show of spurious vivacity.

"Oh, Marty! You home already? The time slipped up on me. I was just going down—"

1. What are the relationships among the four characters in the story?

2. Where are they?

3. What has happened just before this passage?

4. Which character do you think expresses the way the author feels?

5. What do you think will happen after this in the story?

Making Inferences about Opinions

Writers of book or movie reviews or of magazine and newspaper articles often do not tell their opinions directly. You have to infer their opinions (points of view) by "reading between the lines." In the following exercises, infer the writers' points of view from their descriptions and choice of words.

EXERCISE 10

Read the short book reviews below and infer the answers to the questions that follow. Discuss your inferences with another student.

Review 1

A TALE OF TEXAS
by Kurt Wheeler

This modern cowboy story is set in 1949. It follows three young men on a wild ride on horseback out of Texas and into northern Mexico. Their adventure takes them out of twentieth-century America and into a totally different world, where it is still possible to live with horses and nature. There are the bad guys and good guys, as in the classic films, but the book is not just a rewrite of a John Wayne movie. The characters are convincing and the descriptions of the natural world are truly brilliant. The style is ambitious—we are reminded of Faulkner—and it could easily have become terribly stylized. But this author has the skill to make it work. The masterful writing and action-filled plot keep the reader's attention throughout. We hope the second volume that the author promises will be as satisfying as this.

1. What is the reviewer's opinion of this book?

2. How can you tell?

3. From what you have read in this review, do you think that you would like to read this book? Discuss your opinion with another student. Do you agree?

Review 2

AFTER HOURS
by Samantha Trout

This novel, about three people who work for an Internet company in New York, offers a modern twist on one of the oldest themes in literature: the love triangle. The setting is just what you might expect at a "dot-com" company: a large, open office building, equipped with a gym. Almost the whole novel takes place in this office building or at a nearby café. The characters don't seem to have any other life beyond the office, where they talk endlessly about themselves and their grand expectations for the company. In fact, the performance of the company is an important element in the plot. Unfortunately, we can guess from the beginning what the outcome is going to be: This will be another story of a "dot-com" failure as well as romantic failure. Furthermore, the characters are quite predictable and not very likable. All in all, the author never manages to get us interested or involved in their fate, so when the book comes to a tragic ending, we really don't care.

1. What is the reviewer's opinion of this book? How can you tell?

2. From what you have read in this review, do you think that you would like to read this book? Discuss your opinion with another student. Do you agree?

Read the two short news articles below and infer the answers to the questions that follow. Discuss your inferences with another student.

Article 1

Signs of the Times in Britain

"What's your sign?" That question has been a popular conversation starter in England ever since the 1960s, when people began to rediscover the ancient art of reading the stars. For decades, astrology has been gaining in popularity, with astrology columns in all the newspapers, piles of books written on the subject, and a booming business of personal predicting.

One place where astrology has not been appreciated is the academic world. Astrology has not been considered an acceptable subject of study at universities since the seventeenth century, when scientists made a clear division between the study of astrology and the science of astronomy.

Now, however, that might be changing. Researchers in some British universities are taking a closer look at the way human affairs may or may not be influenced by the stars and planets. At the University of Southampton, astrology enthusiasts have set up the Research Group for the Critical Study of Astrology. With funds from this Research Group, doctoral students are studying possible connections between movements in the star charts and various aspects of human life, including fertility and alcoholism.

Some academics, such as Professor George Haldane, at Durham University, wonder if any connections ever will be found between our lives and the stars. But he believes that it could be interesting to look at the way astrology has influenced people, since, over the centuries, people have found meaning in astrology in the same way they have found meaning in poetry or music.

Article 2

Star Pupils in British Universities?

Astrology as the subject of a university course? Until recently, astrology was considered a part of popular culture and no one in the academic world took it very seriously. But some researchers in Britain are trying to change that attitude. With a $12,000 grant, Christopher Bagley, a social psychologist at the University of Southampton, has started the Research Group for the Critical Study of Astrology. He and others like him are pushing for the introduction of university-level courses to study the role of astrology in science, history, and religion.

Most academics, however, and especially scientists, are critical of this trend. "Astrology is in the same category as fairies," says David Minott, professor of science at Cambridge University. He thinks that

universities should spend their money, time, and effort on other, more important matters.

After all, more than 400 years ago, scientists decided that astronomy was the only truly scientific study of the stars and planets. Astrology was discredited as a "pseudoscience," whose theories were based on tradition and mythology, and could not be tested or proved. From that time on, no institution of higher learning in the western world recognized astrology as an acceptable area of study.

The fact that some British universities today may offer courses in astrology is, in the opinion of some scientists, the sign of a dangerous lowering of scientific standards. In their view, universities should not allow themselves to be influenced by the fashions of the moment, but should maintain the clear division that scientists have accepted for centuries between the "pseudoscience" of astrology and the study of the universe according to scientific methods.

1. Are these writers in favor of or against the study of astrology in British universities?

2. How can you tell?

3. What is your point of view on the subject?

UNIT 6   Finding Topics

In order to understand what you are reading, you need to connect it to something you already know. To make this connection, you need to be sure that you know what it is that you are reading about. That is, you need to know the *topic*.

Identifying Topics

In these exercises, you will practice finding the topic of a group of words. The topic is a general word that includes all the other words. Some of the groups include <u>kinds</u> or <u>examples</u> of a more general topic. Other groups of words name the <u>parts</u> of something.

Example: In the groups of words below, one of the words is the topic for all the other words. Circle the topic.

1. roses   flowers   tulips   lilies   geraniums   petunias

The topic is *flowers*. All of the other words are <u>kinds</u> of flowers.

2. roof   house   wall   window   stairs   door

The topic is *house*. All of the other words are <u>parts</u> of a house.

In the following exercises, you should work with another student. By discussing your work, you will learn more from the exercises. While you are working, ask, "What is this about? What is the general idea?"

First, try to do the exercises without using a dictionary. Then, when you have finished, you may look up words you do not know.

EXERCISE 1

In each group of words, one of the words is the topic for all the other words. Work with another student and circle the topic. Do not use your dictionary! Time limit: Three minutes.

1. encyclopedia   dictionary   reference book   atlas   telephone book   catalog
2. anesthesiologist   pediatrician   neurologist   cardiologist   geriatrician   doctor
3. Chicago   Cleveland   Cairo   Carlsbad   cities   Copenhagen
4. tent   water bottle   camping gear   sleeping bag   insect repellent   lantern
5. run   walk   move   stroll   stride   skip
6. aspirin   tetracycline   cough syrup   penicillin   medicine   ibuprofen
7. fertilizing   raking   shoveling   planting   gardening   watering

8. France   Normandy   Brittany   Provence   Alsace   Burgundy
9. fax machine   computer   office   scanner   copy machine   telephone
10. table   menu   chair   waiter   restaurant   meal

EXERCISE 2

In each group of words, the topic is not included. Working with another student, think of a topic and write it on the line. Do not use your dictionary! Time limit: Four minutes.

1. Topic: _____pres_____

   Clinton   Ford   Nixon   Kennedy   Reagan   Johnson

2. Topic: _____piano_____

   strings   hammers   keys   pedals   legs   frame

3. Topic: _____string instruments_____

   violin   viola   guitar   banjo   harp   mandolin

4. Topic: _____computer_____

   modem   screen   keyboard   disk drive   floppy disk   CD rom

5. Topic: _____

   writer   producer   director   actors   camera crew   makeup staff

6. Topic: _____monarch, Eng names_____

   Henry   Elizabeth   George   Victoria   Edward   Mary

7. Topic: _____

   manager   produce manager   cashier   butcher   bagger   cleaner

8. Topic: _____Languages_____

   German   Italian   Basque   Flemish   Spanish   Gaelic

9. Topic: _____

   pineapple   kiwi   papaya   mango   guava   persimmon

10. Topic: _____

    Copernicus   Brahe   Kepler   Galileo   Newton   Sagan

EXERCISE 3

In each group of words, the topic is not included. Working with another student, think of a topic and write it on the line. Do not use your dictionary! Time limit: Four minutes.

1. Topic: _____

   mercury   tin   aluminum   copper   iron   chromium

2. Topic: _____land formations_____

   mountains   plains   hills   cliffs   valleys   plateaus

3. Topic: _____car types_____

sedan   convertible   station wagon   minivan   coupe   sport-utility vehicle

4. Topic: _____cleaning items_____

broom   mop   rag   sponge   vacuum cleaner   scrub brush

5. Topic: _____clothing_____

cotton   polyester   wool   silk   linen   rayon

6. Topic: _____

hair dryer   microwave oven   egg beater   iron   blender   toaster

7. Topic: _____

McKinley   Aconsagua   Everest   Elbrus   Kilimanjaro   Monte Bianco

8. Topic: _____

brakes   tires   accelerator   clutch   steering wheel   seat belts

9. Topic: _____SE Asia_____

Vietnam   Thailand   Cambodia   Laos   Taiwan   North Korea

10. Topic: _____

jazz   rock   folk   religious   classical   reggae

EXERCISE 4

In each group of words, the topic is not included. Working with another student, think of a topic and write it on the line above the words. Then think of another word that fits your topic and write it next to the other words in the group. Do not use your dictionary! Time limit: Five minutes.

1. Topic: _____organs_____

intestines   stomach   liver   kidney   lungs   _____heart_____

2. Topic: _____

butter   milk   cream   yogurt   cheese   _____

3. Topic: _____

planets   meteors   meteorites   asteroids   moons   _____

4. Topic: _____weather_____

snowy   humid   rainy   stormy   breezy   _____dry_____

5. Topic: _____

Quebec   Toronto   Vancouver   Halifax   Victoria   _____

6. Topic: _____parts of tree_____

trunk   branch   root   seed   bark   _____leaves_____

7. Topic: _____shapes_____

circle   oval   pyramid   cube   square   _____triangle_____

8. Topic: _Shoes_

slippers   sandals   moccasins   pumps   sneakers   _high-heels_

9. Topic: _____

Matisse   Gauguin   Monet   Pissaro   Corot   _____

10. Topic: _____

steam   gasoline   oil   wind   water   _____

EXERCISE 5

In each group of words, the topic is not included. Working with another student, think of a topic and write it on the line above the words. Then think of another word that fits your topic and write it next to the other words in the group. Do not use your dictionary! Time limit: Five minutes.

1. Topic: _containers (drinking)_

glass   goblet   mug   bottle   can   _____

2. Topic: _(+) adj_

beautiful   gorgeous   pretty   cute   attractive   _dreamy_

3. Topic: _____

cathedral   church   synagogue   mosque   chapel   _____

4. Topic: _disease_

malaria   tuberculosis   scarlet fever   diphtheria
measles   _____

5. Topic: _games w/balls_

baseball   football   tennis   basketball   handball   _racketball_

6. Topic: _____

editorials   news stories   columns   photographs
business reports   _____

7. Topic: _Island_

Kyushu   Sicily   Tasmania   Jutland   Victoria   _____

8. Topic: _____

laces   sole   heels   straps   lining   _____

9. Topic: _____

Aleutians   Alps   Urals   Cascades   Andes   _____

10. Topic: _religions_

Islam   Catholicism   Judaism   Confuscianism
Taoism   _____

In each group of words, the topic is not included and one item does not belong in the list. Working with another student, think of a topic and write it on the line above the group of words. Then cross out the word that does not fit your topic. (Sometimes there is more than one possible answer.) Do not use your dictionary! Time limit: Four to five minutes.

Example:

Topic: *vegetables*

lettuce   spinach   beans   potatoes   ~~apples~~   cabbage

Apples does not belong. Apples are not vegetables.

1. Topic: _____ grains _____

   rice   wheat   corn   barley   oats   ~~beans~~

2. Topic: _____

   boring   exciting   ~~swimming~~   interesting   surprising   frightening

3. Topic: _____

   twist   waltz   ~~dogtrot~~   swing   tango   lambada

4. Topic: _____ ~~farm~~ (farm animals) _____   animals you can control (# legs / mammals)

   cows   sheep   pigs   ~~mice~~   goats   chickens

5. Topic: _____

   actor   plumber   pilot   mechanic   nurse   ballerina

6. Topic: _____ moveable body joints _____

   wrist   ~~rib~~   shoulder   elbow   knee   hip

7. Topic: _____ cook _____

   steam   bake   roast   boil   fry   ~~stir~~

8. Topic: _____ beach _____

   sunscreen lotion   ball   towel   sunglasses   swimming suit   ~~gloves~~

9. Topic: _____ (cat family) _____

   cat   lion   ~~wolf~~   leopard   tiger   panther

10. Topic: _____ types of houses _____

    palace   apartment   teepee   ~~kitchen~~   mansion   cottage

Discovering Topics of Paragraphs

What Is a Paragraph?

Here are two groups of sentences that look like paragraphs. Read them carefully. Are they paragraphs?

Example a:

In the Trobriand Islands, people do not celebrate birthdays. When a boy is about fourteen or fifteen, he moves out of his parents' house. Each canoe takes about eighteen months to make. Boys and girls may live together for periods of days, weeks, or months. Most islanders have no idea when they were born or how old they are. That way, they have a chance to find out if they are the right people for each other. When it is finally finished, it is named and special ceremonies are held to give it magic powers. This is also about the age that he begins to work on his own garden.

Is this a paragraph? _____

Why or why not? _____

Example b:

In the Trobriand Islands, the yam is both an important food plant and an important part of the culture. Every village has a "yam house" with a giant four-foot yam hanging from the ceiling. It represents wealth and well-being for the village, life and strength for the people. Villagers take great pride in their gardens, especially their yam plants. The yam harvest is one of the high points of the year and also the focus for many traditions. For example, the harvest is always carried out by women. When they are bringing the yams in from the garden all together, no man is supposed to meet them. Any man they meet will be chased, attacked, and treated as a fool.

Is this a paragraph? _____

Why or why not? _____

In a paragraph, all of the sentences are about the same thing; that is, they are all about the same *topic* and they make sense together. Using this definition, we can see that *Example a* is not a paragraph because the sentences are about many different topics. They describe many different aspects of life in the Trobriand Islands, and they do not make sense together. *Example b* is a paragraph because all the sentences are about the same topic. They are all about the importance of yams in the Trobriand Islands, so they make sense together.

Some of these groups of sentences are paragraphs and some are not. Read them carefully and answer the questions.

1.   Iceland is not a place for the ordinary tourist. The landscape, for example, is bare and strange—though many consider it beautiful in its own way. Then, too, the far northern climate is not ideal for tourism. The winter weather is extremely severe and the summers are short and cool, with constant strong winds. The remote location also means that many products have to be imported and so they are expensive. However, the few tourists who do put up with these difficulties are warmly welcomed by the Icelanders.

Is this a paragraph? _____ Y

If it is a paragraph, what is it about? _____

2.   For fewer tourists, lower prices, and more beautiful scenery, head for the Sagres Peninsula. The regional museum has a rich collection of costumes, weapons, and handicrafts. Buses will get you to most places, but for long trips, trains are cheaper and more comfortable. The Portuguese economy has expanded very rapidly in recent years, but it still has many problems. In the fifteenth century, Lisbon was a worldwide center of political power, religion, and culture.

Is this a paragraph? _____ N

If it is a paragraph, what is it about? _____

3.   The two peoples of Belgium—the Flemish and the Walloons—are divided by language, culture, and economics. Hotels in Brussels are expensive, so most young travelers stay in youth hostels or student hotels. In Antwerp, the home of Rubens, you can visit the house where he lived and worked. Throughout the centuries, Belgium has been the scene of many terrible battles between world powers. In many parts of the world, the Belgians are best known for their chocolate and their beer. Ships to England leave either from Oostende or from Zeebrugge.

Is this a paragraph? _____ N

If it is a paragraph, what is it about? _____

4.   To an outsider, Istanbul may at first seem like a Western city. The Western dress, the many new buildings, the traffic problems all make the city seem very modern. But there is another side to this great city—its rich past as the capital of the Ottoman Empire. In the narrow backstreets, the bazaars, and the mosques, this past seems very near and real. And the spectacular mosques are evidence of the city's important role in the history of Islam as well.

Is this a paragraph? _____ Y

If it is a paragraph, what is it about? _____

The Importance of Knowing the Topic

In the following paragraph, the writer does not mention the topic. Read the paragraph and talk about it with another student. Can you infer what it is about?

Some of us have done this hundreds of times—we sometimes think we could do it in our sleep. But if it's your first time, don't worry. It's really a very simple procedure. First, you sort everything into piles. It's better to separate things carefully at this point or you can cause real damage. Then when one pile is ready, let technology do the work. Be sure you follow the directions. And remember that it is better not to do too many things at once. Mistakes can be expensive. Once the first part is done, the next step depends on your equipment. You may be able to put technology to work again. Or you may have to use old-fashioned methods and take everything outside. In any case, it will eventually be time to make piles again and put everything where it belongs. And then you are done— for now. All too soon the time will come to repeat the whole procedure!

Topic: _____

It is difficult to understand what you are reading if you do not know what it is about! Even when there are no difficult words or grammar, you cannot make sense of the sentences if you do not know the topic.

The topic of the paragraph is *doing the laundry*. Knowing the topic is necessary in order to comprehend what you read.

Recognizing the Topic of a Paragraph

When you read a paragraph you should always ask yourself, "What is this about?" That question will lead you to the topic of the paragraph. In the following examples, decide on the topic of each paragraph. The topic should not be too specific—that is, it should cover the whole paragraph and not just a part of it. And the topic should not be too general— that is, it should cover only the sentences in the paragraph and not other possible ideas and sentences. Like a piece of clothing, the topic needs to fit the paragraph just right.

Example a:

What is this paragraph about? Read the paragraph and decide which topic is best.

People have always been interested in bees. This interest may have begun with the honey that bees make. In fact, archaeologists have found evidence that people have been eating honey for many thousands of years. In the more recent past, people were interested in the way bees made honey. They admired the way bees seemed to work so hard. Some languages even developed expressions about people working like bees. In English, for example, we talk about a "busy bee." Now scientists have a new reason to be interested in bees. They have discovered that bees are able to communicate with each other. Research has revealed some surprising facts about this, but there are still many mysteries.

Make a check (✔) after the best topic. Write "too specific" or "too general" after the other topics.

a. Expressions about bees in English _____

b. The story of bees _____

c. People's interest in bees _____

The best topic is *c, people's interest in bees.* It tells best what the paragraph is about. Choice *a, expressions about bees in English,* is too specific. This idea is only a part of the paragraph. Choice *b, the story of bees,* is too general. It includes many possible ideas that are not in the paragraph.

Example b:

What is this paragraph about? Read the paragraph and decide which topic is best.

Communication is also possible among bees through their sense of smell. A group of bees, called a colony, uses smell to protect itself from other bees. This is possible because all the bees in a colony have a common smell. This smell acts like a chemical signal. It warns the group of bees when a bee from a different colony is near. This way, bees from outside cannot enter and disturb a hive (the bee colony's home). If an outsider does try to enter, the bees of that colony will smell it and attack it.

Make a check (✔) after the best topic. Write "too specific" or "too general" after the other topics.

    a. The chemical signals of bees   _____

    b. How bees live   _____

    c. How bees communicate through smell   _____

The best topic is *c, how bees communicate through smell.* Choice *a* is too specific. Choice *b* is too general.

EXERCISE 2

Read each paragraph. Working with another student, decide which topic is the best. On the lines below each paragraph, make a check (✔) after that topic. Write "too specific" or "too general" after the other topics.

Elephants

1.   Elephants are the largest land animals in the world. Whales are the largest sea animals. These two huge animals may, in fact, come from the same biological family. Biologists now believe that the ancestors of elephants once lived in the sea, like whales. There is plenty of evidence to support this idea. For example, the shape of an elephant's head is similar to a whale's. Another similarity is in the fact that both animals are excellent swimmers. Some elephants have chosen to swim for food to islands up to 300 miles away. Like the whale, the elephant uses sounds to show anger or for other kinds of communication. Finally, both female elephants and female whales stay close to other females and help them when they give birth.

    a. How elephants are good swimmers   _____

    b. The largest animals in the world   _____

    c. How elephants and whales are alike   _____

2.   The elephant's trunk is not just a large nose or upper lip. It's an essential and unique feature that serves many purposes for this animal. For one, it is used to make many kinds of sounds. With its trunk, the elephant can communicate anger, fear, or

happiness. The trunk is also used as if it were a kind of hand. At the end of the trunk are two muscles shaped like fingers. These muscles can pick up food and water and carry them to the elephant's mouth. Elephants use their trunks to take dust baths, too, throwing the dust over their backs. If an elephant's trunk is seriously injured, the elephant may die. Without its trunk, it has great difficulty getting enough to eat.

a. The elephant's trunk   _____

b. The elephant's body   _____

c. The elephant's dust baths   _____

3.   The intelligence of the elephant is widely known. We say "the elephant never forgets" in honor of its excellent memory. Elephants are also surprisingly good at solving problems. An Indian farmer who kept elephants discovered this fact, to his misfortune. He had noticed that his elephants were eating his bananas at night. No fence could keep out the elephants, of course, so he decided to tie bells on them. Then he would hear them when they came to eat the bananas and he could chase them away. A few mornings later, however, the bananas were all gone, though he had heard nothing at night. When he checked the elephants, he found that they had played a trick on him. They had filled the bells with mud so they would not make any noise!

a. Facts about elephants   _____

b. How elephants get bananas   _____

c. The intelligence of elephants   _____

EXERCISE 3

Read each paragraph. Working with another student, decide which topic is the best. On the lines below each paragraph, make a check (✔) after that topic. Write "too specific" or "too general" after the other topics.

The Construction of Houses

1.   People usually build their houses out of the materials that are easily available to them. In some areas, most people build their homes out of wood. This is true in parts of North America and in Scandinavia. These areas have large forests, so wood is easy to get and inexpensive. In many other areas of Europe, there are few forests left. Stone and brick are cheaper, so most people build their houses of these materials. In tropical regions, houses are sometimes made from plants that grow there. For example, in parts of Africa or Asia, houses may be made out of bamboo. Finally, in the very coldest areas near the Arctic, people make their homes out of blocks of ice.

a. Materials used for houses   _____

b. The wooden houses of Scandinavia   _____

c. Houses around the world   _____

2.   The differences in climate throughout Europe have resulted in differences in the way houses are built. In hot countries, such as Spain, Greece, or Italy, the houses usually have small windows to keep out the heat. However, in the cooler northern countries, such as Sweden or Holland, people want to let in as much sunlight as possible, so the windows are usually larger. In the southern countries, the houses usually have some kind of outdoor living area—a balcony, terrace, or courtyard—where people can enjoy the cool breeze. In northern countries, on the other hand, houses usually do not have such areas. People in colder climates spend less time outdoors.

a. The architecture of houses   _____

b. Houses in hot and cold countries   _____

c. Houses with small windows   _____

3.   One of the most famous houses in the United States is Monticello. It was the home of Thomas Jefferson, the third president of the United States. Located on a hill near Charlottesville, Virginia, it has a beautiful view of the surrounding countryside. The house is famous, first of all, because it belonged to a president. It is also a fine example of early nineteenth-century American architecture. Jefferson designed it himself in a style he had admired in Italy. Many American buildings of that time, in fact, imitated European styles. But while most were just imitations, his Monticello is lovely in itself. Furthermore, the design combines a graceful style with a typical American concern for comfort and function.

a. The view from Monticello   _____

b. American architecture   _____

c. Reasons for Monticello's fame   _____

Stating the Topic of a Paragraph

Example:

What is the following paragraph about? Read the paragraph and then write the topic on the line below. Think carefully—the topic should not be too specific or too general.

In most industrialized countries, family patterns have changed in recent years. Families used to be large, and most mothers stayed home to take care of the children. They were usually entirely responsible for all the housework, too. Fathers did not often see the children, except to play with them on the weekends. Now that families are smaller and many women are working, this has changed somewhat. Fathers often help with the housework. More importantly, they can be much more involved in the lives of their children. They may feed and dress their children and take them to school in the mornings.

Topic: _____

The topic for this paragraph should include the idea of family patterns and the idea of change. There are a number of ways you could express this. Here are two possibilities: *How family patterns have changed* and *Recent changes in family patterns*. Other answers are also possible if they give the same ideas and are not too specific or too general. For example, *How fathers care for their children* is too specific, and *Families* is too general.

Read each paragraph. Working with another student, decide on a good topic and write it below the paragraph. Be sure your topic is not too general or too specific.

The Importance of Automobile Tires

1.   If you ever get a blowout while you are driving, you should know what to do. A blowout is a sudden flat tire. It can be a very frightening experience, especially if you are traveling at a high speed. If your car gets a blowout, the first thing to do is to hold very tightly to the steering wheel. You can easily lose control of the car if you do not have a good hold on the steering wheel. The next step is to get off the road. You must not try to stop or turn too quickly, however. After you check the traffic, you should move over to the side of the road and slow down gradually. Then you should turn on your flashing lights so other cars will see you.

Topic: _What to do when you have a tire blowout_

2.   Most automobile owners check the gas and oil in their cars regularly. However, they may forget to check something else that is just as important: the tires. Some experts say that about 28 percent of automobiles in the United States have tires that are in poor condition. Some are too worn and others have too much or too little air. Worn tires can lead to a flat tire or a blowout, and sometimes to serious accidents. Tires that are not filled with the correct amount of air can also cause accidents. Thus, it is a good idea to give a quick glance at your tires every time you get into your car. Every month you should check the air pressure more carefully and look closely at the surface of the tires. This way, you may avoid the unpleasant experience of a flat tire or a dangerous blowout.

Topic: _Why you should check your tires regularly_

3.   Tires are one part of the car that need a lot of attention. You need, of course, to check the amount of air in the tire and the amount of wear on the surface of the tire. But that is not enough. You should also bring your car regularly to the mechanic or tire specialist for some other work. First, the mechanic should rotate the tires after a certain number of miles. This means that the tires are removed and then put back on in a different position. The rear tires, for example, are usually moved to the front. The front tires are then moved to the rear and exchanged. That is, the tire that had been on the left front is now on the right rear and the tire that had been on the right front is now on the left rear. Changing the tires like this will prevent them from becoming too worn on one side. For this same reason, the mechanic should also balance the wheels. In balancing the wheels, each wheel is taken off and adjusted to make sure it goes around evenly.

Topic: _The importance of rotating and balancing your tires_

Read each paragraph. Working with another student, decide on a good topic and write it below the paragraph. Be sure your topic is not too general or too specific.

Health Dangers of Flying

1.   Pilots and flight attendants have long known that they become especially forgetful when they fly often with little rest. They lose their car keys, forget their room number at a hotel, or forget the names of people they have just met. People usually think of this loss of short-term memory as part of jet lag, the negative effects that many people feel after long flights. A scientist named Kwangwok Cho, who had to fly across the Atlantic several times in one month, noticed the same problem with his short-term memory. He decided to find out why people with jet lag become especially forgetful. To understand what was happening, Cho did brain scans of people with severe jet lag. He then compared them with brain scans of people without jet lag. In the people with jet lag, there were clear signs of damage to some brain cells. In fact, part of the brain had become smaller. This was what caused the difficulties with short-term memory.

Topic: _The effect of jet lag on the brain_

2.   For many people, sitting still for a long time is one of the worst things about flying. Now doctors are discovering that there are good reasons to be unhappy about sitting still on long flights. In fact, it is not good for you at all: The blood in your legs does not flow well and you are more likely to get a blood clot (a small lump) in your leg. The clot may cause swelling and pain in the leg because the blood cannot flow past it. More serious problems can develop if part of a clot breaks off and travels to the lung. In this case, there is even the risk of death. To avoid risk, doctors recommend moving around as much as possible during a flight. Of course, you cannot stand up often or walk continually around the plane. But you can help the blood flow in your body by doing special exercises at your seat. Many airline companies now include instructions for these exercises in their in-flight magazines.

Topic: _Why sitting still for a long time is not good for you_

3.   In the late 1990s, flight attendants around the world noticed a dramatic increase in "air rage." This is the official term for what happens when someone becomes extremely angry or upset on a plane. These people may become so dangerously violent that the plane has to land somewhere and unload the passengers. Air rage may be the result of several factors. The general worsening of travel conditions in recent years has led to crowded planes and frequent delays. At the same time, airlines have generally reduced the amount of seat space for each passenger, so people are more likely to feel stressed and aggressive. One other factor, however, has nothing to do with the airline industry. Flight attendants say that very often the people who become violent on planes have had too much alcohol to drink, either before the flight or on the plane.

Topic: _The reasons for an increase in air rage_

Topic Sentences

In most paragraphs, the author includes the topic in a topic sentence. This sentence often comes first, but sometimes it is found in the middle or at the end of the paragraph. Finding the topic sentence is important for comprehension. It tells you what the whole paragraph is about.

Example:

Andres Segovia was the first classical guitarist to become known worldwide. Born in Segovia in 1893, he changed the way people think about the guitar. Before the twentieth century, the guitar was not taken very seriously as a classical instrument. Most people thought that the guitar was suitable only for popular music or folk music. Few classical composers wrote music for the guitar, and it was never included in classical concerts. But Segovia changed all this. He believed in the guitar as a classical instrument, and he was a great musician. He used his genius to prove that the guitar could produce beautiful classical music.

Topic: *Andres Segovia*

Topic Sentence: *Andres Segovia was the first classical guitarist to become known worldwide.*

The rest of the sentences in the paragraph give details and explain the author's ideas about the topic.

EXERCISE 6

Each of the paragraphs below is missing the topic sentence. The missing sentences are listed at the end of the exercise (with one extra sentence). Working with another student, read the paragraphs and choose the sentence that fits each paragraph best. Write the letter for the sentence in the empty space.

Facts about Alaska

1. _____.
   The Russians were glad to get rid of this large piece of land so far from Moscow. Many Americans, however, were not happy about buying it. The sale was arranged by William Henry Seward, the American Secretary of State. When people talked about Alaska, they called it "Seward's Folly" or "Seward's Icebox." The price for Alaska was $7,200,000—or about two cents per acre. Though this was a bargain, many thought it was money thrown away. What would America ever do with such a cold land?

2. Do you know what "white out" means, or "ice fog"? These are terms that many Alaskans know well, though other Americans may not. _____
   _____.
   "White out," for example, happens when a very strong, cold wind blows the snow on the ground. The snow fills the air so that you lose all sense of direction. "Ice fog" occurs on very cold (−40°C, or −40°F) days. When the air is this cold, it cannot absorb any moisture, so the water in the air becomes a kind of frozen fog. This fog is very dangerous to drivers or aircraft.

3.   The Yukon River begins in Canada's Yukon Territory. Many other rivers flow into it as it runs from east to west across central Alaska. Some of the rivers are fed by melting glaciers. This gives the Yukon its strange whitish, or milky, color. The river generally freezes in October and melts again in May. Large ice dams sometimes form and cause large-scale flooding. As the Yukon nears the Bering Sea, it breaks into many smaller rivers, forming a delta. This fact makes it impossible for large ships to travel up the river. _____

_____ .

4.   The Alaskan Malamute was originally developed by the Eskimos as a sled dog.

_____

_____ . It is a strong dog, related to and somewhat resembling a wolf. A thick coat of fur protects it even in the coldest weather. The Eskimos use these dogs to pull sleds for them across the Arctic snow and ice. They are intelligent dogs and quickly learn to obey the signals of the sled driver. With their strength and loyalty, they have been known to save people's lives in the Arctic. In spite of their wolf ancestry, they are also extremely gentle and friendly. Their protective nature makes them good companions for children.

Missing topic sentences:

a. That is because Alaska has unique weather that requires special expressions.

b. These days it is popular both as a sled dog and as a family pet.

c. In 1868, the United States bought Alaska from Russia.

d. The Alaskan gold rush in the 1890s nearly doubled the population of the area.

e. The Yukon River's interesting characteristics make it one of Alaska's impressive natural features.

EXERCISE 7

Find the topic of each paragraph and write it below. Then underline the topic sentence. Remember, the topic sentence is not always the first sentence in the paragraph. Compare your work with that of another student. If your answers differ, decide whose is best and correct your work if necessary.

The Hawaiian Islands

1.   The Hawaiian Islands are located in the middle of the Pacific Ocean, far away from any other land. There are eight islands of various sizes, and while they differ from each other in some ways, they share many features. They all have a tropical climate, with temperatures of about 78°F (25.6°C) in the winter and 85°F (29.4°C) in the summer. Rain falls often, but not for long. The islands also share a natural beauty, with mountains and waterfalls, rain forests, and long, sweeping beaches. Their waters are filled with colorful fish, dolphins, and giant sea turtles.

Topic: _____

2.   Until modern times, birds and insects were the only kinds of animals living on the islands, with just a few exceptions. The exceptions were the monk seal (a sea mammal) and a kind of bat (a flying mammal). There were no other mammals until people arrived in about A.D. 500, bringing some animals with them for food. Pigs, for example, arrived this way. Other animals, such as mice, probably traveled to the Hawaiian islands hidden in their boats. The islands, in fact, have an interesting and unusual natural history.

Topic: _____

3.   Each of the islands also has features that are special and unique. For example, the Big Island (Hawaii) is the only one with active volcanoes. Both Mauna Loa and Kilauea on that island occasionally erupt, pouring out hot lava and smoke. The island of Oahu is the site of Honolulu, the modern capital of Hawaii. This island also has one of the world's most famous beaches, Waikiki Beach. And finally, the island of Maui is important to Hawaiians for its role in the history of the islands. In 1800, Kamehameha, the king of Hawaii, established his capital on Maui, where it remained until the early twentieth century.

Topic: _____

EXERCISE 8

Find the topic of each paragraph and write it below. Then underline the topic sentence. Compare your choices with another student. If your answers differ, decide whose is best and correct your work if necessary.

New Discoveries in Psychology

1.   Many people who are good at music are good at languages as well. That should not be surprising, since the study of music and the study of language have a lot in common. Both require you to have a "good ear"—the ability to hear the difference between various sounds. They also require you to reproduce sounds you have heard. Finally, when you learn music or language, you have to learn complex sets of rules. With language, the rules are about grammar and meaning. With music, the rules are about sounds and rhythm. Not surprisingly, researchers have discovered a scientific reason why people are good at music and languages. According to a study done in Germany, you use the same part of the brain for both subjects. This part of the brain is called Broca's area. Scientists have known for some time that it is connected to learning languages. Now they believe that it is also the part of the brain you use when you are learning music.

Topic: _____

2.   Some students become very anxious whenever they have to do a math problem or take a math test. Psychologists call this "math anxiety." Teachers used to think that this happened because the students were not very good at math. Now, however, researchers think that students who get math anxiety are not necessarily bad at math. There is a very different reason for their poor performance on math tests. New studies show that their feelings of anxiety prevent their brains from working well. One area of the brain that is especially affected is the working memory, which holds new information in your mind. This type of memory is essential for doing math problems. But why do students get math anxiety in the first place? That is another important question for teachers and researchers in education.

Topic: _____

3.   A new study has concluded that if you are a positive person with positive feelings, you will live longer. Dr. Debora D. Danner and other psychologists have looked at the writings of a group of 180 women. All of these women had written a short autobiography when they were in their early twenties. There were few negative feelings expressed in these autobiographies, since they were written by women in a religious organization for the director of the organization. However, there was still a wide range in levels of feeling. Some of the writing showed very few feelings at all, while others showed lots of positive feelings, such as happiness, interest, and love. The psychologists then looked at the histories of the women to see how long they lived afterward. The women who expressed the strongest positive feelings also lived the longest. In fact, they lived an average of ten and a half years longer than the women who showed few emotions.

Topic: _____

Understanding Main Ideas

What Is a Main Idea?

The main idea of a paragraph is a statement of the author's idea about the topic. A main idea statement is always a complete sentence that includes both the topic and the ideas that the author wishes to express about the topic.

Topic: Cats

Possible main idea statements about cats:

- Cats are usually very clean animals.
- Cats have very expressive faces.
- Cats are very adaptable animals.

Write three more main idea statements about cats:

- _____

- _____

- _____

Compare your main idea statements with those of another student. You probably have some different ideas. In fact, for every topic there are many possible main ideas. The choice of a main idea depends on what the author wants to say about the topic.

Choose one of these topics and write a main idea statement about it.

- My favorite food

- Growing older

- Travel

Compare your main idea statement with that of another student who wrote about the same topic. Why might they be different?

Finding the Main Idea

The topic sentence of a paragraph often includes both the topic and the main idea, but not always. Sometimes the main idea is expressed in another sentence or in several sentences in the paragraph. In the exercises that follow, some of the paragraphs have topic sentences that include the main idea and some do not.

Example a:

Read the following paragraph. Underline the topic sentence and write the topic on the line below.

When summer brings very hot weather, many people suffer more than they need to. There are a number of ways to make life more comfortable in the heat. For example, you can try to keep your home as cool as possible. It is best to close all the windows and curtains during the hottest part of the day. Then, when it is cooler in the evening, you can open them up again. Also, it is important to keep yourself cool by wearing loose, light clothes. Cotton is the best material for clothes in hot weather. And finally, you should try to stay calm and relaxed. You could even try a nap after lunch, like many people do who live in hot climates. This way you are more rested and ready to enjoy the cool evening hours.

Topic: _____

Is the main idea included in the topic sentence? _____yes_____

The topic is *ways to be comfortable in the heat*. The topic sentence is *There are a number of ways to make life more comfortable in the heat*. The topic sentence does include the main idea because in the paragraph the author writes about ways to be more comfortable in the heat.

Example b:

Read the following paragraph. Underline the topic sentence and write the topic on the line below.

In the 1950s, people thought television had a positive effect on family life. It brought the whole family together in one room. It also put an end to the usual family arguments, since everyone stayed quiet and watched TV. These days, however, psychologists think that watching television may not be so good for family life. They believe that it may be better for the family to have arguments sometimes, instead of being quiet all the time in front of the TV set. When the TV is on, in fact, there is usually little or no communication among the family members. Most of the communication that happens is one way: from the TV program to each individual.

Topic: _____

Is the main idea included in the topic sentence? _____

The topic is *television's effect on family life*. The topic sentence is *These days, however, psychologists think that watching television may not be so good for family life*. The topic sentence does not include the main idea because it does not include all of the author's ideas about this topic. The main idea is *Watching television is not good for family life because it prevents communication among family members*.

Read each paragraph and write the topic on the line below. Then read the paragraph again to find out what the author says about the topic. Circle the letter of the best main idea statement for each paragraph. Compare your work with that of another student.

The Aging Population in Industrialized Countries

1.   In many of the industrialized countries, the population is aging. That is, the average age of the population is older than it was twenty years ago. This fact has encouraged many businesses to develop products and services for older customers. In the medical industry, for example, new medicines and technologies are being developed especially for the health problems of older people. The tourist industry also offers services for the elderly, including special transportation and health services, and trips organized for groups of older people. And finally, there are many different kinds of products designed for the needs of the elderly. These include everything from shoes and shampoos to magazines and furniture.

Topic: _New products & services for the aging pop_

    a. The medical industry is developing new medicines and technology for the health problems of the elderly.

    b. In the industrialized countries, the average age of the population is older than it was twenty years ago.

    (c.) Because of the aging population, many businesses have developed products and services for older customers.

2.   Today, many elderly people in industrialized countries suffer from depression. In the past, most older people lived with or near other members of the family, and they usually had some responsibilities around the home. For example, older women could help take care of the children or prepare meals. Older men could help their sons at work or around the house. These days, married children often prefer to live on their own, sometimes far away from their parents. Thus, older people may be cut off from family ties. They may also feel cut off from the world around them. The many rapid changes that have taken place in technology, entertainment, and travel have led some older people to feel that they do not belong any more.

Topic: _Depression among the elderly_

    (a.) In the industrialized countries, there are several reasons why many elderly people suffer from depression.

    b. Older people used to live with other family members and helped take care of the children.

    c. Some elderly people may feel the world has changed too quickly for them.

3.   The industrialized countries today are all facing a similar economic problem: how to pay the pensions of retired people. The problem is basically the result of changes in the population. Thanks to improved health and medical care, more people are living to an advanced age. That means governments have to spend more on pensions. At the same time, the birth rate has gone down, so there are fewer young people working and paying taxes. Thus, the government receives less money for its pension funds. The situation has become even more serious in some countries because governments in the 1980s and 1990s encouraged people to retire at an early age. The aim was to create more jobs for young people, but governments also had to increase their spending on pensions.

Topic: _____the pensions of retired people_____

a. Because of early retirement, governments had to increase their spending on pensions.

b. Due to population changes, the industrialized countries' governments are having economic problems related to the pensions of retired people.

c. Thanks to improved health and medical care, more people are living to an advanced age.

EXERCISE 2

Some of the paragraphs in this exercise have topic sentences that include the main idea and some do not. Read each paragraph and write the topic on the line below. Then read the paragraph again to find out what the author says about the topic. Write the main idea on the lines below. Remember: The main idea must be a complete sentence! Compare your work with that of another student.

Modern Trends in Management

1.   The "idea box" is a useful concept in management. It was first introduced in the early twentieth century by Kodak in the United States and Michelin in France. The managers of these companies used idea boxes to collect suggestions from employees about improving production. Today, the idea box is not used much in the United States or Europe. However, it is used a lot in Japan. Japanese managers have found it to be a very valuable resource. Employees often know more than managers about the details of production. In the long run, their suggestions can make a real difference to the company. Employees who offer useful ideas may receive extra money in their paychecks.

Topic: _____idea box_____

Main Idea: _____idea box useful for Japan mgt & ee_____

_____

2.   In a recent study of 1,500 business managers in the United States, interviewers asked all kinds of questions about the managers' habits and opinions regarding their working hours. The researchers learned that only 33 percent of the managers worked 40–45 hours a week. The majority of them (57 percent) worked from 46–60 hours and 6 percent worked over 60 hours. Only 2 percent of the managers said they felt satisfied and had enough time to do everything. The rest of the managers felt they did not have enough time for their families or their hobbies. In general, the researchers found that managers in the United States are not happy with their working schedules.

Topic: _____ Study of American mgrs _____

Main Idea: _____ ~ showed they are not happy _____
_____ w/ their working schedules _____

3.   At present, some managers spend much of their working time at home, thanks to modern technology and telecommunication. This is especially true for those who work a lot on computers. They can send their work to the company by fax or by direct computer connections. Managers can keep in touch with their staff through e-mail as well. There are many advantages to working at home, including more flexible hours and better productivity. "Home managers" also save time and money that they would have spent on transportation, business clothes, and lunches.

Topic: _____ Working at home _____

Main Idea: _____ ~ has many advantages for mgr _____
_____ & companies _____

EXERCISE 3

Read each paragraph and write the topic on the line below. Then read the paragraph again to find out what the author says about the topic. Write the main idea on the lines below. Remember: The main idea must be a complete sentence! Compare your work with that of another student.

Panda Bears in China

1.   The giant panda bear is a favorite of children and animal lovers throughout the world. For many people, it also is symbolic of the sad situation for many other kinds of animals. Though so well known and loved, the panda is slowly dying out. At present, there are only about 1,230 wild pandas left in the world. They all live in China, in the forests of the Sichuan and Shaanxi provinces. Pandas used to be common in other areas. However, as the human population increased and the forests shrank, panda territory gradually disappeared. And so did the pandas. Now the Chinese government has created a number of "panda reserves" to protect the pandas. Within these reserves, human settlement and tree cutting will be limited.

Topic: _____ Giant Panda _____

Main Idea: _____ ~ is slowly dying out in China _____

2.   For the whole first year of its life, the panda bear is completely dependent on its mother. The newborn panda is a tiny, helpless little creature. At birth, it looks like a little pink pig, and its eyes remain closed for three to four weeks. Pandas develop fairly slowly, compared to most animals. The babies are completely dependent on their mothers for a long time. In fact, they don't even begin to walk until they are about five months old. The only food they eat for at least a year is their mother's milk. That doesn't stop them from growing, however. Pandas may weigh over fifty-five pounds (twenty-five kilograms) by the time they are a year old.

Topic: _____ Panda 1st year of life _____

Main Idea: _____ completely dependent on mother _____

3.   Chinese scientists recently had a chance to study a wild female panda bear with a newborn baby. She was a very loving mother. For twenty-five days, she never left her baby, not even to find something to eat! She would not let any other panda bears come near. She licked the baby constantly to keep it clean. Any smell might attract natural enemies that would try to eat the little panda. The mother held her baby in her front paws much the way a human does. When it cried, she rocked it back and forth and gave it little comforting pats. The mother continued to care for the young bear for over two years. By that time, the panda no longer needed its mother for food, but it stayed with her and learned about the ways of the forest. Then, after two and a half years, the mother chased the young bear away. It was time for her to have a new baby, and it was time for the young panda to be independent.

Topic: _____ mother panda _____

Main Idea: _____ loving & careful mother _____

Read each paragraph and write the topic on the line below. Then read the paragraph again to find out what the author says about the topic. Write the main idea on the lines below. Remember: The main idea must be a complete sentence! Compare your work with that of another student.

The *Exxon Valdez* Oil Spill

1.   On March 24, 1989, disaster struck in Prince William Sound on the Alaska coast. An enormous ship called the *Exxon Valdez* was carrying about 50 million gallons of petroleum from the Alaskan oil fields. In Prince William Sound, the captain ran the ship aground, the ship's tanks broke open, and about 10.8 million gallons of petroleum poured out. It took three years and over 10,000 workers to clean up the oil. In the court case about the accident, the judges decided that the Exxon Shipping Company was responsible and that it had to pay $900 million in damages. Even that large sum was not enough to pay for cleaning up the Sound. The total cost of all the workers, equipment, and research for the cleanup effort was about $2.5 billion.

Topic: _____

Main Idea: _____

_____

2.   A tourist passing through Prince William Sound today probably would see no sign of the 1989 oil spill. The coast is once more a spectacular, wild place with clean water and beaches. However, to a more expert eye, the consequences of the oil spill are still visible. For one thing, the beaches are even cleaner than normal. The workers used hot water to clean oil off the rocks and sand. But in the process they also killed many kinds of marine plants. Rockweed, for example, is a brown plant that grows on rocks and in shallow water. Before the cleanup, it was very common along that coast, but afterward it almost completely disappeared. Another difference is the decrease in the bird population. Over a half million birds died as a direct result of the oil spill. Certain kinds of ducks and ocean birds were especially unfortunate. Researchers guess that their populations declined by up to 80 percent.

Topic: _____

Main Idea: _____

_____

3.   As scientists study the long-term effects of the *Valdez* oil spill, they are discovering that many kinds of sea animals have suffered. The harbor seal (a marine mammal) is one example. At first, scientists hoped that the seals would stay away from the areas where there was oil. But instead, the seals swam right through the oil and came out on oily beaches. Scientists noted that these seals seemed sick, and in fact many disappeared. At an earlier counting in 1975, there were about 13,000 harbor seals in Prince William Sound. After the spill, there were only about 2,500. Research on the bodies of dead seals showed that they suffered some brain damage. This may have caused the seals to become confused and drown. The oil also seems to have affected the ability of female seals to have healthy babies. In the year after the oil spill, there were many more deaths than usual among baby seals.

Topic: _____

Main Idea: _____

_____

EXERCISE 5

Read each paragraph and write the topic on the line below. Then read the paragraph again to find out what the author says about the topic. Write the main idea on the lines below. Remember: The main idea must be a complete sentence! Compare your work with that of another student.

Errors in Geography

1.   What happens when you ask someone to draw a map of the world? The results can be very interesting. Few people, in fact, have a very accurate idea of what the world looks like. You might expect some errors in the positions of countries. After all, this is a task that requires a certain skill with a pencil and a good memory. But many people do not even know the relative size of continents! They tend to enlarge them or make them smaller, according to their point of view. For this reason, the home continent is often drawn too large. A Brazilian, for example, tends to enlarge the continent of South America, while a Vietnamese enlarges Asia.

Topic: _____

Main Idea: _____

_____

2.   Another common error in hand-drawn maps is the tendency to make Europe too large and Africa too small. People from all parts of the world tend to draw the world this way, including the Africans! There are several factors that may be involved here. One factor may be the influence of old maps made with the "Mercator projection." This technique for drawing maps makes areas nearer the North Pole, including Europe, seem extra large. Other areas in the middle, such as Africa, seem smaller than in reality. However, the Mercator maps also enlarge Greenland and Canada, and people usually do not make mistakes about their size. Thus, a better explanation must lie in people's ideas about the relative importance of the continents. The size of Europe tends to be exaggerated because of its importance in people's minds. Similarly, Africa becomes smaller because people feel it is unimportant.

Topic: _____

Main Idea: _____

_____

3.   Ignorance about the African continent has led to some enormous errors in mapmaking. One of the errors now seems quite incredible. In the late eighteenth century, a European explorer reported seeing mountains in southern Mali. From that report, a mapmaker drew in a long line of mountains. As a result, these "Kong Mountains," as he called them, were drawn on almost all maps of Africa in the nineteenth century. They seemed to be an important feature of the continental geography. European politicians and traders made decisions based on their belief in the existence of these mountains. Finally, in the late 1880s, a French explorer proved that there were no mountains in that part of Africa. Following that discovery, the "Kong Mountains" disappeared from maps of Africa.

Topic: _____

Main Idea: _____

_____

Read each paragraph and write the topic on the line below. Then read the paragraph again to find out what the author says about the topic. Write the main idea on the lines below. Remember: The main idea must be a complete sentence! Compare your work with that of another student.

Hans Christian Andersen

1. The name of Hans Christian Andersen is known around the world. So are the titles of many of his fairy tales, such as "The Ugly Duckling" and "The Little Mermaid." Little is known, however, about the early years of the man who wrote these stories. Born in 1805, in Odense, Denmark, Andersen described his childhood in romantic terms. In reality, he was lonely and unhappy as a child, and desperately poor. His father, a shoemaker, died when he was eleven, and his mother, a washerwoman, was an alcoholic. In spite of these difficult beginnings, Andersen believed that he was special and that he deserved a better life. At the age of fourteen, he packed up his few things and went to Copenhagen to seek his fortune as a writer.

Topic: _____

Main Idea: _____

_____

2. In Copenhagen, Andersen worked hard to become a successful writer. He introduced himself to the best-known writers of his day and to others he thought might help him. He was a strange-looking boy: tall, thin, and awkward, with small eyes, a large nose, and a sad expression. Some people felt sorry for him. Others were impressed by his desperate desire to become a great writer. He got a job at the Royal Theatre and, at the same time, he went back to school, since he had never finished school in Odense. Then, at the age of twenty-one, he published a poem that became very popular. That first taste of public attention made him want more. For the rest of his life, he wrote and wrote without stopping, always hoping to become famous. In all, he wrote thirty-six works for theater, six travel books, six novels, hundreds of poems, and about 170 stories and fairy tales. Some of his novels and plays enjoyed brief success, but the critics often did not like them. Only the fairy tales were immediately recognized as entirely original works of art.

Topic: _____

Main Idea: _____

_____

3.   The first fairy tales that Andersen wrote were published in a cheap little book that he did not take very seriously. This may be the reason why they are so different from his other works. For once, he was not trying to be a great writer. He simply wrote the stories as they came to him. Some were based on folktales he had heard as a child, while others were his own inventions. These stories had the brilliant characters, the action, and the suspense that children love. But what made them special was their informal style, which was completely new at that time. In fact, they were written as though he was telling them at the moment in a voice that was chatty and direct, humorous sometimes and sometimes heartbreaking. By the time Andersen died in 1875, he had indeed become a great writer, loved by children in many countries as well as by famous people and even kings and queens.

Topic: _____

Main Idea: _____

_____

Identifying Patterns of Organization

Try to memorize all of the groups of numbers below. After sixty seconds, your teacher will tell you to turn the page and write the numbers from memory.

a.	15	3	6	9	12
b.	2	1	17	1	9
c.	1	4	7	10	13
d.	19	2	5	6	11
e.	12	4	6	8	10

Try to remember the groups of numbers. Do not look back. Write the numbers here.

a. _____

b. _____

c. _____

d. _____

e. _____

After you have written as many of the numbers as you can remember, look back and check your work.

Did you remember all of the groups of numbers?

Which groups were the easiest to remember?

Did any of the groups have a pattern?

What made the other groups difficult to memorize?

The Importance of Patterns

Since the beginning of history, people have looked for patterns in the world around them. They looked at the mountains and saw the outlines of people's faces. They looked at the stars and saw animals and gods.

Scientists say that it is human nature to look for patterns in what you see. Your brain is always trying to make sense of the world around you. Your brain tries to fit everything into some kind of recognizable shape or pattern that has meaning for you. A pattern makes it easier for you to understand and remember information.

In this chapter, you will learn to recognize five basic patterns that writers often use in developing their ideas in English. Finding the pattern helps you find the main idea and remember the important details. Thus, looking for patterns is a way to improve your comprehension while reading.

Five Patterns of Organization in English

- **List of related ideas or examples**
  In this pattern, the writer states the main idea in the form of a generalization and gives a list of details to support that general statement.

- **Sequence**
  In this pattern, the writer explains the main idea with a series of events or steps that follow one after the other in time order.

- **Comparison/Contrast**
  In this pattern, the writer's main idea is a general statement about two things that are similar and/or different. Specific details about similarities and/or differences are given.

- **Cause/Effect**
  In this pattern, the writer's main idea is that one event or action caused another event or action.

- **Problem/Solution**
  In this pattern, the writer's main idea is a statement of a problem and how it was solved.

Patterns and Their Signal Words

Just as a busy street has signals to guide drivers, writers use signal words to guide the reader. In each pattern, signal words can help you identify the pattern, the main idea, and the important details.

Listing pattern

These are the some of the commonly used signal words for the listing pattern (many others are possible):

a few	one	the main	and
several	another	first	also
numerous	other(s)	second	too
many	for example	third	in addition
a variety of	for instance	last	besides

Example:

In the following paragraph, the signal words are underlined. Working with another student, write the main idea on the lines below. Then write the appropriate detail next to each signal word.

In the past few years, scientists have found several new fuels to replace gasoline for automobiles. <u>One of these</u> fuels is methanol, a form of wood alcohol. It can be used in many cars in almost the same way that gasoline is used. Natural gas is <u>another</u> alternative fuel for cars. However, cars that burn this fuel must be equipped with special tanks of natural gas. <u>A third</u> alternative is electricity. Cars fueled by electricity have no engine at all, though they do have to carry large batteries. <u>A fourth</u> new energy source, and perhaps the most promising, is the hydrogen fuel cell. Hydrogen is available in large quantities, and the fuel cell's only emission is a small amount of water.

Main Idea: _____

_____

Signal Words	Details
One of these	_methanol_____
another	_____
A third	_____
A fourth	_____

The main idea statement for the paragraph in this example is *Scientists have found several new fuels to replace gasoline for automobiles*. The writer used a signal word to point to each of the details—the four new fuels that are mentioned: *methanol, natural gas, electricity,* and *hydrogen fuel cell*.

Read each paragraph and underline the listing signal words. On the lines below, write the main idea, the signal words, and the details. Compare your work with that of another student.

Electronic Mail

1. E-mail (electronic mail) uses computers for communication. It has several important advantages over phones and regular mail. The main advantage of e-mail is that it takes very little time to send and receive messages. From your computer, you can contact people far away (or in the next office). Seconds later, they have your message. If they are at their computer, you can get a response instantly, too. Another reason people like to use e-mail is that for just a few cents you can send a message to someone in another part of the world. In addition, you don't have to worry about the time difference, and your friends or colleagues can send a response at their convenience. Last, e-mail allows you to send a single message to many people at the same time.

Main Idea: _____

_____

Signal Words   **Details**

_____   _____

_____   _____

_____   _____

_____   _____

2. Communicating by e-mail is becoming increasingly popular for many reasons. First, it is a popular way to send messages among people who do not like to use the telephone. Second, it is useful for sending suggestions or requests. The person who receives them has time to think about a response. Also, e-mail messages always look the same, no matter who sends them. This means you don't have to worry about the quality of your letter paper or your handwriting. Furthermore, e-mail messages are uniform. They give no clues to the sender's age, gender, race, or physical condition. In addition, they do not give away the sender's feelings or emotional condition.

Main Idea: _____

_____

Signal Words   **Details**

_____   _____

_____   _____

_____   _____

_____   _____

3.   An advertising executive recently described the many ways that e-mail helps her do her job. First of all, of course, she uses e-mail for communicating with her employees, clients, and business partners. E-mail even allows her to send samples of photographs or illustrations to a client, just by attaching them to an e-mail message. In addition, her employees no longer have to do all of their work in the office. They work at home and send their work to her attached to an e-mail message. And when the advertising company wants to contact a large number of clients, a single e-mail message is sent to them all with the click of a mouse.

Main Idea: _____

_____

Signal Words	Details
_____	_____
_____	_____
_____	_____

EXERCISE 2

Now reread some paragraphs from previous units. This time, notice that the author has used a listing pattern. On the lines below, write the main idea, the signal words, and the details. Compare your work with that of another student.

Locate these paragraphs:

1. Unit 7, Exercise 1, paragraph 1 (page 85)

    Main Idea: _____

    _____

Signal Words	Details
_____	_____
_____	_____
_____	_____

2. Unit 8, Example a (page 97)

    Main Idea: _____

    _____

Signal Words	Details
_____	_____
_____	_____
_____	_____

On a separate sheet of paper, write a paragraph that uses the listing pattern and begins with one of the main idea statements below. Complete the paragraph with sentences that provide supporting details. To guide your reader, use listing signal words for each detail.

Main Idea Statements:

1. Working as a pilot of a jet plane is dangerous for several reasons.

2. In the late twentieth century, there were several important new developments in science and technology.

3. The environment is in danger in many ways.

4. My hometown has many wonderful features.

5. Grandmothers are important to the family for many reasons.

After you have written your paragraph, ask another student to read it. Find out if your ideas were clear and interesting. Then rewrite the paragraph to include any suggestions from your partner.

Sequence pattern

Two kinds of materials are organized in a sequence pattern:

- Events in time order (history, biography)

- Steps in a process (a scientific experiment, directions for making something)

The important point is that things happen in a certain order, and the writer uses signal words to point to events or steps. Sequence signal words include

before	first	at that time	while	at last
during	at first	meanwhile	since	finally
after	in the beginning	in the meantime	later	soon

Other signal words are dates, years, ages, times of day, seasons, and plain numbers.

In the following paragraphs, the signal words are underlined. Working with another student, write the main idea on the lines below. Then write the events or steps next to the appropriate signal word on the lines below.

Example a:

Chronological Order (time)

Franklin D. Roosevelt, the thirty-second president of the United States, served his country for most of his life. He was the only president to be elected four times. He was born in Hyde Park, New York, on <u>January 30, 1882</u>, and he began his studies at Harvard in <u>1903</u>. In <u>1905</u>, he married Eleanor Roosevelt, a distant cousin. <u>During</u> their marriage they had six children. <u>After</u> serving in the New York State Senate, Mr. Roosevelt worked in Washington as Secretary of the Navy until <u>1921</u>. <u>At that time</u>, he became very ill with polio and lost the use of his legs. <u>In 1928</u>, Mr. Roosevelt ran for governor of New York.

<u>After</u> serving two terms as governor, he was elected to the presidency <u>in 1933</u>. President Roosevelt died in office on <u>April 12, 1945</u>.

Main Idea: _____

_____

Signal Words	Events
January 30, 1882	*He was born in Hyde Park, New York.*
1903	
1905	
During	
After	
1921	
At that time	
In 1928	
After	
in 1933	
April 12, 1945	

Example b:

Steps in a Process

Using a digital camera and a computer is an easy and enjoyable way to get good photographs. <u>First</u>, you must install the computer program that is sold with the camera so it will be ready to use. <u>Then</u> take some pictures. <u>After that</u>, connect your camera to the computer using the cables provided with the camera. <u>Next</u>, open the program on the computer and save the pictures on the hard drive or a floppy disk. <u>At this point</u>, you can edit them as desired, using the photo editing tools on the program. You can make them lighter or darker, for example, or you can change the size. <u>Then</u> be sure to save the edited photos, and <u>finally</u>, you are ready to print them.

Main Idea: _____

_____

Signal Words	Steps
First	*install the computer program*
Then	
After that	
Next	
At this point	
Then	
finally	

Read each paragraph and underline the sequence signal words. On the lines below, write the main idea, the signal words, and the events. Compare your work with that of another student.

Famous African-Americans

1.　　As Maya Angelou, an African-American author, was growing up, she learned about abuse and hate, but also about love and support. She was born in 1929 in Long Beach, California, and her parents separated three years later. When she was only eight years old, Maya was abused by her mother's boyfriend. Then she and her brother went to live with her grandmother, who filled her life with love. During her youth, she also discovered her love of literature. In 1945, Maya graduated from a high school in San Francisco and a few months later, she had a baby son, who became the center of her life. In later years, Maya included all of these experiences in her novels, plays, and poems. She has received many honors as a writer. But perhaps her greatest honor came in 1993, when she was invited to write the official poem for the inauguration of President Bill Clinton.

Main Idea: _____

_____

Signal Words	**Events**
_____	_____
_____	_____
_____	_____
_____	_____
_____	_____
_____	_____
_____	_____
_____	_____

2.　　Spike Lee, an African-American film director, is one of the most noted people in his field. He was born in Atlanta, Georgia, in 1957; Spike's middle-class family moved to Brooklyn, New York, when he was two years old. His father, jazz musician Bill Lee, and his mother, Jackie, an art teacher, had five children. The Lees provided a loving and stable home for their family. Spike's interest in movies began as a youngster. After graduating from Morehouse College in Atlanta, he studied filmmaking at New York University. Soon after that, he made his first feature film, *She's Gotta Have It,* with a budget of only $200,000. Since the success of that movie, Lee has written, produced, and directed more than fifteen films. All of them are extremely controversial and extraordinarily popular with both black and white audiences.

Main Idea: _____

_____

Signal Words   **Events**

_____   _____

_____   _____

_____   _____

_____   _____

_____   _____

                        _____

EXERCISE 5

Read this passage and underline the sequence signal words. Then turn the page and try to remember the steps in the process of making a submarine sandwich.

Hot Subs for Lunch

The name may be different in other parts of the world. But in Boston, they are known as "subs," or submarine sandwiches. Their name is due to their shape, long and narrow like a submarine. A sub sandwich is one of the most popular lunch items in town.

The best way to find out about subs is to go to a sub shop. There, these delicious treats are a specialty. You will find huge ovens right behind the counter, because a real sub is served hot.

You wait in line until it is your turn to place your order. The sub sandwich maker usually begins by asking, "What kind of sub do you want?" You might answer, "Large Italian," and the expert goes to work.

First, he takes a large, long bread roll from a plastic bag under the counter. He slices it lengthwise and puts in layers of meat and cheese. For the Italian sub, he'd include Genoa salami, mortadella sausage, other cold meats, and Provolone cheese.

Next, leaving the sandwich open, the sandwich chef places it on a metal tray and slides it into the hot oven. He bakes it until the meat is warm and the roll is toasty. When the cheese has melted a bit, he knows it's time to take it out. Then he calls out, "What do you want on your large Italian?"

When you reply, "Everything," he adds mayonnaise, salt, pepper, olive oil, and a sprinkling of oregano. But that is not all. He also puts in lots of chopped pickles, onions, and hot peppers. Then he tops it off with sliced tomatoes and crunchy chopped iceberg lettuce.

Finally, taking the sandwich in his hand, the sandwich maker folds the two sides together. He carefully cuts it in half and wraps the finished product in waxed paper.

"For here or to go?" he asks. No matter where you eat it, you can be sure that you will enjoy lunch that day!

What are the steps in the process of making a submarine sandwich? They are listed below, but they are out of order. On the lines below, number the steps in the correct order. Do not look back. Then, working with another student, explain how to make a sub sandwich. Remember to use sequence signal words.

____3____ a. He piles sliced meat and cheese on it.

____7____ b. He adds mayonnaise, salt, pepper, and lots more.

____4____ c. He places it on a metal tray.

____9____ d. He wraps it in waxed paper.

____8____ e. He folds the two sides together.

____1____ f. He takes a large, long bread roll from a plastic bag.

____2____ g. He slices the roll in half lengthwise.

____10___ h. He asks, "For here or to go?"

____6____ i. He calls out, "What do you want on your large Italian?"

____5____ j. He allows it to bake until the meat is warm.

EXERCISE 6

Now reread some paragraphs from previous units. This time, notice that the author has used a sequence pattern. On the lines below, write the main idea, the signal words, and the steps or events. Compare your work with that of another student.

Locate these paragraphs:

1. Unit 7, Exercise 4, paragraph 1 (page 90)

   Main Idea: _____

   _____

Signal Words	*Steps*
_____	_____
_____	_____
_____	_____
_____	_____

2. Unit 8, Exercise 6, paragraph 1 (page 105)

   Main Idea: _____

   _____

Signal Words	*Events*
_____	_____
_____	_____
_____	_____
_____	_____

On a separate sheet of paper, write a paragraph that uses the sequence pattern and begins with one of the main idea statements below. Complete the paragraph with sentences describing events or steps. To guide your reader, use sequence signal words for each event or step.

Main Idea Statements:

1. It's easy to make a cup of tea.

2. A trip to another country requires a lot of planning.

3. Learning how to play _____ is a long process. (Add the name of a sport.)

4. My daily schedule is busy and complicated.

5. _____'s musical career began at a very young age. (Add the name of a famous musician.)

After you have written your paragraph, ask another student to read it. Find out if your ideas were clear and interesting. Then rewrite the paragraph to include any suggestions from your partner.

Comparison/Contrast pattern

This pattern is used when the writer wants to explain similarities or differences between two things.

- In a *comparison,* the writer may explain similarities OR similarities and differences.

- In a *contrast,* the writer explains only differences.

Signal words for similarity:

also	as	both	in common
in the same way	like	same	similarly

Signal words for difference:

although	while	different from	more than
however	rather	conversely	less than
but	instead	in contrast	earlier than
yet	unlike	on the other hand	later than

Comparative forms of adjectives and adverbs are also used to signal differences (*older, faster*).

In some passages, you may find that there are two signal words for the same detail. That's because a writer sometimes uses two signal words to make the sentence flow more smoothly.

In the following paragraphs, the comparison/contrast signal words are underlined. Working with another student, write the main idea on the lines below. Then write the appropriate detail next to each signal word.

Example a:

Comparison (Similarities and Differences)

Both New York City and Paris depend on vast subway lines to transport their millions of commuters. In both cities, the subways are often crowded, especially at rush hours. Another likeness is the terrible noise level in the trains. A further similarity is that the two subway systems both cover a wide area at little expense for commuters. However, the differences between the two are quite striking. While subway stations in New York range from plain to ugly, Paris stations are generally attractive. Many of the French stations are filled with works of art. In Paris, the subway trains are clean and they run every few minutes. On the other hand, New York's trains can sometimes be less clean and reliable.

Does this paragraph include similarities, differences, or both? ___Both___

Main Idea: _____

_____

Signal Words	Details
Both	*depend on subways to transport commuters*
both	
Another likeness	
A further similarity	
However	
While	*New York stations are ugly/Paris stations are attractive*
On the other hand	

Example b:

Comparison (Similarities)

The Ukrainian and Japanese cultures are generally very different, but they do have one thing in common. They like to eat pastries filled with meat. The Ukrainian pastries are called *pilmeni* and the Japanese pastries are called *gyoza,* but they are remarkably similar. Both are made of pieces of flat pastry folded around a spicy meat filling. In both countries, people usually eat their pastries with sauce. The Ukrainians use sour cream and the Japanese use soy sauce.

Main Idea: _____

_____

Does this paragraph include similarities, differences, or both? _____

Signal Words	Details
in common	_____
similar	_____
Both	_____
both	_____

Example c:

Contrast (Differences)

When the first baby arrives in a household, everything changes. In the past, the parents needed an alarm clock in the morning, <u>but</u> now the baby decides when they should wake up. Formerly, the parents spent their evenings watching TV or reading, <u>but</u> now all their free time is spent admiring their infant. <u>In contrast</u> to pre-baby days, their life is more carefully planned. <u>While</u> they used to go out to see friends whenever they wanted to, that is no longer possible. If they want to go out without the baby, they must arrange for a babysitter. <u>Unlike</u> the neat and tidy rooms of the past, these days their apartment is full of baby things. Their friends have even noticed a <u>difference</u> in the topic of conversation: It's always about the baby!

Main Idea: _____

_____

Does this paragraph include similarities, differences, or both? _____

Signal Words	Details
but	*in the past, needed alarm clock/now, baby wakes them*
but	_____
In contrast	_____
While	_____
Unlike	_____
difference	_____

EXERCISE 8

Read each paragraph and underline the comparison/contrast signal words. On the lines below, write the main idea, the signal words, and the details. Compare your work with that of another student.

Ideas about Education

1. High school graduates are sometimes nervous about attending college because they fear that everything will be different. In fact, there are some important similarities between college and high school. <u>In both places</u>, academic success depends on being a responsible student. This means attending classes regularly, doing your homework, and

studying new materials carefully. The social situation in college is also like high school. If you had friends in high school, chances are you will have friends in college, too. The activities in college also closely resemble the activities in high school. Musical groups, sports teams, special interest clubs, and other activities are found in both institutions.

Main Idea: _____

_____

Does this paragraph include similarities, differences, or both? _____

Signal Words   **Details**

_____   _____

_____   _____

_____   _____

_____   _____

2.   The University of Bologna in northern Italy is different from most North American universities. One major difference is its age. Founded in the tenth century, it is the oldest university in Europe. Its ancient halls give students an appreciation of history. North American universities, on the other hand, are all relatively new, and students are generally surrounded by more modern buildings. Another difference is the campus. The buildings that make up the University of Bologna are scattered around the center of the city. There is no campus or special university area, as there usually is at North American universities. Unlike the North American university campus, there are no trees or open spaces for students to meet in near this old Italian institution. Instead, students meet on the streets, in cafés, and in the courtyards of the historic buildings.

Main Idea: _____

_____

Does this paragraph include similarities, differences, or both? _____

Signal Words   **Details**

_____   _____

_____   _____

_____   _____

_____   _____

3.   In Russia, there has always been a strong tradition of learning foreign languages. This led to the development of specialized foreign-language schools. These schools teach the same subjects as all other Russian public schools. However, unlike most public schools, many of the subjects are taught in French, German, or English at the foreign-language schools. The students are different, too. Unlike the regular Russian-language schools, students must be selected to attend specialized schools. Quite often

these students come from families with higher levels of education. The greatest difference lies in the language abilities of the students. Students in specialized language schools learn to express themselves fluently in a foreign language.

Main Idea: _____

_____

Does this paragraph include similarities, differences, or both? _____

Signal Words   **Details**

_____   _____

_____   _____

_____   _____

_____   _____

_____   _____

EXERCISE 9

Now reread some paragraphs from previous units. This time, notice that the author has used a comparison/contrast pattern. On the lines below, write the main idea, the signal words, and the details. Compare your work with that of another student.

Locate these paragraphs:

1. Unit 7, Exercise 2, paragraph 1 (page 87)

    Main Idea: _____

    _____

    Does this paragraph include similarities, differences, or both? _____

    Signal Words   **Details**

    _____   _____

    _____   _____

    _____   _____

    _____   _____

    _____   _____

2. Unit 7, Exercise 3, paragraph 2 (page 89)

    Main Idea: _____

    _____

    Does this paragraph include similarities, differences, or both? _____

    Signal Words   **Details**

    _____   _____

    _____   _____

    _____   _____

On a separate sheet of paper, write a paragraph that uses a comparison/contrast pattern and is about one of the following topics. Your main idea statement should let your reader know whether you are writing about similarities, differences, or both. Complete the paragraph with sentences that give details to support the main idea. Use signal words to guide your reader.

Topics:

1. The city you live in and another city

2. Movies and real life

3. Being a student and being a full-time worker

4. Male friends and female friends

5. Business management in your country and another country

After you have written your paragraph, ask another student to read it. Find out if your ideas were clear and interesting. Then rewrite the paragraph to include any suggestions from your partner.

Cause/Effect pattern

Identifying Causes and Effects

Causes and effects are part of our daily lives. Therefore, this pattern is used often by writers of history books, science texts, and novels. It is important to recognize the cause/effect pattern when you read, but it is sometimes more complicated than some of the other patterns.

Example: What happened first? Next?

Steve forgot his umbrella this morning.

Steve got very wet from the rain.

Steve forgot his umbrella first. Then he got wet from the rain. This is shown in the following diagram:

$$\text{forgot umbrella} \xrightarrow{\hspace{2cm}} \text{got wet from the rain}$$
$$\text{(cause)} \quad \text{(time passes)} \quad \text{(effect)}$$

However, a cause/effect sentence is not always written with the cause first!

   a. <u>Because</u> Steve forgot his umbrella, he got wet from the rain.
               (cause)   (effect)

   b. Steve got wet from the rain <u>because</u> he forgot his umbrella.
      (effect)   (cause)

In both sentences, *because* is the signal word. It stays with the part of the sentence that tells the cause, even if the cause comes after the effect in the sentence. In order to understand a cause/effect pattern, always ask, "What happened first?" Then you will know the cause.

A. *Study the following pairs of words and phrases. In each pair, which comes first in time? Which causes which? Working with another student, draw an arrow from the cause to the effect in each pair.*

Example:

viruses ——————————→ infectious diseases

1. AIDS ←——— HIV
2. epidemics ←——— bacteria
3. coughs ←——— colds and flu
4. improperly stored food ——→ food poisoning
5. slow infant development ←— poor nutrition
6. skin cancer ←——— too much exposure to the sun
7. swimming in pools ——→ ear infection
8. heart trouble ←——— diet high in fat
9. lung cancer ←——— cigarette smoking
10. skiing ——→ broken leg

B. *For each pair above, write a sentence. Use a cause/effect signal word based on the directions below. Begin each sentence with the word or phrase in the left-hand column.*

- If the arrow goes from left to right (→), use the following cause/effect signal words. These words are used in sentences where the cause comes first.

cause(s)	lead(s) to	is the cause of	results in
creates	produces	gives rise to	brings about
makes	provokes	contributes to	

- If the arrow goes from right to left (←), use the following cause/effect signal words. These words are used in sentences where the effect comes first.

is due to	is the result of	come(s) from
results from	is produced by	is a consequence of
follows	is caused by	

When a certain effect sometimes happens, but not always, use *can* with the signal word, as in the example below.

Example: *Viruses can cause infectious diseases.*

1. _____
2. _____
3. _____
4. _____
5. _____

6. _____

7. _____

8. _____

9. _____

10. _____

Multiple causes and effects

In many real-life situations, there is not just a single cause and a single effect.

Example a: Sometimes a single cause can produce many effects. Read the following paragraph to find the cause and its effects.

> In 1992, Hurricane Iniki hit the Hawaiian Island of Kauai. As a result, all telephone lines were out of order, the airport was closed, and thousands of homes were damaged. Hotels were washed away, and tourists' holidays were ruined. Many Kauaians lost their jobs.

What is the cause? *Hurricane Iniki*

What are the effects? *telephones out of order, airport closed, homes damaged, hotels washed away, holidays ruined, jobs lost*

Example b: Sometimes a single effect is the result of several causes. Read the following paragraph to find the effect and its causes.

> The Frozen Yogurt Company closed its shop in the center of town. There really was no other choice. The poor economy meant fewer customers and higher prices for supplies. Bills for electricity and water seemed to go up every month. And then the landlord decided to double the rent.

What is the effect? *The Frozen Yogurt Company closed*

What are the causes? *poor economy; fewer customers; higher prices for supplies; higher electric, water, and rent bills.*

Example c: Sometimes a single cause leads to an effect that becomes the cause of another effect and so forth. This could be called a "chain of events," with all the causes and effects linked together. Notice how one thing leads to another in this paragraph.

> During the war in Vietnam in the 1970s, many villages were destroyed. People were left homeless, so they moved to the city. The cities were often overcrowded, with little hope for a good life. This led many Vietnamese to leave their homeland and move to the United States. As a result, many schools and colleges in the United States expanded their English language programs.

Chain of events:

War in Vietnam → Villages were destroyed → People were homeless → People moved to cities → Cities became crowded, no hope → Vietnamese moved to the United States → United States needed more English language programs

A. *Here are two causes that have multiple possible effects. Working with another student, write the letters of the effects that could go with each cause. Some of the effects can be used twice, and there are many possible answers. Be prepared to explain your answers.*

Causes:

Cause 1: *Learning a new language*

Possible effects: _a b e f g h i j_

_____

Cause 2: *Living in a new city*

Possible effects: _a b c d f i j_

_____

Possible effects:

a. Having many headaches

b. Meeting interesting people

c. Feeling in danger

d. Spending a lot of money

e. Going to the language lab

f. Feeling confused

g. Understanding others' ideas

h. Doing homework

i. Finding a new job

j. Getting married

B. *Here are two effects that have multiple possible causes. Working with another student, write the letters of the causes that could go with each effect. There are many possible answers. Be prepared to explain your answers.*

Effects:

Effect 1: *Many animals have become extinct.*

Possible causes: _a b c e h_

_____

Effect 2: *Many cities are overcrowded.*

Possible causes: _d f g_

_____

Possible causes:

a. Smaller rain forests

b. Use of chemical fertilizers

c. Carbon dioxide emissions

d. Lack of job opportunities on farms

e. Polluted rivers

f. Wars

g. High birth rates

h. Too many hunters

Read each paragraph. On the lines below, write the main idea and the cause(s) and effect(s). Remember, you may find a single cause and single effect, multiple causes, multiple effects, or a chain of events. Compare your work with that of another student.

How Diseases Spread

1. When people move from one city or country to another, the spread of diseases may result. People often bring in germs that may not have been present there before. These new germs can spread quickly and cause previously unknown diseases. If a germ is completely new to a region, people who already live there have no natural protection against it. As a result, they become ill more easily and die more often. In turn, newcomers may catch diseases that were not present where they came from. If they go back, they may carry the disease with them and bring about an epidemic there, too.

Main Idea: _____

_____

Cause(s):   **Effect(s):**

_____   _____

_____   _____

_____   _____

2. Changes in heating systems of buildings can also lead to disease. In the 1970s, there was a worldwide shortage of heating oil. As a result, hotels in the United States lowered the temperature in their heating systems in order to save fuel. This lower temperature led to the growth of a deadly germ that grows in heating pipes. When the heated air was blown into the rooms of a hotel, it carried the germs. Many visitors became ill and several died.

Main Idea: _____

_____

Cause(s):   **Effect(s):**

_____   _____

_____   _____

_____   _____

3. C Pollution of the oceans can also result in the spread of disease. Chemicals from fertilizers (such as phosphates and nitrates) and human waste eventually flow into the oceans. These pollutants result in the increased growth of tiny plants called *algae*. e These plants provide a home for cholera, a deadly disease. The infected algae can stick C to ships, which then carry the cholera germs all around the world. For instance, germs of the disease recently rode on ships going from India to South America. There, thousands of people have died from the resulting epidemic of cholera. e

Main Idea: _____

_____

Cause(s):   *Effect(s):*

_____   _____

_____   _____

_____   _____

EXERCISE 14

Now reread some paragraphs from previous units. This time, notice that the author has used a cause/effect pattern. On the lines below, write the main idea, the causes, and the effects. Remember, you may find a single cause and single effect, multiple causes, multiple effects, or a chain of events. Compare your work with that of another student.

Locate these paragraphs:

1. Unit 7, Exercise 5, paragraph 1 (page 91)

   Main Idea: _____

   _____

   Cause(s):   *Effect(s):*

   _____   _____

   _____   _____

   _____   _____

2. Unit 8, Exercise 5, paragraph 3 (pages 104)

   Main Idea: _____

   _____

   Cause(s):   *Effect(s):*

   _____   _____

   _____   _____

   _____   _____

   _____   _____

On a separate sheet of paper, write a paragraph that uses the cause/effect pattern and is about one of the following topics. Complete the paragraph with sentences that include causes and effects. To guide your reader, use signal words for each cause or effect.

Topics:

1. An earthquake in Mexico

2. The AIDS epidemic around the world

3. An election in your country

4. The Internet

5. Doing your homework assignment at the last minute

After you have written your paragraph, ask another student to read it. Find out if your ideas were clear and interesting. Then rewrite the paragraph to include any suggestions from your reader.

Problem/Solution pattern

Every day, people face a variety of problems, small and large.

Who will take care of our plants while we are out of town?
How can we stop our neighbors from being noisy late at night?
How can we pay the rent and also pay our doctor bills?
Can governments find a place to store harmful radioactive waste from nuclear power plants?

The problem/solution pattern is important because it is found in almost every kind of text: in science, history, and social science textbooks, and in novels, newspapers, and magazines. In the problem/solution pattern, the topic sentence usually states a problem to be solved. Often, this is followed by a description of the problem. Then there is either a suggestion for how to solve the problem or a description of how someone solved it.

Signal words and the problem/solution pattern

Unlike the previous four patterns of organization, the writer may use many different kinds of signal words in a problem/solution passage. For this reason, this pattern can be more difficult to recognize than other patterns. One way to recognize a problem/solution pattern is to look for the word *problem* or one of its synonyms in the topic sentence. These synonyms include: *situation, difficulty, trouble, crisis, dilemma, predicament, issue,* and *quandary.* Another way to recognize the pattern is by noticing that the passage begins with a question that states a problem. In some cases, however, the only way to recognize the problem/solution pattern is by reading the whole paragraph or passage.

In the following paragraph, the problem is underlined. What is the solution? Using a complete sentence, write the solution on the line below. Then complete the main idea statement.

<u>How can you keep fruits and vegetables fresh in a hot climate when you do not have a refrigerator?</u> A teacher in Nigeria has invented a new, nonelectric cooler that does not need ice. It is a simple device made of a small clay pot that fits inside a larger pot, with wet sand between them and a damp cloth on top. This cooler can keep eggplants, tomatoes, and peppers fresh for three weeks or more. Since the device does not require electricity and it costs little to make, it could be extremely useful in developing countries, where transporting and storing fresh produce is difficult. The Nigerian teacher has won a $75,000 prize for his work. He plans to make and distribute the coolers in Nigeria and other African countries.

Problem: *How can you keep fruits and vegetables fresh in a hot climate when you do not have a refrigerator?*

Solution: _____

Main Idea: *You can keep fruits and vegetables fresh in a hot climate if you* _____

_____

EXERCISE 16

Read each paragraph. Then, on the lines below, write the problem, the solution, and the main idea. Remember to write complete sentences. Compare your work with that of another student.

Staying Healthy

1.   As people get older, they usually begin to experience physical problems. They often begin to lose their eyesight, their hearing, and their memory, and they become less able to get around. Getting older is a fact of life, of course, and there is nothing you can do to stop the years from passing. However, some scientists at Tufts University in Boston have discovered that there may be a way to prevent some of the physical problems associated with aging. In experiments with rats whose age was the same as humans at sixty-five to seventy-five, the scientists fed the animals half a cup of blueberries every day. After eight weeks, the rats showed improved physical skills. They also showed improved short-term memory, as demonstrated by the fact that they could find their way through mazes more quickly. In fact, blueberries contain antioxidants, which slow the aging process. One leading scientist says he now eats blueberries every day.

Problem: _____

Solution: _____

Main Idea: _____

_____

2.   In the United States and many industrialized countries, asthma is a serious health problem for many children, especially in cities. When a person has an asthma attack, the bronchial tubes that bring air to the lungs become blocked and it becomes very difficult to breathe. Doctors have long believed that the ozone in automobile exhaust causes asthma in children. The summer Olympics in Atlanta, Georgia, provided some evidence to support this theory, because city officials closed the downtown area to all automobile traffic for seventeen days. During those days, only half the usual number of children in the area were taken to doctors or hospitals because of asthma attacks. A recent scientific report confirms the evidence of Atlanta and says that many asthma attacks could be prevented by reducing pollution from automobiles. This could be possible if more people took buses or trains to work instead of using their cars.

Problem: _____

Solution: _____

Main Idea: _____

_____

3.   Two men from Munich faced an unexpected predicament last weekend. They were hiking in the Italian Alps when a heavy snowstorm began. It was snowing so hard and there was so much wind that it was impossible to see where they were going, and they lost their way. The men were not dressed for snowy weather, so they were in serious danger of freezing to death. Fortunately, one of the men remembered a story he had read as a child and he suggested that they make a kind of cave in the snow to protect themselves from the wind. They were near some rocks, so they decided to dig a cave in the deep snow near the rocks. They spent the night in their cave. During the night they even managed to build a small fire, and they jumped around to stay warm. In the morning, the snow had stopped and they were able to find their way down the mountain. The idea of digging a cave probably saved their lives.

Problem: _____

Solution: _____

Main Idea: _____

_____

Read each paragraph. Then, on the lines below, write the problem, the solution, and the main idea. Remember to write complete sentences. Compare your work with that of another student.

Ideas for Business

1.   In the 1980s, Kansas City, Missouri, like many other cities in the Midwest, was growing rapidly. New businesses and industries were moving into the area and the city government needed to build an industrial park for new factories and warehouses. The problem was deciding where to put it. There was no empty space near the city, and the government did not want to force people to move from their houses or farms. At the same time, limestone mines were closing down in many parts of the country. For over a hundred years the area around Kansas City, in fact, had been a center of limestone mining. The mining companies had dug large mines fifty to sixty feet below the ground and built roads and railroads to carry out the limestone. Now the city government realized it could use these empty mines for an industrial park. There was plenty of space—20 million square feet. There were also roads and railroads already in place. After the mines were cleaned and painted, they were ready to use. In a few years, about 400 businesses employing over 4,000 people moved into the underground industrial parks.

Problem: _____

Solution: _____

Main Idea: _____

_____

2.   The Amazon rain forest in Brazil is in trouble. This rain forest is a uniquely rich and diverse environment. It is a resource for the people who live there and for the environment of the planet as a whole. However, every year large parts of it are cut down by companies so they can do business. Agribusinesses (very large farm companies) are clearing the land for their cattle ranches or soybean farms, and multinational lumber companies are cutting trees to sell for wood. The native people and many environmentalists are concerned about the situation. They understand that the economy of Brazil needs to grow and that people need jobs, but they believe that the rain forest should be protected. They propose a different kind of business that would help the economy but not damage the forest. A number of these new businesses are already working in the rain forest. They harvest and sell products that grow naturally in the rain forest environment. One of these products is a berry called

guarana that is used to make a beverage similar to Pepsi, Coke, and other cola drinks. The Brazilians have made a deal with the Pepsi-Cola Company to introduce this beverage in North America. By selling a natural product, Brazilians will build a stronger economy without endangering the rain forest.

Problem: _____

Solution: _____

Main Idea: _____

_____

3.   In many places in the United States, factories, farms, and military bases have produced dangerous levels of pollution in the ground. The usual method for cleaning up ground pollution is very expensive and complicated. Big machines dig out all of the polluted earth and transfer it to large trucks, which then carry it to an official dumping place. This dumping place then has to be carefully closed off so that the pollution cannot escape into water supplies. Scientists now believe that there may be a better and less expensive way to clean up ground pollution by using trees and plants. They have identified hundreds of species of trees and plants that can eliminate certain polluting substances. This new method of removing ground pollution has been tried out successfully in Detroit on a plot of land with lead pollution. Scientists removed four feet of the polluted soil to another area and planted sunflowers and Indian mustard in it. At the end of the project, the lead had been reduced by 43 percent and the scientists had spent less than half as much as the cost of the usual cleanup process.

Problem: _____

Solution: _____

Main Idea: _____

_____

EXERCISE 18

Think of some problems and solutions that you know about. These could be problems in your own life, in your hometown, or general world problems. Choose one of the problems. On a separate sheet of paper, write a paragraph in which you state the problem in a topic sentence, describe the problem, and explain how it was solved or could be solved.

After you have written your paragraph, ask another student to read it. Find out if your ideas were clear and interesting. Then rewrite the paragraph to include any suggestions from your partner.

Recognizing patterns

Each of the sentences below is written in one of the five patterns. Working with another student, decide which pattern you think is being used in each sentence. Write the name of the pattern in front of the sentence.

Use these abbreviations:

**L—Listing   S—Sequence   PS—Problem/Solution
CC—Comparison/Contrast   CE—Cause/Effect**

S 1. Nicole and Brigette woke up very early on the morning of the international roller-skating competition and ate a quick breakfast.

CC 2. The roller-skating rink in Miami was much larger than the rink in their home town in France.

L 3. Among the competitors, there were skaters from Japan, Korea, Australia, Russia, Argentina, and many other countries.

CE 4. Since the competition was taking place in the United States, the largest group of competitors was American.

PS 5. Lola, the Argentinean skater, broke her skate during practice, so her coach had to bring her extra pair of skates to the rink.

S 6. The competition began in mid-morning with free-skating for couples, and the first scores were posted after lunch.

CE 7. A young Korean couple won this category because they worked so perfectly together.

CC 8. Nicole and Brigette felt that the French couple had given a much more lively performance than the Korean couple.

S 9. After they had finished competing, the girls stayed to watch the men's speed skating event.

PS
(CE) 10. Brigette couldn't find Nicole in the crowd, so she climbed up on a table to look for her.

Each paragraph below has a different pattern and a missing sentence. The missing sentences are listed at the end of the exercise with an extra sentence. Working with another student, decide which pattern is used in each paragraph and which sentence fits best. Then write the letter of the missing sentence and the name of the pattern below each paragraph.

Use these abbreviations:

> L—Listing   S—Sequence   PS—Problem/Solution
> CC—Comparison/Contrast   CE—Cause/Effect

1.   For the tourist in Italy, Bologna has many advantages over the more popular city of Florence. There are far fewer tourists in Bologna. This means that museums and monuments are much less crowded. Since there are few foreigners, you can also get a much better idea of how Italians live. Furthermore, the Bolognese tend to be more friendly to visitors, in contrast to some Florentines, who can be quite rude.

Sentence: __d__   Pattern: __CC__

2.   Bologna's Etruscan origins go back at least 2,400 years. It became a Roman city in the second century B.C. With the fall of the Roman Empire, it came under Byzantine rule. Then it fell to the armies of northern barbarians called the Longobards. Bologna became an independent city-state in about 1000. In 1507, the city came under the rule of the Roman Catholic Church. This ended with the arrival of Napoleon and the French army in 1796. Then, in 1859, the city joined the Kingdom of Savoy, which became the Kingdom of Italy in 1861.

Sentence: __a__   Pattern: __S__

3.   In the 1990s, the people of Bologna felt that something was missing in the city. It did not have a good central library. There were many small libraries in different neighborhoods of the city, but none in the center. A large central library could also serve as a center for cultural and intellectual activity. The big question was where to put this new library. There are strict laws in Italy against tearing down old buildings, and in the center of Bologna most of the buildings are old. The only possibility was to take an old building and turn it into a library. In the end, the city government decided to use the "Sala Borsa," a sixteenth-century building that once housed the financial exchange of the city. It took many years of work to plan and complete the renovation, but in 2001, the new library opened and immediately became very popular.

Sentence: __b__   Pattern: __PS__

4.   A number of historical factors led to a progressive, or leftist, city government in Bologna after World War II. The Bolognese had undoubtedly been influenced by several centuries of sometimes brutal rule under the Roman Catholic Church. Because of that experience, they learned to distrust the Church and all established power. This distrust was an important factor in the strong progressive movement that developed in

Bologna in the early twentieth century. Many Bolognese were also angered by the behavior of the conservative parties in Italy, which supported Fascism and the Nazi occupation. As a result, when Fascism and World War II came to an end and Italians could vote again, a large majority voted for the leftist parties.

Sentence: _e_   Pattern: _CE_

5.   In their fondness for Bologna, the Bolognese have given their city a number of nicknames. To some, it is known as Bologna "the red." This name comes in part from the strong leftist political tendencies of the city. To others, it is Bologna "the wise" because of its university, the oldest in Europe and still an important intellectual and cultural center. And finally, some like to think of Bologna as "the fat," a paradise for food lovers. And indeed, the local cooking tends toward richness and plenty—delicate stomachs, be careful!

Sentence: _f_   Pattern: _L_

Missing sentences:

a. In 1816, Bologna was once again ruled by the Church, with the help of the Austrian Empire.

b. In the center of Bologna it was not possible to build something new without tearing down something old.

c. Many Bolognese spend time drinking strong Italian coffee at one of the many outdoor cafés.

d. Unlike Florence's narrow, noisy streets, Bologna's streets are lined with porticos that make them far more pleasant for walking.

e. Medieval Bologna was an independent city-state, which caused the Bolognese to develop a long-lasting love of independence and self-government.

f. It also comes from the many red-toned buildings in Bologna that give the city a unique coloring.

EXERCISE 21

Each paragraph below has a different pattern and a missing sentence. The missing sentences are listed at the end of the exercise, with an extra sentence. Working with another student, decide which pattern is used for each paragraph and which sentence fits best. Then write the letter of the missing sentence and the name of the pattern below each paragraph.

Use these abbreviations:

L—Listing   S—Sequence   PS—Problem/Solution
CC—Comparison/Contrast   CE—Cause/Effect

1.   Archaeologists believe that the first people to eat corn lived in central Mexico 5,000 years ago. They gathered a kind of corn that grew wild in much of Central America. Throughout the following centuries, the cultivation of corn made possible the great Indian civilizations, from the Aztec to the Zuni. By the time Columbus and

other Europeans arrived in the late fifteenth century, corn was cultivated all over North and South America. Curious about this new grain, Columbus brought some seeds back to Europe. Within a century, people were growing corn in many parts of Europe, Asia, and Africa.

Sentence: _f_   Pattern: _S_

2.   The cultivation of corn in the United States has changed dramatically in the past century. Farmers used to grow corn in small fields of a few acres, but now corn farms may be as large as 6,000 acres. Before the age of machines, farmers had to pick each ear of corn by hand. Now, however, huge harvesting machines can pick hundreds of acres of corn in a day. While corn growing used to be a way of life for many families, now it is big business.

Sentence: _e_   Pattern: _CC_

3.   In modern life, corn has many uses. Corn is also hidden in many other foods: cookies, bread, or beef. A large part of the corn production in the United States, in fact, goes to feed beef cattle. But corn is not just a food. It is also used in the production of all kinds of things, from glue to hand lotion and paint. Recently, manufacturers have begun to use corn to make a new type of plastic for garbage bags. In many places, cars are now powered by a mixture that contains ethanol, a fuel made from corn.

Sentence: _b_   Pattern: _L_

4.   Genetic engineering has brought about some important changes in the production of corn. It has allowed scientists to develop plants that produce larger and more numerous ears of corn. This makes it possible for farmers to harvest far more corn per acre of land. Through genetic engineering, scientists have also developed types of corn that resist certain diseases. Scientists are also working on kinds of corn that can be cultivated in very dry or hot areas. All these changes mean that corn will be able to feed more people.

Sentence: _a_   Pattern: _CE_

5.   B.t. corn is a new kind of corn that has been developed through genetic engineering. This corn contains B.t., a natural insecticide that is found in the soil. This insecticide protects it against harmful insects. The United States government permitted several large farm companies in the United States to plant B.t. corn, but only for animal food. However, when the B.t. corn was picked, it was mixed in with the corn that is used by companies that make corn meal and tortillas for supermarkets and fast-food restaurants. Faced with this predicament, the government took quick action. Soon the locations of the B.t. corn were discovered, and the corn meal and tortillas were taken from the supermarket shelves. The farms that had mixed up the corn were fined, and stronger controls were put in place so that this would not happen again.

Sentence: _c_   Pattern: _PS_

Missing sentences:

a. Consequently, farmers will save millions of tons of corn that are lost to disease every year.

b. For example, we eat corn in many forms, from popcorn to corn oil, corn flour, and corn syrup.

c. No one knew if this genetically engineered corn was safe for people, so it had to be kept separate from other corn.

d. For the Hopi Indians, corn is a symbol of life.

e. It took a family several long days of hot, hard work to harvest a few acres of corn.

f. Before a thousand years had passed, they had learned to cultivate corn.

EXERCISE 22

Each paragraph below has a different pattern and a missing sentence. The missing sentences are listed at the end of the exercise, with an extra sentence. Working with another student, decide which pattern is used for each paragraph and which sentence fits best. Then write the letter of the missing sentence and the name of the pattern below each paragraph.

Use these abbreviations:

L—Listing   S—Sequence   PS—Problem/Solution
CC—Comparison/Contrast   CE—Cause/Effect

1.   Sir Isaac Newton was born in Woolesthorpe, England, in 1642. He began his studies at Trinity College, Cambridge University, in 1661. In 1665, when the plague (a terrible disease) struck England, Newton left the university and returned home. The next few years in Woolsthorpe were the most productive in his life. However, his most famous book, *Principia,* was not published until 1682. In honor of his work, he was made director of the English Mint in 1699. Sir Isaac Newton died in 1727 and is buried in Westminster Abbey.

Sentence: *e*   Pattern: *S*

2.   Isaac Newton worked on many important scientific problems of his day. His best-known written work is *Principia,* the book that explained his law of universal gravitation. He is famous as well for his development of the laws of motion. He also made important discoveries about optics and the nature of color. His other work included experiments and writings on astronomy, chemistry, and logic.

Sentence: *C*   Pattern: *L*

3.   Ever since Aristotle first wrote about it, scientists had argued about the nature of light. Is white light made up of the primary colors (red, blue, green, yellow), they asked, or is white light the primary color that can be changed by various other colors? Newton answered this question in his first paper to the foremost group of scholars and scientists of his time. In a dark room, he passed sunlight through a prism (a piece of glass shaped like a triangle). The white light divided itself into light beams of the primary colors. Then he passed the light beam of one of the primary colors (red) through another prism. The red beam did not divide into anything else; it remained

red. This is how Newton proved that light is composed of the primary colors, and they cannot be further divided.

Sentence: _a_   Pattern: _PS_

4.   Newton did most of his best work between 1665 and 1668, during his stay in Woolsthorpe. Many historians and scientists have wondered how he managed to produce so many brilliant ideas in such a short time. It is probable that he had begun to develop his theories earlier while at the university, and that the peace and quiet of Woolsthorpe allowed him to develop those ideas. No one will ever know exactly what inspired his most creative thinking. It is certain, however, that many of today's scientific advances are the result of his genius.

Sentence: _b_   Pattern: _CE_

5.   Although both men were geniuses, Isaac Newton and Albert Einstein have very little else in common. True, they both did their best work before the age of twenty-six. However, that is the only similarity between them. Newton cared about the public's opinion of him, and he did not like improper behavior. Einstein, on the other hand, enjoyed being different and did not care what others thought. Newton spent his later years in a comfortable job with the government, while Einstein remained a full-time scientist.

Sentence: _d_   Pattern: _CC_

Missing sentences:

a. He did a simple experiment.

b. Popular belief says that a falling apple gave Newton the idea of the law of universal gravitation.

c. In addition, he invented differential and integral calculus.

d. Newton was described as a man who never smiled, but Einstein was well known for his sense of humor.

e. In fact, by the age of twenty-six, he had already completed most of his best scientific work.

f. Present-day physicists have discovered limits to the mechanical universe that Newton described.

In every essay, book chapter, or magazine, it is possible to find a single overall pattern for the whole text. However, individual paragraphs in the text may have different patterns. Read this article and then answer the questions that follow. When you have finished, compare your work with that of another student.

Water Sports in Hawaii

If you enjoy water sports, Hawaii is the place for you! With its warm climate and warm water, it is possible to be on the water or in the water all year round. Many different sports are popular on the islands. Anyone of any age can go swimming at one of the many beautiful Hawaiian beaches. Or you can choose sport fishing from the shore or from a boat. Many people enjoy sailing, but if you prefer, you can go canoeing or windsurfing. Other sports that are especially popular on the islands are surfing, snorkeling, and scuba diving.

Surfing, the islands' most famous sport, started in Hawaii many years ago. The Hawaiians called it "he'enalu," which means "to slide on a wave." Long before the arrival of the Europeans, the Hawaiians would ride on the waves on long, narrow wooden boards. When the first Europeans came to the islands, they were amazed by these surfing Hawaiians. Since that time, surfing has become a very popular sport not only in Hawaii, but also on the California coast and in Australia, among other places.

Surfing is a sport that requires you to be a good swimmer. You must also have an excellent sense of balance. To go surfing, you must swim out from the beach with your surfboard under your arm. When you get to the place where the waves begin to break, you have to wait for the right moment—the moment of calm just before a wave arrives. Then you need to try to stand up on the board as the wave begins to rise under you. At the same time, you must try to steer the board with your feet so you stay on top of the wave. The important thing is to keep your balance and not fall. If you can manage this, you will have an exciting ride all the way in to the shore.

Two additional popular sports in Hawaii are scuba diving and snorkeling. These sports allow you to look at what is under the surface of the ocean. Of the two, scuba diving allows you to see the most interesting undersea sights because you can go farther underwater. "SCUBA" means "Self-Contained Underwater Breathing Apparatus," which is the equipment used for breathing and swimming far under water. In Hawaii, you must take special courses to learn how to scuba dive because it can be dangerous. If you are less adventuresome, you might try snorkeling instead of scuba diving. Less equipment is needed to snorkel—just a face mask, a breathing tube (snorkel), and flippers for your feet. Unlike scuba diving, snorkeling is easy to learn and does not require any special instruction. You breathe through the snorkel, float on the surface of the water, and look down through the mask. Often, fish will come close to you and eat out of your hand.

The ocean around the Hawaiian Islands is clean, clear, and full of hundreds of kinds of colorful fish. The undersea world is made even more colorful by the coral reefs, large structures produced by small marine organisms over many, many years. Among the red, gold, white, and light purple reefs, you may also see larger fish and sea turtles. Whether you choose surfing, scuba diving, or snorkeling, you will understand why Hawaii is known as a perfect place to enjoy water sports.

1. What is the overall pattern of this reading?

2. What are some signal words that helped you decide on this pattern?

3. What are the patterns in each of these paragraphs? Explain your answers.

Paragraph 1: __L_____

_____

_____

Paragraph 2: __S_____

_____

_____

Paragraph 3: __S_____

_____

_____

Paragraph 4: __C/C_____

_____

_____

Paragraph 5: __L_____

_____

_____

UNIT **10** Summarizing

What Is Summarizing?

Summarizing is the process of retelling the important parts of a passage in a much shorter form. It is an important reading skill. When you are able to summarize a passage, you can be confident that you have understood it.

Summarizing is also a good study skill. Often you must read, understand, and remember information from several textbook chapters. When you write summaries of your reading, the summaries can help you review for examinations.

Summarizing is also useful in completing written reports. When you are assigned to write a research report, you usually include information from several sources. By summarizing such information, you can make your report richer and clearer.

A good summary

- includes the main ideas and the major supporting points of what you have read.

- does *not* include minor details or repeated details.

- does *not* include your own ideas or opinions.

- is much shorter than the original.

Summary words

A summary word (or phrase) names a general idea that has several examples or parts. Summary words and phrases are very helpful in summarizing.

Example:

One morning, Ayako decided to make some egg salad. First, she boiled the water. Then she added a drop of vinegar and six eggs. She boiled them for ten minutes. After that, she placed the eggs in some cold water for half an hour to cool them. Then she peeled the eggs and chopped them. Finally, she added some mayonnaise and chopped celery, and the salad was ready. The <u>whole process</u> had taken about an hour.

<u>Whole process</u> is a summary phrase that refers to all the steps in making egg salad.

Write a summary word or phrase for each list. Work with another student.

1. <u>sports</u>
   baseball
   basketball
   football
   swimming
   tennis

2. <u>planets</u>
   Mars
   Uranus
   Jupiter
   Saturn
   Mercury

3. <u>contagious diseases</u>
   malaria
   tuberculosis
   scarlet fever
   diphtheria
   measles

4. <u>business</u>
   personnel department
   marketing department
   executive suite
   warehouse
   cafeteria

5. <u>planting a tree</u>
   get a shovel
   dig a hole in the ground
   put lots of water in the hole
   unwrap the roots of the tree
   place the roots in the hole
   be sure the tree is straight
   cover the roots with lots of soil
   stamp down the soil
   add more water

6. <u>getting ready BDay party</u>
   clean the house
   buy some chips and salsa
   make some pizza
   bake a cake and decorate it
   wrap the presents
   set the table
   cool the drinks

7. _____

   Every body continues in a state of rest or of motion at a constant speed in a straight line unless it is disturbed by a force acting on it.

   A force is required to accelerate a body. The strength of the force is directly proportional to the mass of the body.

   To every action there is an equal and opposite reaction. The action is on one body, the reaction on another.

8. _places of worship_

cathedral

church

temple

mosque

chapel

9. _parts of speech_

verb

noun

adjective

pronoun

adverb

10. _snorkeling_

put your mask around your neck

hold your flippers in one hand

walk into the surf until the water is about two feet deep

sit down with your back to the waves

put your flippers on your feet

stand up and turn around to face the waves

place the breathing tube in your mouth

adjust your mask

start swimming

be sure to keep the end of the air tube above the surface of the water

Summarizing a Sentence

When you summarize a sentence, you make it much shorter. You can do this by using summary words and phrases to take the place of groups of words about the same topic. You should leave out descriptive words such as adjectives or adverbs, and keep only the words that tell the main point of the sentence. Use as few words as possible. The summary of a sentence should still be a complete sentence.

Example: The tall cowboy put the saddle on his horse, untied him from the fence, waved good-bye, and rode off into the sunset.

Summary: *The cowboy left.*

You can leave out the word *tall* since that is a descriptive word (adjective). All of the cowboy's actions (put the saddle on his horse, untied him, waved good-bye, and rode off) can be summarized in one summary word: *left.*

The cowboy left is a complete sentence.

Summarize these sentences using summary words and phrases. Remember that the sentence summary must be a complete sentence. Work with another student.

1. After she turned on the oven, Yuki mixed the sugar, flour, eggs, milk, oil, and vanilla in the mixer, poured the batter into the buttered pans, and put the cake in the oven.

   Summary: _Yuki baked a cake_____

2. As the bus rolled into her hometown, Liz looked around at the familiar streets and shops that she had not seen for two years.

   Summary: _Liz comes home._____

3. Geraldo put on his coat, picked up his briefcase from the table near the door, put out the cat, and got ready for his ten-minute walk to the bus stop.

   Summary: _Geraldo left._____

4. When the Chen family returned from their vacation, they found the back door broken open, the television set missing, and all the food in their freezer gone.

   Summary: _The Chen's were robbed_____

5. In Natasha's library you can find mysteries, novels, biographies, travel books, how-to manuals, science fiction thrillers, and reference books.

   Summary: _Natasha has lots of books. (variety of ~)_____

6. With her new credit card, Piper bought groceries at the supermarket, shoes at the department store, and a new set of tires for her sports car at the auto supply store.

   Summary: _Piper bought many things 4 herself._____

7. During the summer along the Charles River in Boston, you can go walking, in-line skating, jogging, hiking, and bicycling, or you can have a picnic while listening to an outdoor concert or watching a movie.

   Summary: _You can do many things along the river_____
   _in Boston._____

8. After clearing away the old leaves and branches, Jeff dug up the hard ground, mixed in fertilizer and new soil, raked it all smooth, and planted the seeds.

   Summary: _Jeff planted a garden._____

9. When they heard the weather forecast, the islanders closed the windows, put tape across the glass, moved all of their plants and chairs indoors, and bought many bottles of fresh water.

Summary: _The islanders got ready for a storm._

10. Anna put her pens and pencils neatly in a row, turned on the radio, stacked her English books on the desk, got herself a soda, and sat down in her desk chair.

Summary: _Anna prepares to study._

Summarizing a Paragraph

A paragraph summary should be as short as possible, and it must be a complete sentence. The summary should express the main point in as few words as possible. Follow these steps:

Step 1. Read the paragraph all the way through to be sure you understand it.

Step 2. Check to see if the paragraph contains a topic sentence.

- If the paragraph has a topic sentence, does it state the main idea of the paragraph? If so, you can use it for your summary. Just make the topic sentence shorter by using summary words and phrases and taking out descriptive words.

- If the topic sentence is not a good statement of the main idea, write a main idea statement and then make it shorter using summary words and phrases and leaving out descriptive words.

Example:

Shopping malls have produced a revolution in shopping and living habits in many industrialized countries. Before 1950, there were no malls, but now almost every city or region in industrialized countries has at least one. In fact, shopping malls have become a part of daily life. Many people even think of them as social centers. In a way, malls have taken the place of the main streets of a town or city. Shops and services that were once spread over several city blocks are now in one place at the mall. Everyone can save time by doing their shopping at the mall. And people young and old, with time on their hands, often say, "Let's go to the mall!"

Topic sentence: _Shopping malls have produced a revolution in shopping and living habits in many industrialized countries._

Summary: _Shopping malls have changed the cultures of many industrialized countries._

Read and summarize each of the following paragraphs, using as few words as possible. Follow the steps explained on page 145, and remember that your summary must be a complete sentence. Work with another student.

Shopping Malls in the United States

1.   Although every shopping mall is a bit different in design, shoppers often feel comfortable in a new mall. That is because malls share certain features. You can almost always find most of the following: a department store, a pharmacy, a toy store, a bookshop, clothing shops for all ages, shoe shops, a bank, and places to eat. These businesses are all under one roof. Most malls are enclosed, so that shoppers never have to go outdoors once they get to the mall. Some malls also have doors to shops on the outside of the mall. Usually a mall is surrounded by a large parking area.

Summary: _All malls have some common features._

2.   Malls are not all exactly alike, however. In a suburb of a large city, the local mall may be large and beautiful. It may be several stories high, housing as many as fifty businesses. These can range from small specialty shops to large luxury department stores. The roofs of these malls are sometimes made of glass and there may be a courtyard with plants and fountains. In a poor, rural town, however, the local mall may be plain and rather small. It may offer only essential shopping and services, such as a supermarket, a pizza parlor, a card and gift shop, a Laundromat, and a bank. All the shops are generally on one level, and the interior of the mall is plain and undecorated.

Summary: _City malls are big... town malls are ..._

3.   While shopping malls have changed life in the modern world, not all of their effects have been positive. Most of the shops and services found in malls are parts of large corporations. These businesses take away customers from smaller shops in nearby towns, forcing many of them to close. That has led to fewer individually owned businesses and less local control over jobs. In addition, malls are harmful to the environment. They are often built on land that is important to the survival of birds and wild animals. Wherever they are built, they cover large areas with buildings and parking lots—instead of trees or grass. Thus, they contribute to the general loss of nature and rainwater to refill underground aquifers. And finally, malls are usually built far away from the city or town center. This means that people must drive their car to the mall, resulting in increased air pollution and heavy traffic on nearby roads.

Summary: _Malls can also have negative effects._

Read and summarize each of the following paragraphs using as few words as possible. Follow the steps explained on page 145, and remember that your summary must be a complete sentence. Work with another student.

The *Challenger* Disaster

1.   By 1984, NASA, the United States space program, had carried out many successful flights of the space shuttle. In fact, Americans were beginning to take the whole NASA program for granted. Then the president announced that the next shuttle would carry a school teacher into space. Hundreds of teachers from all parts of the country applied for the job. They all wanted to be "the first teacher in space." During the next year, these adventurous educators were tested and examined and trained. At last, the choice was announced. A teacher from New Hampshire, Christa MacAuliffe, would be the first teacher-astronaut.

Summary: _____

2.   Many months of preparation and training followed the announcement. First, Christa went through intensive physical training. She had to be in top condition for the flight. Then she learned how to operate some of the delicate instruments on the *Challenger* space shuttle. Christa planned special lessons which she would teach from space. Finally, she trained with the other astronauts, so they could work as a team in space.

Summary: _Christa had lots of training._

3.   Almost everyone knows what happened on that terrible day in January 1986. Early in the morning, the *Challenger* crew had a good breakfast and discussed their plans. They made sure they understood all of the work they would be doing during the flight. Later, they boarded a special van that carried them to the shuttle. The weather was rather cold, and some NASA officials wondered if they should put off the flight. After some discussion, they decided to go ahead. The *Challenger* took off over the Atlantic Ocean in Florida. Minutes later, it exploded in the air. All of the crew members, including Christa MacAuliffe, died in the explosion.

Summary: _The challenger exploded, and the crew died._

Summarizing Short Passages

Step 1. Read the passage all the way through.

Step 2. Go back to the beginning and check to see if each paragraph contains a topic sentence.

- If the paragraph has a topic sentence, does it state the main idea of the paragraph? If so, you can use it for your summary. Just make the topic sentence shorter by using summary words and phrases and taking out descriptive words.

- If the topic sentence is not a good statement of the main idea, write a main idea statement and then make it shorter using summary words and phrases and leaving out descriptive words.

Step 3. Put the sentences from the paragraphs together to form a one-paragraph summary. The summary paragraph should express the main point of the whole passage. You may need to include some signal words and revise some of the sentences in order to tie all of the ideas together and express the main point.

Example: Reread the three paragraphs in Exercise 3 (page 146). Write your summaries for those paragraphs on the lines below.

Paragraph 1: _____

Paragraph 2: _____

Paragraph 3: _____

Three possible summaries for the paragraphs are:

Paragraph 1: *All shopping malls have similar features.*_____

Paragraph 2: *Malls vary in luxury according to the neighborhood around them.*_____

Paragraph 3: *Malls can have negative effects on their local areas.*_____

Now tie your sentences together in one short paragraph. Use only the words that are necessary. Write your summary below.

The example sentences above can be combined to summarize the entire passage. For instance: *All shopping malls have similar features, though they vary in luxury according to their surrounding neighborhood. Malls often have negative effects on the surrounding area.*

EXERCISE 5

Reread the three paragraphs in Exercise 4 (page 147). Write your summaries for those paragraphs on the lines below.

Paragraph 1: _____

Paragraph 2: _____

Paragraph 3: _____

Now tie these sentences together in one short paragraph. Use only the words that are absolutely necessary. Write your summary below.

Working with another student, summarize this short passage. Remember to begin by reading the passage all the way through. When you have finished your summary, compare your work with that of another pair of students.

An Exciting Way to Visit the Wilderness

People who are looking for outdoor adventure often go to Maine. This state in the northeastern United States contains large areas of wilderness and many rivers. There you can enjoy a popular sport: white-water rafting. In the past, this sport was practiced only in the western states. But now, several outdoor travel companies offer weekend rafting trips in Maine. They provide guide service, equipment, and even food, and they welcome people who have had no experience at all. Thus, city residents, too, can get a taste of wilderness. All they need to bring with them is a desire for adventure.

"White water" is the water of a river when it moves very fast over rocky areas. As the water fills with air bubbles, it looks white. The areas of white water are the most exciting areas for rafters—and also the most dangerous. In fact, rafting guides must always be on the lookout for white water. And rafters must be ready to swim because the raft can tip over in white water. For that reason, rafters must wear special life vests that will keep them afloat.

Rafting is not a sport that everyone can do. It often requires great physical strength. Sometimes, at very rocky parts of the river, rafters will need to walk for a while. They may also have to carry their rubber rafts at times. Fortunately, though, the rafts are very light. Paddling the boats is easy because they are going downriver. But everyone on the raft has to be alert for changes in the river current. They cannot simply sit and enjoy the wonderful wild scenery.

Most rafting companies offer overnight trips that combine with camping. This kind of trip is ideal for a family with children over twelve. Several rafts of people will start out from a base camp. Their food supplies, sleeping bags, tents, and other necessities are sometimes packed onto the rafts. Or all the supplies might be brought by car to the next campsite. The guide often is also the cook for the group of rafters and may be quite a good chef. After a day of rafting, in any case, the food tastes good and sleep comes easily.

Write one sentence to summarize each paragraph.

Paragraph 1: _____

Paragraph 2: _____

Paragraph 3: _____

Paragraph 4: _____

Now tie these sentences together in one short paragraph. Use only the words that are absolutely necessary. Write your summary below.

Working with another student, summarize this short passage. Remember to begin by reading the passage all the way through. When you have finished your summary, compare your work with that of another pair of students.

The Invasion of Alien Species

In many parts of the world, alien species are harming the environment and causing other problems. An alien species is a species of plant or animal that has moved from its original home to a new area. Sometimes people have purposely introduced the new species; sometimes it arrives accidentally, as a side effect of international trade. In its new location, the alien species has no natural enemies, so it can grow and multiply without limit. Over time—sometimes decades, sometimes a few years—the new species takes living space and food away from the native plants and animals. The result can mean drastic change in the natural landscape and problems for people.

The tiger mosquito is an example of an alien species. This kind of mosquito is common in Asia, but in recent years it has moved to parts of southern Europe. Scientists believe that the eggs of this insect probably arrived inside some car tires that were filled with water. In a few years, the mosquitoes multiplied and spread over large areas of Italy and other countries. Tiger mosquitoes can reproduce faster than the common European mosquito, so they quickly replaced a large percentage of the native mosquitoes. Though they do not cause serious disease in humans, tiger mosquitoes are a serious nuisance. They are far more aggressive than common European mosquitoes, and the effects of their bites are worse.

Another example of a different kind of animal that has recently moved to another continent is the zebra mussel. This small shellfish was first discovered in the Great Lakes of North America in 1986. It may have come over from Russia on a cargo ship. In a very few years, zebra mussels had spread over all the Great Lakes and into many important rivers. They have grown into thick masses, covering many areas of lakes or river bottoms. They have also covered and closed up pipes of power stations and water treatment centers. Government officials say that the mussels have caused many millions of dollars worth of damage.

Among the many examples of alien species of mammals that have caused damage is the Indian mongoose. This animal was brought to Hawaii in the 1800s to kill rats in sugarcane fields. Since then, they have grown in numbers so that today they are a major threat to bird life on the islands. One of the mongoose's favorite foods, in fact, is birds' eggs. Thus, the mongoose has caused millions of dollars worth of damage to poultry farmers in Hawaii, and it has greatly reduced the numbers of many native bird species. Many of these species, which are unique to the islands, are now at risk of extinction.

Write one sentence to summarize each paragraph.

Paragraph 1: _____

Paragraph 2: _____

Paragraph 3: _____

Paragraph 4: _____

Now tle these sentences together in one short paragraph. Use only the words that are necessary. Write your summary below.

Summarizing Longer Passages

When you summarize an essay, textbook chapter, or article with many paragraphs, follow these steps:

Step 1. Read the essay, chapter, or article all the way through.

Step 2. Divide the reading material into logical parts and write a topic for each part. All of the paragraphs in a part should be about the same topic. For example, if paragraph 1 to paragraph 3 are about the same topic, they would be part one. Part two would start with paragraph 4, and so forth.

Step 3. Write a sentence that summarizes all the paragraphs in each part. This is the same as writing the summary of a short passage.

Step 4. Put all of the summary sentences together to form one paragraph summary, using signal words.

EXERCISE 8

You have already read "The Iceman" from the introduction to Reading Faster. Now summarize it by following the steps below.

Step 1. Read the passage all the way through.

The Iceman

1   On a September day in 1991, two Germans were climbing the mountains between Austria and Italy. High up on a mountain pass, they found the body of a man lying on the ice. At that height (10,499 feet, or 3,200 meters), the ice is usually permanent, but 1991 had been an especially warm year. The mountain ice had melted more than usual and so the body had come to the surface.

2   It was lying face downward. The skeleton was in perfect condition, except for a wound in the head. There was still skin on the bones and the remains of some clothes. The hands were still holding the wooden handle of an ax and on the feet there were very simple leather and cloth boots. Nearby was a pair of gloves made of tree bark and a holder for arrows.

3   Who was this man? How and when had he died? Everybody had a different answer to these questions. Some people thought that it was from this century, perhaps the body of a soldier who died in World War I, since several soldiers had already been found in the area. A Swiss woman believed it might be her father, who had died in those mountains twenty years before and whose body had never been found. The scientists who rushed to look at the body thought it was probably much older, maybe even a thousand years old.

4   Before they could be sure about this, however, they needed to bring the body down the mountain and study it in their laboratories. The question was, who did it belong to? It was lying almost exactly on the border between Italy and Austria and of course both countries wanted the Iceman, as he was called. For some time the Austrians kept the body, while the Italians and Austrians argued, but later it was moved to Italy. It now lies in a special refrigerated room in the South Tyrol Museum in Bolzano.

5   With modern dating techniques, the scientists soon learned that the Iceman was about 5,300 years old. Born in about 3300 B.C., he lived during the Bronze Age in Europe. At first scientists thought he was probably a hunter who had died from an accident in the high mountains. More recent evidence, however, tells a different story. A new kind of X-ray shows an arrowhead still stuck in his shoulder. It left only a tiny hole in his skin, but it caused internal damage and bleeding. He almost certainly died from this wound, and not from the wound on the back of his head. This means that he was probably in some kind of a battle. It may have been part of a larger war, or he may have been fighting bandits. He may even have been a bandit himself.

6   By studying his clothes and tools, scientists have already learned a great deal from the Iceman about the times he lived in. We may never know the full story of how he died, but he has given us important clues to the history of those distant times.

Step 2. Divide the passage into logical parts. Write a topic for each part.
(There may be fewer than five parts.)

Part 1: Paragraphs __*1*__ – _____   Topic:

Part 2: Paragraphs _____ – _____   Topic:

Part 3: Paragraphs _____ – _____   Topic:

Part 4: Paragraphs _____ – _____   Topic:

Part 5: Paragraphs _____ – _____   Topic:

Step 3. Write one sentence to summarize each part.

Part 1:

_____

_____

Part 2:

_____

_____

Part 3:

_____

_____

Part 4:

_____

_____

Part 5:

_____

_____

Step 4. In the space below, combine the summary sentences together into a single paragraph, using signal words to show the relationship between ideas. Use as few words as possible. Compare your work with that of another student.

Summarize "How Men and Women Cope with Stress" by following the steps below.

Step 1. Read the passage all the way through.

How Men and Women Cope with Stress

1   Researchers in the psychology department at the University of California at Los Angeles (UCLA) have discovered a major difference in the way men and women respond to stress. This difference may explain why men are more likely to suffer from stress-related disorders. Their work was published in the *Psychological Review* of the American Psychological Association in July 2000. It was based on the analysis of hundreds of biological and behavioral studies of response to stress by thousands of humans and

2 animal subjects.

    In the past, women were not included in stress research because researchers believed that monthly changes in female hormones would lead to inconsistent responses. But in 1995, a new law in the United States required that federally funded research include both men and women, and since then, the number of women represented in stress studies has increased substantially. Researchers are now beginning to realize that men and women use different coping mechanisms when dealing with stress.

3   Until now, psychological research has maintained that both men and women have the same "fight-or-flight" reaction to stress. In other words, individuals either react with aggressive behavior, such as verbal or physical conflict ("fight"), or they react by withdrawing from the stressful situation ("flight"). This is a survival mechanism that humans learned thousands of years ago when living in the wild with dangerous animals. However, according to the principal investigator in the new research, Shelley E. Taylor, the research team found that men and women have quite different biological and behavioral responses to stress. While men often react to stress in the fight-or-flight response, women often have another kind of reaction. Their response, which is similar in other species as well, could be called "tend and befriend." That is, they often react to stressful conditions by protecting and nurturing their young ("tend"), and by looking for social contact and support from others—especially other females ("befriend").

4   Scientists have long known that in the fight-or-flight reaction to stress, an important role is played by certain hormones that are released by the body, including one called adrenaline. The UCLA research team suggests that the female tend-or-befriend response is also based on a hormone. This hormone, called oxytocin, has been studied in the context of childbirth, but now it is being studied for its role in the response of both men and women to stress. Dr. Taylor explained that "animals and people with high levels of oxytocin are calmer, more relaxed, more social, and less anxious." While men also secrete oxytocin, its effects are reduced by male hormones. This means that in stressful situations, oxytocin has more of an effect on women.

5   In terms of everyday behavior, the UCLA study found that women are far more likely than men to seek social contact when they are feeling stressed. They may phone relatives or friends, or ask directions if they are lost. This difference in seeking social support is one of the most basic differences between men's and women's behavior, according to Dr. Taylor.

6   One of the studies analyzed by Dr. Taylor's team showed how fathers and mothers included in the study responded differently when they came home to their family after a stressful day at work. The typical father wanted to be left alone to enjoy some peace and quiet, or if work was especially stressful, he might react harshly to his children. For a typical mother in this study, coping with a bad day at work meant focusing her attention on her children and their needs.

7   Other researchers looked at how well women functioned after the death of their husband. The death of a spouse is thought to be the worst cause of stress that people can face. They found that women who had close friends and confidantes were more likely to survive the experience without a negative effect on their health or feeling of vitality.

8   The differences in responding to stress may explain the fact that women have a lower incidence of stress-related disorders such as hypertension, aggressive behavior, or alcohol and drug abuse. The tend-and-befriend regulatory system may protect women against stress, and this may explain why women on average live about seven and a half years longer than men.

***Step 2. Divide the passage into logical parts. Write a topic for each part.
(There may be fewer than seven parts.)***

Part 1: Paragraphs __1__ – _____   Topic:

Part 2: Paragraphs _____ – _____   Topic:

Part 3: Paragraphs _____ – _____   Topic:

Part 4: Paragraphs _____ – _____   Topic:

Part 5: Paragraphs _____ – _____   Topic:

Part 6: Paragraphs _____ – _____   Topic:

Part 7: Paragraphs _____ – _____   Topic:

Step 3. Write one sentence to summarize each part.

Part 1:

_____

_____

Part 2:

_____

_____

Part 3:

_____

_____

Part 4:

_____

_____

Part 5:

_____

_____

Part 6:

_____

_____

Part 7:

_____

_____

Step 4. In the space below, combine the sentences together into a single paragraph, using signal words to show the relationship between ideas. Use as few words as possible. Compare your work with that of another student.

You have already read the article below, from Unit 1. Now summarize it by following the steps below.

Step 1. Read the passage all the way through.

Educating Girls Is a Real Lifesaver

by Victoria Brittain and Larry Elliott

1 Clare Short knows it. Every development economist knows it. The World Bank knows it: The education of girls is the surest way to reduce poverty. If there is to be a serious effort to improve the lot of the billions of people deprived of the basic ingredients of a decent life, schools in poor countries have to be full of girls as well as boys.

2 The reason is simple. All the evidence shows that taking girls out of the fields and homes, and putting them behind desks, raises economic productivity, lowers infant and maternal mortality, reduces fertility rates, and improves environmental management. Countries that have pursued gender equality over the past three to four decades have grown faster and become more equal.

3 Why, then, are 90 million primary school-age girls around the world not in school? For the same reason that when Charles Dickens was writing *David Copperfield* 150 years ago girls were absent from the British education system: Men in power mostly prefer it that way, or are not interested enough in changing the situation to commit energy and money to doing so. Or perhaps they do not quite believe the mountains of studies that have established beyond question the link between the eradication of poverty and those years in a schoolroom by ranks of girls.

4 The countries with the poorest record for having women in positions of power or influence have the worst figures for girls' education. High-profile intervention by organizations such as the World Bank has begun successfully with several countries, and more of the same will probably be needed to bring change in conservative, male-run states.

5 Even if there were no development payoff from gender equality in schools, the education of girls would still be a cause worth fighting for. Education is a human right, and the denial of it to girls, in the systematic way it is denied in some feudal societies, is a scar on the community in the twenty-first century.

6 To be born a girl in a rural area in Nepal, Pakistan, Indonesia, Morocco, Togo, or Sudan—half a dozen of the most shameful performers—means being doomed to a life without school, education, or clean water, marriage and babies coming too early, too many births, children who die of preventable diseases, backbreaking work in the fields, subordination to husband and his family, and an early death. Sexual exploitation is also a danger for a female deprived of education. The uneducated woman transmits to her children the same doomed life.

7 Every year, almost 12 million children under the age of five needlessly die of infectious diseases associated with poverty. But each additional year spent by their mothers in primary school lowers the risk of premature child deaths by about 8 percent. In Pakistan, an extra year of school for 1,000 girls could prevent sixty infant deaths.

8 There are places that show how different things can be. In the southern Indian state of Kerala—communist in politics, Christian in ideology—where literacy is almost universal, the infant mortality rate is the lowest in the developing world. Schooling is the route to lowering infant mortality.

9 Each extra year of school also reduces the birthrate and cuts maternal deaths. In Brazil, illiterate women have an average of 6.5 children, whereas those with secondary education have 2.5.

10 With women and girls being the main farmers in Africa and southern Asia, their education offers a chance to develop more efficient farming practices, improve output, and raise awareness of the ecological needs of the land with tree planting and crop rotation. With malnutrition at the level it is in these regions, and environmental degradation posing a threat that exacerbates the global warming affecting us all, the world community cannot afford to ignore this avenue of change.

Step 2. Divide the passage into logical parts. Write a topic for each part. (There may be fewer than seven parts.)

Part 1: Paragraphs _1_ – _____   Topic: _____

Part 2: Paragraphs _____ – _____   Topic: _____

Part 3: Paragraphs _____ – _____   Topic: _____

Part 4: Paragraphs _____ – _____   Topic: _____

Part 5: Paragraphs _____ – _____   Topic: _____

Part 6: Paragraphs _____ – _____   Topic: _____

Part 7: Paragraphs _____ – _____   Topic: _____

Step 3. Write one sentence to summarize each part.

Part 1:

_____

_____

Part 2:

_____

_____

Part 3:

_____

_____

Part 4:

_____

_____

Part 5:

_____

_____

Part 6:

_____

_____

Part 7:

_____

_____

Step 4. In the space below, combine the summary sentences into a single paragraph, using signal words to show the relationship between ideas. Use as few words as possible. Compare your work with that of another student.

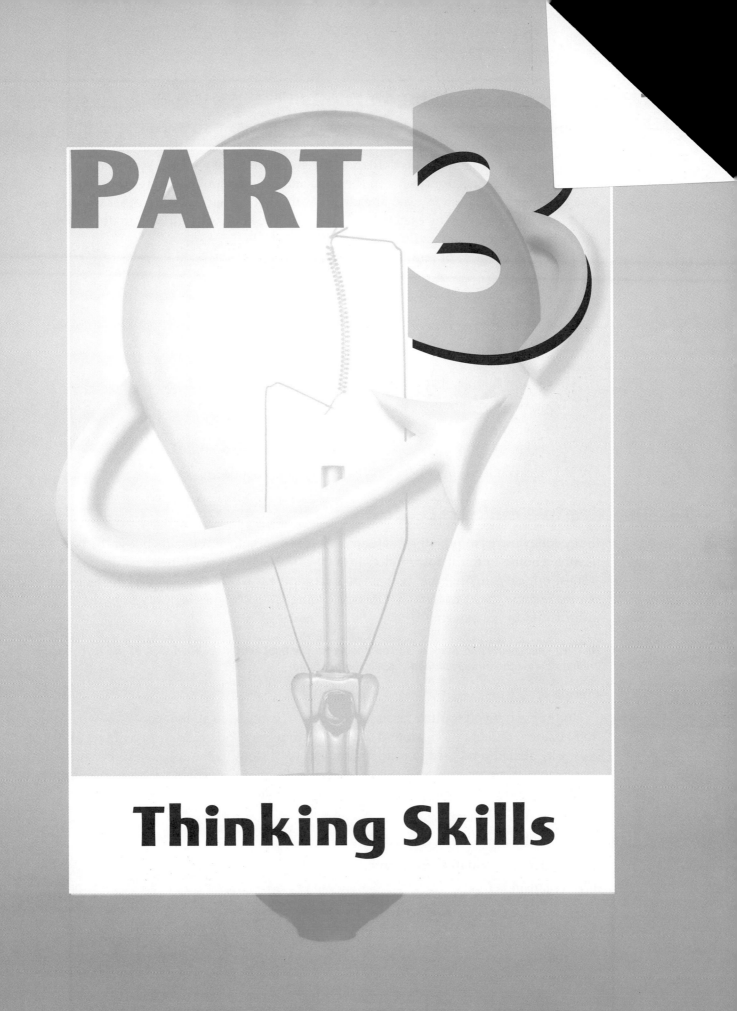

PART 3

Thinking Skills

Introduction to Thinking in English

If you want to read well in English, you must think in English as you read. If you think in another language and translate into English, you will always have difficulty with comprehension. Understanding the words and the grammar is not enough. You need to be able to make logical connections between the ideas and information in your reading. This means using the information you already know to reach a conclusion. In other words, you need to think logically. The exercises in this part of the book will help you to develop your ability to connect ideas and think logically in English.

Here is an example of one kind of logical thinking:

Question:	Is Ned taller than Will?
Known information:	Ned is taller than Peter.
	Peter is taller than Will.
Logical conclusion:	Ned is taller than Will.

Here is an example of another kind of logical thinking:

Question:	Are whales warm-blooded?
Known information:	Whales are mammals.
	Mammals are warm-blooded.
Logical conclusion:	Whales are warm-blooded.

Practice in Thinking Logically

In the following examples, the final sentence is not complete. You will choose the best possible ending from the four choices listed below the paragraph. When you do this, you will use critical thinking; that is, you will look for the ways that each ending may or may not make sense in the paragraph. The best ending always follows logically from the information in the paragraph.

Read the paragraph and think of a good ending for the final sentence. Then look at the four possible endings below the paragraph and choose the best one.

Example a:

In the past, if you wanted to eat Japanese food, you had to go to Japan. Now, you can find Japanese restaurants all around the world, from New York to Rome or Sydney. In the same way, Italian food used to be found only in Italy. Now, Italian restaurants can be found everywhere, from Moscow to Tokyo or São Paulo. People everywhere are learning to enjoy the foods of other countries. Someday, it may be possible to eat

a. Italian food in Tokyo.

b. only traditional food in each country.

c. every kind of food in every country.

d. only Japanese food.

Which is the best ending? Why is it logical? Why are the other choices not possible?

Ending *a* does not follow the ideas in the paragraph logically because the words *someday* and *may be possible* in the last sentence suggests that it is not yet possible to eat Italian food in Tokyo. However, we know from the paragraph that people already eat Italian food in Tokyo. So *a* is not correct.

Ending *b* does not follow logically because we know from the paragraph that many different kinds of food are already available in many countries.

Ending *c* is correct because the main idea of the paragraph states that different national foods are being eaten in many countries, so it is logical to think that someday every kind of food may be found in every country.

Ending *d* is not correct because it is the opposite of what the paragraph says.

Example b:

The "Potato Famine" was a terrible period in Irish history. In the early nineteenth century, many Irish people were very poor. They had little to eat except potatoes. Then, in the 1830s, a disease killed most of the potato plants in Ireland. With no potatoes to eat, millions of Irish people

a. bought other vegetables.

b. ate meat instead.

c. were much happier.

d. died of hunger.

Which is the best ending? Why is it logical? Why are the other choices not possible?

Compare your choice with that of another student. Explain how you got your answer.

Example c:

Coca-Cola was invented in the United States at the beginning of the twentieth century. By the 1950s and 1960s, it had become a popular drink and a kind of symbol of American culture. In the next decade, the Coca-Cola company began exporting to Europe and other countries. The drink was soon in great demand around the world, but shipping costs made it very expensive. That is no longer the case. There are now Coca-Cola factories in many countries. In most places, a can of Coca-Cola is no more expensive than other drinks. In fact, market research recently discovered something surprising. The country where a can of Coca-Cola now costs the most is

a. the United States.

b. Switzerland.

c. China.

d. Australia.

Which is the best ending? Why is it logical? Why are the other choices not possible?

Compare your choice with that of another student. Explain how you got your answer.

- Do these Thinking Skills exercises in sets of five.

- Do not translate from another language while you are reading. Words in another language can confuse you and prevent you from following the ideas in English. Guess the meanings of unknown words.

- Look for the main idea of the paragraph. The correct ending will follow logically from the main idea.

- Work quickly! Your first guess is usually your best guess.

Thinking in English Exercises

These exercises have been divided into three levels of difficulty.

- Level one (Exercises 1–25): The paragraphs at this level are short; the vocabulary and most of the sentences are not complex.

- Level two (Exercises 26–50): The paragraphs at this level are slightly longer and more complex than those in Level One.

- Level three (Exercises 51–75): At this level, the paragraphs are longer, the sentences may be more complex, and the vocabulary is more challenging.

Read each paragraph and think of a good ending to the final sentence. Then look at the four possible endings below the paragraph and choose the best one.

Level one

1. Fog is a major cause of accidents on highways in some areas. Every year many thousands of people lose their lives because fog can dangerously reduce visibility. The drivers cannot see very far ahead, so they

    a. do not have time to avoid accidents.
    b. go faster to avoid accidents.
    c. have more time to read the signs.
    d. do not have time to have accidents.

2. Scotland is famous for its golf courses, and many Scottish people think of golf as a truly Scottish sport. The game did not start in Scotland, however. It was first played in Holland in the fourteenth century and only later did it become

    a. popular with the Dutch.
    b. popular in Scotland.
    c. a real sport.
    d. an Olympic sport.

3.   When Christopher Columbus sailed west from Spain in 1492, he dreamed of reaching Asia. He did not know there were other continents between Europe and Asia or that the land he found was America. He never realized his mistake, and when he died he still believed that the land he had found was

   a. Asia.
   b. America.
   c. Spain.
   d. another continent.

4.   In the past, many people in western Ireland and the Scottish Highlands spoke Gaelic as their first language. Now only a few people speak Gaelic as their first language. These people are mostly from the older generation. The younger people

   a. hardly understand any English.
   b. don't like to speak with strangers.
   c. often don't even understand Gaelic.
   d. don't often speak with the older generation.

5.   When Europeans came to North America in 1620, the forests were full of bears. There were more than half a million of these wild animals. Then the Europeans began to cut down the forests and hunt the bears. By 1900, there were very few bears left. In recent years, however, the bear population has begun to multiply again. There are now at least 200,000 bears, thanks to better

   a. hunting methods.
   b. roads and communication.
   c. laws to protect them.
   d. laws to protect Europeans.

6.   Some of the most famous classical composers died quite young. Among these were Schubert and Mozart, who both died in their thirties. Not all great composers had short lives, however. Bach lived until the age of sixty-five and Haydn until the age of sixty-nine, and others, like Verdi and Strauss,

   a. died at a very young age.
   b. lived on into their eighties.
   c. died while playing the piano.
   d. lived in the twentieth century.

7.   The dog was the first domesticated animal. Very early in human history, people realized that a dog could help with hunting and could protect them against dangerous wild animals. They also realized that dogs were good company, and so they began to keep them as pets. We can say that the dog is man's best friend and his

   a. worst enemy.
   b. only friend.
   c. latest friend.
   d. oldest friend.

8.   For many years, alligator skin was popular in the United States for making fashionable shoes and handbags. From 1870 to 1965, at least 10 million alligators were killed in the United States for their skins. Then, in 1967, the government passed laws against hunting alligators. After that, the alligator population began to grow again. Now there are

    a. no more alligators in the United States.
    b. fewer alligators than there were in 1967.
    c. more alligator skins for making shoes and purses.
    d. nearly 2 million alligators in the United States.

9.   The tulip is a popular flower in gardens around the world. Though Holland is now famous for its tulips, the flowers originally came from Turkey. They were brought to Holland in the seventeenth century and immediately became very fashionable. The Dutch merchants who imported them became wealthy, since they sold the tulips to the

    a. Dutch at very high prices.
    b. Turks at very high prices.
    c. Turks at very low prices.
    d. Dutch at very low prices.

10.   The yew tree grows very slowly and can live for hundreds of years. In southern England one year, a terrible storm blew down many tall, old yew trees. Some of these beautiful trees were more than 300 years old. New yew trees have been planted, but they will

    a. grow more quickly.
    b. only live for a few years.
    c. be tall and beautiful only after many years.
    d. never be as beautiful as the old trees.

11.   In the past, North American forests were full of chestnut trees. People used chestnuts in cooking in many different ways. They also loved to cook chestnuts over a fire and eat them plain. Then in the early 1900s, a disease killed almost all the trees. Now it is hard to find fresh chestnuts in U.S. markets, and most chestnuts for sale are usually

    a. from North America.
    b. diseased.
    c. roasted over a fire.
    d. imported from Europe.

12.   Evergreen trees do not lose their leaves in the autumn like many other kinds of trees. The fact that they do not seem to die in winter gives them special meaning in some places. In Italy, for example, evergreen trees are associated with the idea of life after death. For this reason, Italians often plant evergreens

    a. in cemeteries.
    b. along streets.
    c. in long lines.
    d. in gardens.

13.   Until recently, the kiwi fruit was rare in most countries of the world. All the kiwis came from New Zealand, which meant they were transported a great distance and were expensive. Now many countries grow kiwis. The supply of this fruit has greatly increased, and so it

   a. has become even more expensive.
   b. is harder to get.
   c. is found only in New Zealand.
   d. has become less expensive.

14.   There are many ways to cook eggs. You can fry them, boil them, scramble them, put them in an omelette, or use them to make a cake. If the eggs are very fresh, you can even eat them without cooking them. Whatever way you choose to eat your eggs, however, you must

   a. always break the shell first.
   b. always cook them.
   c. never cook them.
   d. never break the shell.

15.   Chocolate is one of the most popular sweets in the world. It is eaten in candy, cakes, cookies, and puddings. In some places, however, it is also eaten in a non-sweet form. The Mexicans, for example, make a chicken dish with a spicy chocolate sauce. This sauce does not include any

   a. chocolate.
   b. vitamins.
   c. sweetener.
   d. candy.

16.   Legumes are a category of vegetables that includes beans, lentils, and peas. In many parts of the world, legumes are an important basic food. They usually do not cost much, and they are full of protein, vitamins, and minerals. People in the United States and Canada generally do not eat many legumes. Instead, they spend a lot of money on meat. Meat has protein, too, but it also has a lot of unhealthy fat and cholesterol. In fact, many North Americans would be healthier if they

   a. ate more meat.
   b. ate more legumes.
   c. were richer.
   d. spent less money on food.

17.   Pigs have long been the most common animal for meat in many parts of the world. The reason for this is economic. The pig produces meat more efficiently than any other animal. For every 100 pounds of food that it eats, a pig produces 20 pounds of meat. In comparison, beef cattle produce

   a. more than 30 pounds of meat per 100 pounds of food.
   b. twice as much meat per 100 pounds of food.
   c. only about 7 pounds of meat per 100 pounds of food.
   d. nearly double the amount of meat per 100 pounds of food.

18. Vitamins are very important for good health. One vitamin that you need to have regularly is vitamin C. Some fruits and vegetables rich in this vitamin are oranges, lemons, and grapefruits, as well as red peppers, broccoli, and tomatoes. However, vitamin C can be destroyed by heat, so it is a good idea

   a. to eat only cooked fruits and vegetables.
   b. to eat only vegetables that have vitamin C.
   c. to eat lots of uncooked fruits and vegetables.
   d. never to eat uncooked fruits and vegetables.

19. Some birds fly great distances every year. In the fall, they leave their homes in the north and fly thousands of miles south. Then, in the spring, they return to the north, to exactly the same place. Scientists do not really know how they do this. They believe that these birds must have

   a. some way of speaking.
   b. an especially rich diet.
   c. a kind of map in their heads.
   d. special feathers on their wings.

20. We usually do not think of the night sky as a colorful scene. You don't see much color, in fact, if you look at the stars with just your eyes. However, scientists with special equipment now have a different picture of what is in the sky at night. A new series of photographs shows

   a. no colors in the night sky.
   b. bright colors in the night sky.
   c. that the night sky has little color.
   d. lots of new stars in the night sky.

21. Many people are very afraid of snakes. It is true that poisonous snakes can make you ill or even kill you, but there are actually very few poisonous snakes. Most snakes are harmless. In fact, they usually are afraid of people. If you meet a snake in your garden, it will probably

   a. bite you.
   b. slide quickly away.
   c. stay and watch you.
   d. come closer.

22. When people began to try to create a "flying machine" in the eighteenth century, they used hot-air balloons. These balloons went up into the air but then could not be controlled. They went wherever the wind was blowing. The idea of a real flying machine remained a dream for a long time. That dream finally came true in 1903, when Wilbur and Orville Wright

   a. invented a new kind of engine.
   b. made their first successful flight in an airplane.
   c. flew across the Atlantic Ocean.
   d. invented the hot-air balloon.

23.   In a traditional children's song, a star is compared to a "diamond in the sky." Some scientists are now saying that there may be real diamonds among the stars of the universe. These diamonds are certainly interesting for the scientists. However, they are probably not going to make anyone rich, because

a. only children can see them.
b. only the scientists know where they are.
c. they are too expensive.
d. they are too far away.

24.   Exercising in your home may be good for your health, but it may not be good for your children. Each year, about 25,000 children in the United States are hurt by exercise equipment. The exercise bicycle is the most common cause of injury. Many children have lost a finger or a toe in the wheels of these bicycles. So if you have an exercise bicycle, you should

a. let your children use it, too.
b. stop using it immediately.
c. use it every day.
d. not let your children play with it.

25.   Long before airplanes were invented, people wanted to be able to fly. Early scientists studied birds' wings to see how they worked. Then they built wings of feathers, but when they tried to fly they never

a. spread their wings enough.
b. stayed up in the air for long.
c. hurt themselves.
d. fell to the ground.

Level two

26.   What would you do if you got lost in a desert? You should first of all look for water to drink. But deserts are very dry, with no lakes or rivers. Where can you find water? The answer is simple: in desert plants. In fact, the most common desert plant, the cactus, contains lots of good water. With the right method and some simple tools, you

a. can get only a few drops of water a day.
b. will get water that is undrinkable.
c. will be able to find some bottled water.
d. can get about a quart of good water a day.

27.   Do you know what to do if someone falls off a small boat? First, you should throw out a life ring to the person in the water so he or she does not drown. Then you should try to turn back and get closer with the boat, trying not to lose sight of the person in the water. When you get close to the person, you should help him or her climb back into the boat. This is not always easy, especially if

a. the weather is warm.
b. the person is hurt or cold.
c. you do not know how to swim.
d. the person is a good swimmer.

28.　　The game of croquet was probably invented in France. In the thirteenth century, French villagers played something they called "paille-maille." From there, the game traveled to Ireland, where they called it "crooky." In the mid-nineteenth century, some people in England began playing "croaky." It quickly became popular in many countries, from

a. the United States to India and Australia.
b. the south coast of England to the north of Scotland.
c. one village to another.
d. the Middle Ages to our modern age.

29.　　In 1585, Sir Walter Raleigh tried to start the first English settlement in North America, but it was not successful. Many settlers became sick and others died of hunger or in battles with the Native Americans. When another ship from England arrived at the settlement a few years later, the newcomers found that

a. the settlement had grown.
b. the settlers were not glad to see it.
c. all the settlers had died.
d. all the settlers were healthy.

30.　　The one-cent coin in the United States has a picture of Abraham Lincoln on it. Lincoln, the sixteenth president of the United States, was one of the country's greatest presidents. He came from a poor family, and as a young man, he had to work very hard. This was the reason why the government decided to put Lincoln's picture on the smallest coin. It would remind everyone that in America

a. someone from a poor family could become president.
b. someone from a poor family could never become president.
c. most of the presidents have come from poor families.
d. there have been no presidents from poor families.

31.　　Many people are afraid of going to the dentist. There are a number of reasons for this fear. One reason is that the patient cannot see what the dentist is doing. Another reason is that the patient, who is lying back, may feel very helpless. People also may be influenced by the general belief that dentists cause pain and are therefore scary. And finally, many people

a. like seeing the dentist's shiny instruments.
b. do not like to brush their teeth very often.
c. are afraid of going to the doctor as well.
d. are afraid of the dentist's instruments.

32.　　The Japanese love to eat raw fish. Dishes of uncooked fish, called sushi or sashimi, are prepared at most Japanese restaurants. Japanese cooks use many kinds of fish or shellfish for these dishes. Whatever kind of fish they use, however, it must always be very fresh. To prove that a fish is fresh, some restaurants will show the fish to customers

a. and then cook it on a grill.
b. when it is still alive.
c. when it has been cooked.
d. after they have eaten it.

33.   The gasoline burned in car engines is the main cause of air pollution in many cities. In order to reduce pollution, the number of cars on the roads must be reduced. This is only possible if fewer people drive their cars every day. Thus, if city governments want to improve the quality of the air in their city, they need to improve the

a. highway system.
b. quality of life in the city.
c. connections between cities.
d. public transportation system.

34.   Imagine a baby about five months old. It can cry and smile, and it can eat and sleep. Did you know a baby can also count? According to new psychological research, a small baby can even add and subtract small numbers of objects. People generally think that these abilities are learned much later, but in fact they are

a. not present until adulthood.
b. learned only by five-month-old babies.
c. already present in small babies.
d. very difficult for children to learn.

35.   Children who are left-handed tend to have more accidents than right-handed children. Doctors have two theories to explain this fact. One theory says that left-handed children may simply fall and bump into things more often. Another theory, however, explains the accidents very differently. According to this theory, the problem is not with the children, but with the world around them. Most things, such as doors, cars, and toys are

a. designed for right-handed people.
b. designed for left-handed people.
c. not designed for people to use.
d. made by people without children.

36.   One of the most important principles in biology is that all living things must come from other living things. This principle was not discovered until the eighteenth century. Before that, people believed that life could come from nonliving matter. For example, they thought that worms could come from meat. Then an Italian scientist named Francesco Redi tried an experiment. He covered some meat with a cloth so that flies could not land on it. When no worms grew on the meat, he knew that the worms really came from

a. scientists.
b. the cloth.
c. fly eggs.
d. the meat.

37.   Sixty-five million years ago, the dinosaurs all suddenly disappeared from the earth. Until recently, scientists did not understand why this happened, but then, in Mexico, they discovered a huge circle more than 100 miles/160.9 kilometers wide. This circle was caused by some very large object, probably a meteor, that hit the earth and caused changes in the earth's climate and sea levels. These changes may have

    a. helped the dinosaurs live longer.
    b. been necessary for the dinosaurs.
    c. killed the dinosaurs in Mexico.
    d. been disastrous for the dinosaurs.

38.   Frogs are not generally known for being good parents. The female frog usually lays her eggs and then goes away, and male frogs never go near the eggs or the babies. However, one kind of tropical frog is known to be an especially caring parent. These frogs, both male and female, stay with the eggs until the baby frogs are born. Then the mother and father carry the babies on their backs to a special kind of water plant. The parents put one baby frog in each of the flowers of this plant, and every day

    a. the babies grow larger.
    b. the babies swim further.
    c. they bring food to the babies.
    d. they swim around the babies.

39.   Scientists wondered for a long time just how whales are related to land mammals, especially the largest land mammal, the elephant. They believed there must have been some kind of in-between mammal that lived partly in the sea and partly on the land. They had no evidence for such an animal, however, until the discovery of the bones of an animal scientists have called "Pakicetus." This large mammal, which was alive 50 million years ago,

    a. could not swim but it could run very fast.
    b. lived on the land but found its food in the water.
    c. was totally different from both elephants and whales.
    d. lived in the deep ocean water and ate mostly fish.

40.   "Every time you eat a sweet, drink green tea." This is what some Japanese mothers used to tell their children. Modern dentists never took this advice very seriously until just recently. Research now shows that green tea really does help your teeth. It contains something that naturally kills the bacteria that damage teeth. This discovery was made by a Japanese-American chemist, who is planning to make and sell

    a. green tea toothpaste.
    b. a new kind of sweet.
    c. green toothbrushes.
    d. a sweet toothpaste.

41.   An albino is an animal (or a person) that is born without any color. Albinos have pale, whitish fur, feathers, or hair, and pink skin and eyes. Albinos are very rare in nature because they usually do not live very long. One reason for this is that they often become blind and cannot take care of themselves. Another reason is simply the color. In most regions, a white animal

a. is not noticed by other animals, and so it is not disturbed.
b. can hide well in the snow all winter.
c. can easily find other animals and kill them.
d. is easily seen and caught by larger animals.

42.   In 1990, 80,000 pairs of Nike athletic shoes fell off a ship in the Pacific Ocean. Ocean scientists were very interested when they heard about this. They asked anyone who found a pair of these shoes to report the finding so they could learn where the shoes landed. In all, 1,300 pairs of shoes were reported along the coast of the United States and Canada. These reports gave the scientists important information about

a. certain rare sea birds over the Pacific Ocean.
b. the movement of ocean currents.
c. how to get free shoes.
d. shipping routes in the Pacific Ocean.

43.   For centuries, men who work as coal miners have had many health problems. The worst of these problems is a disease called "Black Lung," which is caused by the coal dust in the mines. Until very recently, about one in every five miners in the United States got this disease. For these men, it meant poor health and a shorter life. Then, in 1969, a new law forced the coal companies to improve the working conditions for miners. Since then,

a. many more miners have gotten "Black Lung."
b. the conditions in the mines have worsened.
c. there have been many fewer miners in the mines.
d. fewer miners have gotten "Black Lung."

44.   The connection between sunlight and cancer has been known for a long time. Now there is no doubt that getting a sunburn increases the risk of skin cancer. For this reason, doctors today advise everyone, especially young people, to avoid staying in the sun for a long time. If you do spend time in the sun, doctors say you should use some protective sunscreen. A recent study shows, however, that this advice is not being followed. In fact, many young people

a. stay out of the sun.
b. do not use sunscreen.
c. use sunscreen.
d. do not want to get cancer.

45.   Many scientists, including Charles Darwin, have wondered why we cry tears. What is the biological or evolutionary purpose of tears? We could just as well cry without any tears falling, but, in fact, our eyes fill with tears. Scientists have proposed many theories about tears, but none of these theories has been proven. In evolutionary terms,

   a. the reason for tears remains a mystery.
   b. Darwin explained the origin of tears.
   c. there are many reasons for crying with tears.
   d. only Darwin studied the origin of tears.

46.   Theoretical physicists are known for their bad luck with equipment. Other scientists like to say that something breaks whenever a theoretical physicist walks into the room. One physicist, Wolfgang Pauli, was especially famous for the unfortunate effect he had on laboratory equipment. A scientist in Göttingen, Germany, told about the time some equipment in his laboratory suddenly broke for no clear reason. Later, he heard that on that day Pauli had been traveling by train through Germany. In fact, the train had stopped at the station in Göttingen

   a. long after the equipment had broken.
   b. long before the equipment broke.
   c. at the same moment that the equipment broke.
   d. long enough for Pauli to change to another train.

47.   The Chinese were the first people to make books. They discovered how to make paper and how to print books in about A.D. 1200. At that time, there was almost no contact between Europe and China. One of the few Europeans to travel that far east was Marco Polo, an Italian. He visited China in the thirteenth century and may have seen some books. However, he did not bring the idea of making books back home with him. Europeans, in fact,

   a. learned how to make books from Marco Polo.
   b. never learned how to make books.
   c. did not start making books until much later.
   d. started making books before the Chinese.

48.   A bird feeder can provide you with an interesting new hobby—bird-watching. Winter is the best time for this hobby, since then the birds have trouble finding other food. If you put the feeder near a window, you can watch them from inside your home. However, once you start feeding the birds, you should continue until spring. If you stop in the middle of winter, the birds

   a. will have more to eat.
   b. may stay near the house.
   c. may get cold.
   d. may die of hunger.

49. Over 15 million people cross the twenty-five-mile-wide English Channel every year. Some of these people go across in airplanes and some by ferry boat. These days, many others drive or take the train through the "Chunnel," the tunnel that connects England and France. The idea of building a tunnel goes back to the nineteenth century, but it only became a serious possibility late in the twentieth century. The reasons for this were partly technical and partly political. Until recently, most English people wanted England to remain separate. They did not want to

   a. live on an island anymore.
   b. travel by boat to get to other European countries.
   c. be connected directly with the rest of Europe.
   d. learn other European languages.

50. According to Eugene Morton, a scientist, all animal sounds have certain things in common. Animals tend to make low, loud sounds when they are angry and to make high, softer sounds when they are fearful or friendly. Human beings can, of course, make many more kinds of sounds than most animals, but Morton believes that even human speech has the same features as other animal sounds. According to his theory, if you say, "I love you," your voice will be

   a. naturally high.
   b. usually very loud.
   c. naturally low.
   d. usually angry.

Level three

51. Scientists believe that the first Americans came from northeast Asia. These people were probably hunters from what is now northern China, Japan, or Siberia. Many thousands of years ago, they crossed over from Asia to what is now Alaska. From there, they spread throughout North and South America. The first evidence for this theory was found in Chile in 1936, when scientists found the teeth of some very early Indians. These teeth proved to be very similar to the teeth of people in

   a. America today.
   b. northeast Asia today.
   c. the 1930s.
   d. very early times.

52. We all know that monkeys are smart animals, but sometimes their intelligence is surprising and entertaining. A psychologist once wanted to see just how smart a monkey was. He hung a banana high up in a monkey's cage and placed several large boxes and a stick nearby. He wanted to see if the monkey could use the boxes and the stick to get the banana. The monkey looked at the banana, the boxes, and the stick. Then it took the psychologist's hand and led him to where the banana was hanging. It jumped up onto his shoulders and

   a. looked at the banana.
   b. reached the banana from there.
   c. jumped down onto one of the boxes.
   d. hit him with the stick.

53.   Unlike plastic, which is artificial, rubber is a natural product. It is made from latex, a white liquid found in certain plants, especially the Para rubber tree. This tree originally came from the Amazon forests in Brazil. The Indians of that area used the latex from the rubber tree to make statues, cups, and shoes. When latex was discovered by Europeans, they soon found many uses for it. For example, an Englishman named Charles Mackintosh invented a way to make waterproof rainwear with latex. His method is no longer used, but even today, many people in England

a. call a raincoat an "overcoat."
b. do not like to use latex.
c. call a raincoat a "mackintosh."
d. like to plant rubber trees.

54.   After simple animal skins, wool is probably the oldest material used for making clothing. We do not know exactly when people started to make woolen clothing, but it was probably quite early in human history. The wool was made from the hair of whatever kind of animal people had available. Most of the time these were sheep, but in some desert areas people made cloth from camel hair. In other areas, they used goat hair, and in the mountains of South America, they used the hair from llamas. All these kinds of wool have one thing in common: They protect a person's body from outside changes in temperature. Woolen clothing keeps

a. the body warm in summer and cool in winter.
b. insects away from the body.
c. the body cool in summer and warm in winter.
d. hair on a person's body.

55.   Farmers in most of the industrialized countries grow cash crops today. This means that they usually grow and sell large amounts of only a few crops, such as soy, wheat, or corn. They use the money to buy what they need for their families and farms. In the past, farming was quite different. Most farmers used to grow many different kinds of crops and also raise cows, pigs, chickens, and other animals. They sometimes sold extra farm products or animals, but

a. they usually kept most of the farm products for their families.
b. they preferred to sell all of the farm products for cash.
c. people in the city needed food from the farms, too.
d. they did not grow soy in those days.

56.   In many countries, textbooks for children in elementary school give a false picture of women's lives. They often show women only as mothers and housewives. The women are seen caring for their families or doing simple tasks around the home. In reality, in many countries, the majority of women work outside the home. They may also have children and do housework, but at the same time, they have jobs. Their lives can be quite complicated as they try to balance their responsibilities at home and at work. Their situation is nothing like the situations shown in the school books. Some educators believe that these books

   a. do not help girls prepare for their future.
   b. give girls a good idea of their future.
   c. show women in many complex situations.
   d. do not show enough pictures of women.

57.   Supermarket managers have all kinds of tricks to encourage people to spend money. Their aim is to slow people down as they move through the supermarket. To do this, they place colorful displays in surprising places to catch the customers' attention. They also make the aisles (walkways) near the cash registers narrower, so customers will not be able to move quickly with their shopping carts. Sometimes the floor is even slightly uphill for people moving toward the cash registers. The idea behind these tricks is simple: If you make customers go slowly, they will

   a. get angry and go home.
   b. buy a few extra items.
   c. buy healthier food.
   d. decide not to buy anything more.

58.   The guppy is a small fish that people often keep in bowls or tanks in their homes. In their bowls, guppies are harmless, but in the wild, the story is different. When some guppy owners in Nevada grew tired of their fish, they threw them in a small lake. The guppies then multiplied rapidly and ate all the food in the lake, so that there was none left for the native fish, which disappeared. The same thing has happened in a number of other lakes in the western United States, and now at least one species of fish—the white river spring fish—is almost extinct. Thus, even a little fish like the guppy

   a. can survive in lakes and rivers.
   b. is sold in pet stores throughout the United States.
   c. sometimes improves the ecology of lakes.
   d. can cause big changes in the ecology of lakes.

59.   Imagine what it would be like to wake up and find yourself locked in a metal box. This is what happened to a man in South Africa who had been in a car accident. The doctors thought he was dead, so he was put in the metal box. He remained there, unconscious, for two days. Then he woke up and called for help. The people who heard him were afraid at first, but when they realized that he was alive, they let him out of the box. He was happy to be alive and free, but his happiness did not last long because his girlfriend refused to see him. She did not believe that he was really alive and said that

a. he must be a ghost returning from the dead.
b. she wanted to marry him as soon as possible.
c. he should go back into the box.
d. he must be still asleep and dreaming.

60.   Sociologists and psychologists have argued for centuries about how a person's character is formed. The argument has long been known as "nature versus nurture," describing the two main opposing theories. The first theory says that character is formed genetically before birth. According to this theory, nature—through genetics—determines what a person will be like. The other theory says, on the contrary, that a newborn baby has no definite character. The child's character develops as he or she grows up, and the development of that character is influenced by the child's family and social environment. Thus, according to the second theory, the most important factors are

a. natural and genetic.
b. scientific and theoretical.
c. psychological and physical.
d. cultural and social.

61.   The problem of pollution has turned up on every continent on earth—even Antarctica. Winter Quarters Bay, on Antarctica, is the site of an important scientific station. Though the population here is never more than a few thousand people, this bay is as polluted as many city harbors. The reason is that for a long time, people at the station dumped garbage into the water. However, that has stopped now because of an international agreement. According to the agreement, scientific communities in Antarctica must

a. dump all their garbage into the bay.
b. take all their garbage away from Antarctica.
c. close down all their scientific stations.
d. stop polluting the air in Antarctica.

62.   Four out of five people suffer from back pain at some time in their working lives. In the United States, it is the most expensive health problem in the workplace. In all, it costs people up to $60 billion in medical expenses and lost working time. Back pain is bad for business as well—it is the cause of 40 percent of all lost work days. That means a total of about 93 million sick days a year in the United States. Doctors now believe that exercise is the best treatment for many kinds of back pain. For this reason, some companies

   a. do not let their employees exercise too much.
   b. send their employees to specialized doctors.
   c. tell their employees to get more rest.
   d. have started exercise programs for employees.

63.   Lichen are one of the few kinds of life that can survive in the mountains of Antarctica. These tiny plants live in small holes in the rocks. Outside, the extreme cold and strong winds prevent any life at all from surviving. Inside the holes, these lichen manage to find enough water and warmth to keep alive, even though they are frozen much of the time. This fact means that the lichen function extremely slowly and live a very long time. Scientists believe that a lichen may remain alive for thousands of years. If this is true, the lichen may

   a. be among the oldest forms of life on earth.
   b. live only for a few years before they die.
   c. not survive another Antarctic winter.
   d. be one of the newest forms of life on earth.

64.   The Celts were never an empire or a nation, just groups of tribes. They came out of central Europe in about 1000 B.C. By 300 B.C., they had spread over all of Europe, from Turkey to Spain to the British Isles. Later they were conquered by the Romans and by various Germanic tribes, but many Celtic legends stayed alive and are still familiar to us today. The best known of these is the story of King Arthur and the Round Table. There is some evidence that Arthur may really have been a Celtic leader in the early sixth century. Even if he never lived, his story almost certainly has Celtic origins, since it includes

   a. many typically British elements.
   b. very few elements that could be Celtic.
   c. some traditionally European historical figures.
   d. many typically Celtic elements.

65.   For the Japanese, a bath is not just a way to get clean. It is also a way to relax and recover from a stressful day. In Japan, in fact, people like to take very long, hot baths. While they are in the bathtub, they like to listen to music or read books. However, reading in the bathtub can be a problem sometimes, as water and books do not get along very well. With this problem in mind, a Japanese company has begun selling special "bath" books. These books

   a. are made entirely of paper.
   b. have plastic pages.
   c. do not break when they fall.
   d. are printed in English.

66.   Monticello, the home of Thomas Jefferson, is much admired today for its wonderful views of the Virginia countryside. It is located on the top of a high hill— "Monticello" means "little mountain" in Italian. In Jefferson's time, however, people thought he was a little crazy to build a house on a hilltop. In those days, people did not care so much about views. They cared more about comfort, so they usually built their houses in places they could get to easily. For that reason, most houses were built

   a. on top of mountains.
   b. out of brick.
   c. in low areas.
   d. far from cities.

67.   Anthropologists used to believe that romantic love was invented by Europeans in the Middle Ages. By romantic love, they mean an intense attraction and longing to be with the loved person. Some anthropologists believed that this kind of love spread from the West to other cultures only recently. Others thought that it may have existed in some other cultures, but only among the rich and privileged. Now, however, most anthropologists agree that romantic love has probably always existed among humans. It is not surprising, then, that stories of romance, like Romeo and Juliet,

   a. exist only in the West.
   b. exist only in books and plays.
   c. are unusual outside of the West.
   d. are found in many cultures.

68.   At Ashkelon, in Israel, archaeologists have found a very large dog cemetery. The cemetery dates from the fifth century B.C., when that area was part of the Persian Empire. So far, about 1,000 dog graves have been found in the cemetery. Archaeologists are not certain about the reason for so many graves, but they believe that dogs must have been very important for the people there. In fact, all of the dogs died of natural causes and were buried very carefully. Perhaps

   a. dogs were important in the religion of these people.
   b. these people ate dog meat when they could not find other meat.
   c. there were not many cats in that part of the Persian Empire.
   d. these people wanted to get rid of all their dogs.

69.   Why do we grow old? This is a question that people have asked since the beginning of history. Now biologists are looking for scientific answers to this question. They think that aging is part of our genetic program. From the evolutionary point of view this makes sense. A person who can no longer have children is not useful to the species, so he or she

   a. grows old and dies.
   b. lives a long life.
   c. stops having children.
   d. has a genetic program.

70.   Almost every language has some topic areas that are especially rich in vocabulary and idiomatic expressions. For example, the Inuit people who live in the far north of Alaska and Canada have many different ways to describe snow. The Irish, on the other hand, have a wide variety of ways to describe a green landscape. Other examples can be found in language relating to food. For instance, the French and Italian languages are rich in vocabulary for talking about wine, while American English has many ways to indicate how a steak should be cooked. We can conclude from all this that the development of a language is

   a. influenced by only weather and geography.
   b. influenced by both environment and culture.
   c. not influenced by any factors outside the language itself.
   d. independent of all cultural factors.

71.   Texas is famous for its cattle farms, but another kind of farm is growing much faster: ostrich farms. Not long ago, ostrich farms were rare, but there are now thousands of them in the United States, many of them in Texas. It's easy to see why so many farmers are interested in these large birds. The price of ostrich meat is many times higher than the price of beef, which makes the birds extremely valuable: A pair of young adult ostriches are worth over $40,000, and an ostrich egg may be worth up to $1,500. Since a female ostrich may lay up to eighty eggs a year,

   a. farmers may not be able to make much profit.
   b. ostrich farming is not a very profitable business.
   c. farmers may prefer to raise cattle.
   d. ostrich farmers can make a large profit quickly.

72.   What is the world's largest living creature? It may be a fungus that scientists have discovered in the state of Wisconsin. This fungus is huge—it spreads over about thirty-seven acres and is still growing. This may seem like a science fiction nightmare, but in fact the fungus lives underground in the woods and does not disturb its environment. It also grows very slowly, having taken 1,500 years to reach its present size. Scientists used to think that this fungus was made up of many different fungi. Now, with DNA testing, they have definite proof that it is really

   a. just one individual fungus.
   b. separate fungi living close together.
   c. dead material.
   d. a science fiction nightmare.

73. After Columbus traveled to the Americas, Europeans began to import many kinds of products from the New World. Some of the products are well known, such as coffee, cocoa, tobacco, tomatoes, corn, potatoes, pumpkins, beans, and strawberries, but other products are little known today. For two centuries, one of the most important New World exports was the cochineal. This small red insect was used for making red cloth. It is still used for this purpose today, and some insects are still exported from the Americas. However, with the invention of chemical colorants, the cochineal has

   a. regained its commercial importance.
   b. become extinct.
   c. lost its commercial importance.
   d. lost its brilliant red coloring.

74. Immigration in the United States continues at a steady pace in the twenty-first century, with hundreds of thousands of legal immigrants every year and many more illegal immigrants. The immigrants of the early twentieth century came mostly from Europe, but today's immigrants come from many different parts of the world and many different cultural and racial backgrounds. Like the earlier immigrants, however, they have a strong desire to work and do well in their new homeland. For this reason, many people feel that the U.S. government should not shut its doors to the newcomers. Immigrants have helped the country grow in the past, and now the United States

   a. needs better laws to keep out immigrants.
   b. could benefit from them again.
   c. does not need people from other countries.
   d. could benefit only from European immigrants.

75. In many parts of England, hedges are an important part of the countryside. (A hedge is a kind of fence made of bushes or trees.) An English botanist, Max Hooper, studied the English hedges and discovered some interesting facts about them. First, he determined that the older the hedge, the more species of bushes and trees it contained. Second, he concluded that a hedge usually starts with one species and gains a species with each century. Using this rule, which became known as "Hooper's Rule," people have studied hedges in England and discovered that many of them are very old. Quite a few of them have more than ten species, which means that they

   a. may be 1,000 years old.
   b. may be only 100 years old.
   c. will be made of bushes and trees.
   d. must be English.

PART 4

Reading Faster

Introduction to Reading Faster

There are two important reasons for learning to read faster:

- You can read more in less time.

- You can improve your comprehension.

How is it possible to improve your comprehension when you read faster? The answer is very simple: When you read slowly, you read one word at a time. The words seem separated like the words below. Is it easier or harder to understand these sentences?

> What really happens when we read? Some people think we read one word at a time. They think we read a word, understand it, and then move on to the next word.

Reading separate words makes it harder to understand. The separate words become separate pieces of information that you must remember. By the time you get to the end of a sentence, you may have forgotten the beginning!

When you read faster, you understand better because your brain can make connections and put the words together. They are no longer single words, but groups of words that form ideas. These ideas are easier to remember than a lot of single words. It is also easier to connect these smaller ideas together to get the general idea of what you are reading. This is why your comprehension actually improves with faster reading.

How to Read Faster: Four Steps

By following these four steps you can increase your reading speed. Many students have doubled their speed in one semester! This means that if they began with a reading rate of 100 wpm (words per minute), they were able to read 200 wpm at the end.

Step 1. Check your reading habits.

Certain bad habits may be slowing you down. Do you

a. try to pronounce each word as you read? Pronunciation is not necessary for comprehension. In fact, if you try to say the words, even silently, you will probably understand less.

b. usually move your lips while you read silently? If you do, you will never be able to read faster than 200 words per minute, the fastest speed at which English can be spoken. This is not fast enough for good reading comprehension.

c. follow the words in the text with your finger or a pencil while you read? This is another habit that can slow you down. It also limits the way you read because you cannot skip around. Pointing at the words forces your eyes to follow the lines of text too closely. *Your eyes should follow your thoughts, not your finger!*

d. translate into your native language as you read in English? Do you often write translations of words in the English text? These habits will slow down your reading speed and will interfere with your ability to think in English.

Step 2. Skip over unknown words.

In order to read more quickly, good readers usually skip over words they do not know. They also skip over many other words that are not important for the general meaning. In fact, you can get the important ideas from a text even with many words missing.

Example a: In this passage, every eighth word is missing. Do not try to guess the missing words. Read the passage and answer the comprehension questions below the passage.

Dear Joan,

   I'm sorry not to have written sooner. I have been very busy since I _____ back from vacation. There has been so _____ to do at work lately! Almost every _____ I have to stay late. I've even _____ going in to the office on Saturdays, _____.

   I've had no time to relax at _____ either. Every free moment has been taken _____ by work on the house. The roof _____ in very bad condition after the big _____. If I'd known how busy I'd be _____ work, I might have waited.

   Anyway, it's _____ finished now. So at last I can _____ you to come over some weekend with _____ family. We could all take a walk _____ Mt. Grey.

   Judy sends her love. We _____ to see you all soon.

                                        Love, George

1. Why has George not written sooner?

2. What has he been doing in his free time?

3. What does George suggest to Joan?

Example b: In this passage, every fifth word is missing. Again, do not try to guess the missing words. Read the passage and answer the questions below.

   Grace Simmons is only fourteen, and she speaks no French, but she is famous in Paris. She has become a _____ model for a well-known _____ designer. Grace is from _____, Michigan. Her father is _____ car salesperson and her _____ is a teacher. Grace _____ very unhappy as a _____ girl because she was _____ tall—almost six feet. _____ other children laughed at _____ all the time and _____ had very few friends. _____ she was eleven years _____, Grace's mother took her _____ a modeling school. There _____ tall girls at the _____, so she finally felt _____. When she was younger, _____ had often been teased _____ her height. Her Korean _____ and her American father _____ her special looks and _____ were really quite extraordinary. _____ as a fashion model, _____ looks have brought her _____ fame and money.

1. Why was Grace unhappy as a child?

2. When did her life change for the better?

3. How did she become rich and famous?

How many of the questions in Examples a and b were you able to answer? You probably could answer all of them. You did not need to read every word in order to understand!

Step 3. Do reading sprints.

Sprints (short-distance runs at fast speeds) are often used by runners who want to improve their speed. Reading sprints can help you break old habits and improve your reading speed. You should do them regularly, in class and on your own. To do reading sprints, follow the directions below and write your answers on a separate piece of paper. You will need your pleasure reading book and a good clock or watch so you can time yourself.

1. Write the title of your book: _____

2. Mark with a pencil where you are starting to read in your book. Make a note of your starting time and read for five minutes. How many pages did you read? _____

3. Now count the same number of pages ahead and mark the place as you did before. (For example, if you read one and a half pages in five minutes, count ahead one and a half pages.) Mark the place in the margin with a pencil.

4. Try to read the new pages in only *four* minutes. If you do not succeed the first time, keep trying until you do (using new pages each time). You will need to force your eyes to move faster along the page. You may also have to skip over some words. Do not worry about your comprehension at this point. It is normal to feel that you understand less when you are concentrating on speed. Better comprehension will come later.

5. Now count the same number of pages ahead and mark the place as you did before. Try to read these pages in *three* minutes. If you do not succeed, try again with new pages.

6. Next, try to read the same number of pages in *two* minutes. Keep trying until you succeed. You may be able to catch only a few words from the text. This does not matter. The important thing is to make your eyes move quickly and understand *something* from the text.

7. Finally, make a note of where you are starting, and read again for five minutes.

8. How many pages did you read this time? _____
    How does this compare with your first five-minute reading before doing the sprints?

Many students find that they read faster the second time, after the sprints. Slow reading is often a matter of habit. Your eyes are used to moving across the page at a certain speed from when you were first learning to read in English. When you do reading sprints, you realize that your eyes can, in fact, move more quickly. At first, reading faster may seem difficult and tiring, but with practice, it will get easier and your comprehension will improve.

Note: Since you may find that you don't remember what you read during the sprints, you may want to go back to your pleasure reading book and reread those pages afterward.

Step 4. Practice reading faster by timing yourself.

To increase your reading speed, you need to practice reading against the clock. Many students find that they have a reading rate between 50 and 200 words per minute. Reading at less than 200 words per minute means that you are almost certainly reading word by word and having trouble understanding.

When you read against the clock, be sure to record the exact time you start and finish reading the passage.

Use the example on the next page to practice timing yourself and to find out your reading rate.

The Iceman
Starting time _____

On a September day in 1991, two Germans were climbing the mountains between Austria and Italy. High up on a mountain pass, they found the body of a man lying on the ice. At that height (10,499 feet, or 3,200 meters), the ice is usually permanent, but 1991 had been an especially warm year. The mountain ice had melted more than usual and so the body had come to the surface.

It was lying face downward. The skeleton was in perfect condition, except for a wound in the head. There was still skin on the bones and the remains of some clothes. The hands were still holding the wooden handle of an ax and on the feet there were very simple leather and cloth boots. Nearby was a pair of gloves made of tree bark and a holder for arrows.

Who was this man? How and when had he died? Everybody had a different answer to these questions. Some people thought that he was from this century, perhaps the body of a soldier who died in World War I, since several soldiers had already been found in the area. A Swiss woman believed it might be her father, who had died in those mountains twenty years before and whose body had never been found. The scientists who rushed to look at the body thought it was probably much older, maybe even a thousand years old.

Before they could be sure about this, however, they needed to bring the body down the mountain and study it in their laboratories. The question was, who did it belong to? It was lying almost exactly on the border between Italy and Austria and of course both countries wanted the Iceman, as he was called. For some time the Austrians kept the body, while the Italians and Austrians argued, but later it was moved to Italy. It now lies in a special refrigerated room in the South Tyrol Museum in Bolzano.

With modern dating techniques, the scientists soon learned that the Iceman was about 5,300 years old. Born in about 3300 B.C., he lived during the Bronze Age in Europe. At first scientists thought he was probably a hunter who had died from an accident in the high mountains. More recent evidence, however, tells a different story. A new kind of X-ray shows an arrowhead still stuck in his shoulder. It left only a tiny hole in his skin, but it caused internal damage and bleeding. He almost certainly died from this wound, and not from the wound on the back of his head. This means that he was probably in some kind of a battle. It may have been part of a larger war, or he may have been fighting bandits. He may even have been a bandit himself.

By studying his clothes and tools, scientists have already learned a great deal from the Iceman about the times he lived in. We may never know the full story of how he died, but he has given us important clues to the history of those distant times.

Finishing time _____
Subtract your starting time −_____
Your reading time _____

Answer the questions on the following page. Do not look back at the passage.

Circle the letter of the best answer for each item.

1. This passage is about
   a. a soldier who died in World War I.
   b. mountaintop discoveries.
   c. how men lived in the distant past.
   d. a frozen body found in the mountains.

2. The Iceman was found by
   a. some Austrian scientists.
   b. a Swiss woman.
   c. two German mountain climbers.
   d. soldiers in the army of Frederick of Austria.

3. The body was in good condition because
   a. it had always been frozen.
   b. the scientists took good care of it.
   c. the air was very dry.
   d. it had just fallen there.

4. When the Iceman was found, the body
   a. was in poor condition.
   b. still had some clothes on.
   c. was underground.
   d. was in several pieces.

5. When the body was first found
   a. everyone thought it must be twenty years old.
   b. everyone had a different theory about it.
   c. no one had any idea about where it came from.
   d. scientists were sure it was thousands of years old.

6. The Italians and Austrians were arguing about
   a. who should keep the Iceman.
   b. the age of the Iceman.
   c. how the Iceman died.
   d. why the Iceman was fighting.

7. After examing the body, the scientists said the Iceman was
   a. a German soldier.
   b. a few centuries old.
   c. over 5,000 years old.
   d. an Italian from Bolzano.

8. Scientists now think that the Iceman was killed by
   a. a fall in the mountains.
   b. the cold weather.
   c. another man with arrows.
   d. a wild animal.

Check your answers in the Answer Key. If you have any incorrect answers, reread the passage to find the correct answers.

Now find your reading rate by looking up your reading time for "The Iceman" in the Reading Rate Table on page 188.

Guidelines for Reading Faster

1. Set a reading rate goal for yourself. If you have a personal goal, you will push yourself more to reach that goal.

    Your current reading rate: _____ wpm.

    Your personal goal: _____ wpm.

2. Answer the questions **without looking back** at the text.

3. Check your answers. If you have some incorrect answers, look back at the text to find out why.

4. Find your reading rate on the Reading Rate Table on the next page.

5. Record your reading rate, comprehension score (the number of correct answers), and the date on the Progress Chart for Reading Faster on page 189.

6. After you have read four or five passages, note any changes in your reading rate or comprehension score. Your aim should be to gradually increase your reading rate, while keeping your comprehension score at six or seven correct answers.

    *   If your reading rate stays the same, that means you need to push yourself more.

    *   If you miss more than three questions, you might be pushing yourself too much. Try to slow down a little and concentrate better.

Reading Rate Table

All of the passages are about 500 words long.

Reading Time (Minutes: Seconds)	Rate (Words per Minute)	Reading Time (Minutes: Seconds)	Rate (Words per Minute)
:30 sec	1,000 wpm	2:10	231
:35	857	2:15	222
:40	750	**2:20**	215
:45	668	2:25	207
:50	597	2:30	200
:55	545	2:35	194
1:00	500	2:40	188
1:05	463	2:45	182
1:10	429	2:50	176
1:15	400	2:55	172
1:20	375	3:00	166
1:25	353	3:15	154
1:30	333	3:30	143
1:35	316	3:45	135
1:40	300	4:00	125
1:45	286	4:15	117
1:50	273	**4:30**	111
1:55	261	4:45	105
2:00	250	5:00	100
2:05	240		

Progress Chart for Reading Faster

Mark the box corresponding to your reading rate. Write the number of correct answers at the top of this chart.

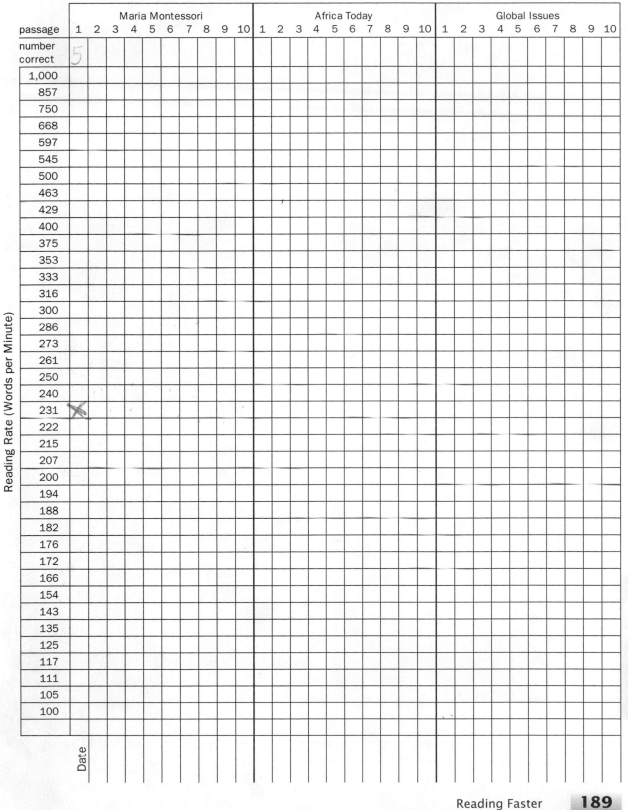

passage	Maria Montessori										Africa Today										Global Issues									
	1	2	3	4	5	6	7	8	9	10	1	2	3	4	5	6	7	8	9	10	1	2	3	4	5	6	7	8	9	10
number correct	5																													
1,000																														
857																														
750																														
668																														
597																														
545																														
500																														
463																														
429																														
400																														
375																														
353																														
333																														
316																														
300																														
286																														
273																														
261																														
250																														
240																														
231	✗																													
222																														
215																														
207																														
200																														
194																														
188																														
182																														
176																														
172																														
166																														
154																														
143																														
135																														
125																														
117																														
111																														
105																														
100																														
Date																														

Reading Rate (Words per Minute)

About the reading faster passages

The Reading Faster Passages are divided into three topics:

Maria Montessori: ten passages about her life and influence.

Africa Today: ten passages about life today in various African countries.

Global Issues: ten passages about problems that the whole world faces.

After you have practiced reading faster with these passages, you may want to read them again and discuss them with your classmates.

UNIT 1   Maria Montessori

Time yourself as you read the following passages. Read each passage and answer the questions on the following page. Do not look back at the passage as you answer the questions.

1. Childhood

Starting time _____

When Maria Montessori was born in Italy in 1870, her future seemed certain. Women did not have careers in those days, nor did they attend college. People generally believed that women were not very intelligent and not capable of complex thought, so Maria, it seemed, had little choice. Like her mother and most women of her day, she would become a mother and a housewife.

She did, in fact, become a mother, but otherwise, her life took a very different course. She became a doctor—the first woman doctor in Italy. With her brilliant medical studies and research, she proved that women could indeed think and work as well as men. Later, she became internationally famous as the inventor of the Montessori method of teaching. To this day, Montessori schools around the world follow her method.

She was born in Chiaravalle, near Ancona, Italy. Her father, Alessandro Montessori, was a government official in the state-run tobacco industry. In his youth, he had fought for the liberation and unification of Italy. Well-educated himself, he wanted the best for his daughter. However, he was also conservative and did not approve of her unusual choices. Only later, when she became famous, did he change his mind and become proud of her.

Maria's mother never had any doubts about her daughter. She supported all of Maria's decisions and helped her through many difficult times. Her own life was ordinary enough, but she wanted her daughter's life to be different. It was she who gave Maria the optimism and the ideals necessary for success. She also taught Maria not to be afraid of hard work. Even as a small girl, Maria always had her share of housework to do. And finally, Maria's mother gave her a sense of responsibility toward others. This was an important factor in her later work as a doctor and as an educator.

The Montessori family moved several times when Maria was young. When she was five, they went to live in Rome, and there she started primary school. Only an average student at that time, Maria did not seem very ambitious. Nor did she sympathize with the competitive behavior of some of her classmates. When she won a prize in the first grade, it was for good behavior. In second grade, she won another prize for sewing and needlework. So far, her interests and achievements were the same as those of any other girl of her time.

However, something in Maria's character stood out among the other children and she was often the leader in their games. Self-confident and strong-willed, she came to believe that her life was somehow going to be different. At the age of ten, when she became dangerously ill, that belief in herself was already strong. She told her mother she couldn't die because she had too much to do in life.

Finishing time _____   Reading time _____

Circle the best answer for each item. Do not look back at the passage.

1. This passage is about

    a. Maria Montessori's parents.
    b. girls in the nineteenth century.
    c. Maria Montessori's background and childhood.
    d. Maria Montessori's education.

2. We can infer from this passage that before Maria,

    a. many Italian women had studied medicine.
    b. Italian women didn't go to doctors.
    c. Italian women often became lawyers.
    d. no Italian women had ever studied medicine.

3. Maria Montessori

    a. was like most other women of her time.
    b. did not attend college.
    c. became a mother and a housewife.
    d. was not like most other women of her time.

4. Maria's father

    a. worked as a government official.
    b. ran a tobacco company.
    c. worked in a hospital.
    d. was an officer in the army.

5. The most important influence on Maria's development was probably her

    a. teacher.
    b. mother.
    c. father.
    d. illness.

6. Maria's mother believed in

    a. hard work and helping others.
    b. leaving the work for others.
    c. giving others hard work to do.
    d. helping her husband at work.

7. In primary school, Maria was

    a. a very brilliant student.
    b. a most unusual girl.
    c. not a very brilliant student.
    d. a terrible student.

8. As a child, Maria felt that

    a. her life was going to be short.
    b. she was going to be different from others.
    c. she was going to be just like others.
    d. her life was going to be very long.

2. Going Her Own Way

When she was twelve, Maria made her first important decision about the course of her life. She decided that she wanted to continue her education. Most girls from middle-class families chose to stay home after primary school, though some attended private Catholic "finishing" schools. There they learned a little about music, art, needlework, and how to make polite conversation. This was not the sort of education that interested Maria—or her mother. By this time, she had begun to take her studies more seriously. She read constantly and brought her books everywhere. One time she even brought her math book to the theater and tried to study in the dark.

Maria knew that she wanted to go on learning in a serious way. That meant attending the public high school, something that very few girls did. In Italy at the time, there were two types of high schools: the "classical" schools and the "technical" schools. In the classical schools, the students followed a very traditional program of studies, with courses in Latin and Greek language and literature, and Italian literature and history. The few girls who continued studying after primary school usually chose these schools.

Maria, however, wanted to attend a technical school. The technical schools were more modern than the classical schools and they offered courses in modern languages, mathematics, science, and accounting. Most people—including Maria's father—believed that girls would never be able to understand these subjects. Furthermore, they did not think it was proper for girls to study them.

Maria did not care if it was proper or not. Math and science were the subjects that interested her most. But before she could sign up for the technical school, she had to win her father's approval. She finally did, with her mother's help, though for many years after, there was tension in the family. Maria's father continued to oppose her plans, while her mother helped her.

In 1883, at age thirteen, Maria entered the "Regia Scuola Tecnica Michelangelo Buonarroti" in Rome. Her experience at this school is difficult for us to imagine. Though the courses included modern subjects, the teaching methods were very traditional. Learning consisted of memorizing long lists of facts and repeating them back to the teacher. Students were not supposed to ask questions or think for themselves in any way. Teachers were very demanding, discipline in the classroom was strict, and punishment was severe for those who failed to achieve or were disobedient.

It took a strong character to survive these methods. Everyone predicted that Maria would fail, but instead she succeeded brilliantly. She proved, with her high marks in math and science, that girls, too, could think about complex subjects. For a while, Maria wanted to be an engineer like many of her male school companions, but by the time she finished school, she had changed her mind. She had become very interested in biology and she wanted to study medicine. It didn't matter to her that no woman in Italy had ever studied medicine before.

Circle the best answer for each item. Do not look back at the passage.

1. This passage is about

   a. Maria's high school years. *(circled)*
   b. technical schools in Italy.
   c. high school courses.
   d. Maria's favorite courses.

2. Maria wanted to attend

   a. a private "finishing" school.
   b. a school with Latin and Greek.
   c. a technical high school. *(circled)*
   d. a school for art and music.

3. In those days, most Italian girls

   a. went to classical schools.
   b. went to "finishing" schools. — PP1
   c. did not go to high school. — PP1 — most stay at home *(circled)*
   d. went to technical schools.

4. You can infer from this pasage that

   a. girls usually attended private primary schools.
   b. only boys usually attended technical schools. *(circled)*
   c. girls did not like going to school.
   d. only girls attended classical schools.

5. Maria's father probably

   a. had very modern views about women.   TP4
   b. had very traditional views about women. *(circled)*
   c. had no opinion about women.
   d. thought women could not learn Latin.

6. High school teachers in Italy in those days were

   a. very modern.
   b. very intelligent.   TP5
   c. quite scientific.
   d. quite strict. *(circled)*

7. Many of Maria's school companions wanted to become

   a. engineers. *(circled)*
   b. teachers.   last TP
   c. biologists.
   d. technicians.

8. In her high school years, Maria showed that she was

   a. afraid of criticism.
   b. eager to please her father.
   c. serious about learning. *(circled)*
   d. not interested in science.

3. Starting at the University Starting time _____

The first step toward becoming a doctor was easy for Maria. In a short time, she had completed the premedical program at the University of Rome and passed her exams. Then she was ready to begin studying at the university's department of clinical medicine. The university, however, was not ready for her. There had never been a woman in the department and the professors did not want one.

No one knows how Maria managed to convince the university to accept her. She spoke with the head of the medical faculty, Professor Baccelli, who was also an important politician. He wanted to reform the Italian school system and universities, but he did not want women to study medicine, so he was no help. There were reports that she also spoke with Pope Leo XIII and that he helped her, though this story may not be true. It may only be one of the many legends that later surrounded Maria.

In any case, in 1892, Maria began to attend classes in clinical medicine. She was not received well by her fellow students. They laughed at her and made unpleasant comments about women doctors. The presence of a woman in their classes, especiallly an intelligent woman like Maria, clearly disturbed them. They did not like the fact that she received better grades than many of them, and they also did not like the way she took her studies so seriously. In fact, many medical students at that time wanted to become doctors only because that would improve their position in society. They were not interested in learning about medicine or in working as doctors.

Maria felt very differently about her studies. She was very interested, first of all, in the subjects themselves. Then, too, she wanted to lead a useful life and she believed she could do this best as a doctor. With these beliefs to strengthen her, she paid no attention to the other students. If someone was rude to her at the university, she just stared back at him. In time, her fellow students came to respect her strong nerves as well as her ability.

Only once did Maria have any doubts about her career. That was when she began to attend anatomy classes. These classes came as a terrible shock to her. Women in those days were not used to looking at or talking about people's body parts. Both women and men, in fact, wore clothes that almost completely covered their bodies. Women, especially, were never supposed to talk about or even think about bodily functions.

So Maria was extremely embarrassed the first time she had to examine a naked body. She also hated the idea of working with dead bodies. When she went home after the first anatomy lesson, she felt so awful that she got sick to her stomach. She later wrote that she was ready at that point to quit studying medicine.

But she did not quit. The next day she went back. Somehow she managed to control her feelings and continue.

Finishing time _____   Reading time _____

Circle the best answer for each item. Do not look back at the passage.

1. This passage is about

   a. how medicine was taught in Italian universities.
   b. Maria's feelings about medicine.
   c. Maria's first experiences at medical school.
   d. how Maria got into the university.

2. Some people thought that Pope Leo XIII

   a. helped Maria with her studies.
   b. had studied medicine when he was at university.
   c. wanted to reform the university system.
   d. helped Maria get accepted into medical school.

3. Many of Maria's fellow students showed that they

   a. liked having a woman in their classes.
   b. did not like having Maria in their classes.
   c. were interested in a woman like Maria.
   d. were interested in their medical studies.

4. As a student, Maria

   a. was less intelligent than her fellow students.
   b. got the same grades as her fellow students.
   c. performed better than many of her fellow students.
   d. got lower grades than most of her fellow students.

5. You can infer from this passage that doctors in Italy

   a. had a high social status.
   b. were laughed at by the public.
   c. had a low social status.
   d. were often very religious.

6. As a medical student, Maria

   a. didn't take her studies very seriously.
   b. was too upset to study seriously.
   c. took her studies very seriously.
   d. was only interested in her social status.

7. At first, Maria found the anatomy classes very

   a. interesting.
   b. upsetting.
   c. easy.
   d. amusing.

8. From this passage, it seems that Maria

   a. never really wanted to become a doctor.
   b. never doubted her decision to become a doctor.
   c. was interested only in getting good grades.
   d. rarely had doubts about becoming a doctor.

4. Success at the University

Starting time _____

As a woman student at the university, Maria had to follow many special rules. Young women could never be alone in public in Italy, which meant that she always had to find someone to walk with her to classes. She was also not supposed to have very close contact with the male students, so she had to wait to enter the lecture hall until they were all in their seats. And finally, she couldn't work on the dead bodies in the anatomy lab together with male students. Instead, she had separate sessions alone in the evenings.

As the only woman, Maria was inevitably very visible. Before long, however, she began to attract a different kind of attention. Her professors began to be impressed by her seriousness and her ability. As a result, at the end of her second year she won a large scholarship, the Rolli Prize, which gave Maria enough money to be financially independent. This was important because her father had threatened to cut off all financial support. He still opposed her choice of careers, though her mother continued to support her.

After her first success, Maria went on to others. The next year she won a tough competition for a position as an assistant in a hospital in Rome. Then, in her fourth and last year, her final lecture was received with great applause. All the people in the audience stood up to congratulate her, including her father, who had decided at the last minute to attend the lecture. He, too, was impressed by his daughter's knowledge and authority. That was the beginning of a change in his attitude toward his daughter's career.

Maria's final assignment at the university was to write a thesis on an original topic. She completed her thesis—on a psychiatric subject—in the spring of 1896. After discussing it with the examiners, she was given her degree with high honors on July 10, 1886. Since Maria was the first woman graduate, a special diploma had to be written out for her. The traditional wording had to be changed so that it no longer referred only to the male sex.

The new doctor was much talked about in Rome. Maria's mother was often stopped on the streets and questioned about this extraordinary daughter. Maria couldn't go for a walk anywhere without feeling noticed. People were surprised to see that she was an attractive young woman, quite modest and feminine. They probably had expected an older, more severe kind of person, and they must have wondered how such a delicate-looking woman could work with dead and naked bodies. Or how she could have the courage to speak in public about such difficult scientific matters!

Maria was famous, but sometimes she wondered about this fame. Were people really interested in her ability and intelligence? Or were they simply curious because she was different? She was sure about one thing, however. It had taken a great deal of courage and determination to succeed.

Finishing time _____   Reading time _____

Circle the best answer for each item. Do not look back at the passage.

1. This passage is about

   a. Maria's successes at the university.
   b. the position of women in Italian universities.
   c. how Maria's father changed his mind.
   d. Maria's courage and determination.

2. At the university, Maria

   a. worked with other female students.
   b. was treated like all the male students.
   c. worked closely with all the male students.
   d. had less freedom than the male students.

3. Maria won the Rolli Prize because

   a. she was a woman.
   b. of her ability.
   c. of her father.
   d. she needed money.

4. Maria's final lecture was

   a. much applauded.
   b. not applauded.
   c. poorly attended.
   d. about the economy.

5. After the final lecture, Maria's father

   a. began to think she shouldn't have a career.
   b. was always proud of his daughter.
   c. began to change his mind about her career.
   d. didn't want her to have a career.

6. Maria's diploma had to be rewritten because

   a. she had won high honors.
   b. she was a woman.
   c. she had studied medicine.
   d. it didn't mention her family.

7. People in Rome thought a woman doctor would

   a. be especially attractive.
   b. not be as old as Maria.
   c. be more courageous than Maria.
   d. not be attractive like Maria.

8. You can infer from this passage that

   a. many Italian women spoke in public.
   b. Italian women generally did not speak in public.
   c. most Italian men liked to speak in public.
   d. Italian women liked to listen to public speaking.

5. The Young Doctor Starting time _____

Only two months after graduating, Maria was faced with a new and different kind of challenge. She was invited to be a delegate to the International Woman's Congress in Berlin. At the congress, she was a great success once again. She gave two speeches—about education for women and about the condition of working women in Italy. Both speeches were received with great enthusiasm. Newspaper reporters from all over Europe interviewed her and praised her in their articles. They described the young doctor from Italy as both intelligent and charming. They were amazed, too, that she had used no notes for her long speeches.

When she returned from Berlin, Maria settled down to serious work in Rome. She continued to work in several hospitals, including a women's hospital and a children's hospital. She also had some private patients. Some of these patients wrote letters of thanks that Maria's mother kept for many years. From these letters, it is clear that Maria was no ordinary doctor. She often stayed for hours with her patients, particularly those who could not afford nursing help. One time, for example, Maria arrived at the home of the young mother of very sick baby twins. She saw at once that the mother was desperately tired, so Maria sent her to bed. Then she bathed the babies, prepared their food, and stayed with them all day. The mother believed that Maria's special care saved her children's lives.

Along with her hospital work, Maria continued to do research at a psychiatric clinic. She became more and more involved in this research, especially when it concerned children. She was particularly interested in the case of the so-called "idiot children." These children with severe developmental problems could not function at home or at school. No one knew what to do with them, so they were locked up in hospitals. There they were treated like little animals and they behaved like animals.

Maria believed that it might be possible to do something for these children. She spent many hours watching them in the hospital. One thing she noticed was that at feeding time, they often played with bits of food. She also noticed how terribly bare their rooms were. They had nothing to look at, nothing to touch or play with—until their food arrived. The fact that they played with bits of food was a positive sign, Maria thought. It showed that they could respond to something, that their minds were not completely closed off. Maybe what they needed was more opportunity to play, so they could use their minds more.

The question of the "idiot children" came to occupy Maria's thinking more and more. She refused to accept that they were unteachable, as other doctors said. Somehow, she felt, it must be possible to reach these children. With the right kind of teaching, she believed that she could help them become human again.

Finishing time _____   Reading time _____

Circle the best answer for each item. Do not look back at the passage.

1. This passage is about

    a. Maria's research at a psychiatric clinic.
    b. the responsibilities of an Italian doctor.
    c. Maria's social life after she finished her studies.
    d. Maria's work after she finished her studies.

2. You can infer from this passage that

    a. most public speakers used notes for their speeches.
    b. Maria usually used notes for her speeches.
    c. most public speakers did not use notes for their speeches.
    d. Maria did not like to give interviews to reporters.

3. Maria worked

    a. only with private patients.
    b. at hospitals and with private patients.
    c. only in hospitals with poor patients.
    d. as a nurse in private homes.

4. When Maria went to visit a patient, she

    a. usually sent them to the hospital.
    b. often stayed for dinner.
    c. often stayed to help nurse the patient.
    d. was sometimes too busy to stay long.

5. We can infer from this passage that Maria

    a. was much liked by her patients.
    b. did not have many patients.
    c. was not much liked by her patients.
    d. did not like to go to her patients.

6. Maria's research involved

    a. patients who had problems with children.
    b. treating many children like animals.
    c. giving food to the "idiot children."
    d. children with developmental problems.

7. The "idiot children" were sent to hospitals because

    a. they would get better food there.
    b. they were happier there with other children.
    c. no one knew what to do with them.
    d. they could be studied better there.

8. Maria believed that these children

    a. did not want to play.
    b. were hopeless cases.
    c. needed to play more.
    d. needed to be fed more.

6. Maria Becomes a School Director

Starting time _____

Maria continued to work for several years in the public hospitals in Rome, as well as with private patients. In her free time, however, she began to study what was known about children with developmental problems. She was particularly interested in the work of a French doctor, Edouard Seguin, who had developed special methods for teaching these children. He had started a school for them in Paris, where he taught them many skills that people thought they would never be able to learn. Dr. Seguin's ideas about teaching these children were very close to Maria's own ideas. She decided that she needed to know more about educational theory in general, so she read everything on the subject that she could find, and she attended a course at the university.

As Maria began to have clearer ideas about the education of children with developmental problems, she expressed those ideas in writing. Her articles attracted much attention and she was invited to give speeches as well. In 1898, in Turin, she spoke before an enthusiastic audience at the National Teachers Congress. In this speech, she argued that Italy should have special schools for children with developmental problems. In these schools, they could become useful members of society, she said, and would no longer be condemned to waste their lives in hospitals or on the streets as criminals.

Among the teachers and among the Italian people there was strong support for Maria's idea of special schools. An organization called the National League for the Education of Retarded Children was started to raise money for them. Maria gave many speeches for the league and became one of its directors. She was soon widely known as an expert on children's developmental problems, and in 1898, she received an award for her research and her work in the hospitals.

In 1899, the league had enough money and support to open a school in Rome. It was called the Orthophrenic School and Maria was chosen as its first director. This was a great honor for such a young doctor and an extraordinary achievement for a woman of any age. But with her ideas, her experience, and her strong personality, Maria was clearly the best person for the job.

The Orthophrenic School was an unusual institution in many ways. Its goal was to educate not only children with developmental problems, but also teachers from the regular schools. They would then return to their classes better prepared to deal with problem children. At the end of its first year, the school gave a public demonstration that was attended by many important doctors, professors, and politicians. They were all amazed at how much the children had learned in such a short time.

On August 31, 1900, when Maria celebrated her thirtieth birthday, her father gave her an enormous book that he had put together, with 200 newspaper articles about Maria that had been published over the years. Now at least Maria would have no doubts about his love and support.

Finishing time _____   Reading time _____

Circle the best answer for each item. Do not look back at the passage.

1. This passage is about

   a. how Maria finally won her father's love and suppport.
   b. an organization for children with developmental problems.
   c. how Maria became the director of the Orthophrenic School.
   d. the Orthophrenic School for children with developmental problems.

2. Maria was interested in Seguin because of his

   a. work with private patients.
   b. support for teachers and schools.
   c. theories about how to change society.
   d. ideas about teaching children.

3. The organization Maria worked for

   a. wanted special schools for problem children.
   b. had already started many special schools.
   c. organized courses about educational theory.
   d. was founded by Edouard Seguin.

4. You can infer from this passage that in Italy children with development problems

   a. did not become useful members of society.
   b. were not allowed to go out in the streets.
   c. were usually treated well in the schools.
   d. usually became useful members of society.

5. By 1898, Maria was well known

   a. as a politician.
   b. for her articles and speeches.
   c. as a children's doctor.
   d. as a university professor.

6. You can infer from this passage that in Italy there

   a. weren't many young women directors of schools.
   b. were many young women directors of schools.
   c. weren't many young women teachers.
   d. were many young women who gave speeches.

7. The new school was unusual because it taught

   a. many new skills.
   b. retarded children to read.
   c. both children and teachers.
   d. teachers how to be useful.

8. On her thirtieth birthday, Maria's father showed that he

   a. had many doubts about the new school.
   b. had many doubts about his daughter.
   c. was very proud of his daughter.
   d. was very proud of his book.

7. Big Changes

Starting time _____

While she was the director of the Orthophrenic School, Maria worked closely with the children. At night she studied her notes and designed new materials for children with particular problems. There was one girl, for example, who seemed unable to learn how to sew. Maria invented a weaving exercise so that her hands could practice the in-and-out movement of sewing. When the girl next tried sewing, she was far more successful.

In fact, Maria found that the children generally learned a task more easily if they could first practice some of the skills with simple exercises. She soon discovered that the same approach helped them learn reading and writing. Some of the children at the Orthophrenic School even managed to pass the regular state elementary school examinations. This seemed like a miracle to many people. For Maria, however, the success of her methods brought new questions. She wondered if they would work as well with normal children in regular schools. Teachers in the Italian schools had always relied on repetition as their main teaching method, and many children had learned little that way.

At this point in her career, Maria made a decision that surprised everyone. In 1901, she left the Orthophrenic school and went back to the university as a student of education. No one could imagine why she would want to leave her position as director of the school. At the time, she simply said that she had to learn more about education, but this explanation was probably only part of the truth.

The details of Maria's personal life are surrounded by mystery, but one thing is sure. While she was working at the Orthophrenic School, she had a romance with one of her fellow doctors, Dr. Giuseppe Montesano. He had worked in hospitals with Maria and then had become co-director of the Orthophrenic School. Maria and Giuseppe were together day after day, and eventually their relationship had become more than professional.

By 1898, Maria was expecting a baby, a fact that she kept secret from everyone. It is hard to imagine how she hid her changing shape during that busy period, but somehow she did. When her son Mario was born, she gave him to another family to raise. She did not marry Giuseppe, perhaps because his family was against it. In any case, Giuseppe married someone else in 1900, and that may have been the real reason for Maria's decision to leave the school.

With Maria's love of children, it may seem surprising that she gave her son to another family. However, in those days, it was shameful for an unmarried woman to have a child. Maria may not have cared about scandal, but her mother probably did, and if the public had known about her son, Maria's career would probably have ended. The fact that Maria did not bring up her son may have influenced her later life and work. Having missed the experience of caring for her son, she may have cared even more about helping other children.

Finishing time _____   Reading time _____

Circle the best answer for each item. Do not look back at the passage.

1. This passage is about

   a. Maria's romance with Montesano.
   b. how Maria taught retarded children.
   c. the end of Maria's career.
   d. important changes in Maria's life.

2. Maria got ideas for new materials by

   a. reading books.
   b. working with the children.
   c. doing sewing exercises.
   d. talking with other teachers.

3. The Italian schools usually made children

   a. repeat tasks again and again.
   b. prepare for a task with simple exercises.
   c. do lots of sewing and weaving.
   d. read their notes every night.

4. You can infer from this passage that Italian children

   a. all passed the elementary school examinations.
   b. did a lot of homework.
   c. had to take examinations in elementary school.
   d. all learned to read and write.

5. Maria said she left the school so she

   a. would have time for her son.
   b. could study education.
   c. could have her baby.
   d. would be better respected.

6. When Maria decided to leave the school,

   a. most people were surprised.
   b. no one was very surprised.
   c. people thought it was a good idea.
   d. she told everyone the reason why.

7. Maria worked closely with Giuseppe Montesano

   a. at the university.
   b. at the school.
   c. in his office.
   d. at home.

8. The fact that Maria had a child probably made her

   a. less interested in children.
   b. want to get married.
   c. want to have more children.
   d. more interested in children.

8. The Children's House Starting time _____

After several years as a student, in 1904 Maria became a professor of educational theory and methods at the University of Rome. She was also very involved in this period in a movement to change the Italian school system. Her earlier experience had shown her how poorly the schools functioned for children with problems. Now she believed that they functioned poorly for many normal children as well.

Then, in 1906, a group of bankers decided to fix up some apartment buildings in a very poor area of Rome. They wanted to create nursery schools for the children who lived in the buildings and since Maria was well known for her work with children, they asked her to become the director of these schools. Some of her friends thought that as a doctor and university professor, she should not work in a nursery school. Maria, however, saw this as a perfect opportunity to try out some of her theories.

The first school, opened on January 6, 1907, was called "La Casa dei Bambini," the Children's House. The bankers had given Maria a large room and an assistant—and not much else. Friends and supporters gave her some small tables and chairs, a few toys, paper, and pencils, and she brought in the materials she had designed for the Orthophrenic School. Later she also brought in some plants and pictures, and even several small animals in cages.

On opening day, there were about fifty children from three to five years old. They were all frightened and some were crying miserably. Then, as they got over their fear, some children became violent, while others refused to talk. Before long, though, as Maria introduced her activities, their behavior began to change. The violent children calmed down and the silent ones began to communicate. They all became more sociable and cooperative, and soon all were enthusiastic about the school.

Maria noticed that the children seemed to prefer her materials to the ordinary toys. Also, they were far more interested in doing the activities than in being rewarded for them. She was amazed sometimes at their ability to concentrate on what they were doing. Once, for example, a little girl was playing with a set of blocks of different shapes that fit into holes of the same shape. She did not notice when Maria told the children to sing and march around the room. She did not even notice when her chair was picked up and set on a table. She just kept on fitting the blocks into the holes. When she had done this forty-two times, she suddenly stopped and smiled. She was done.

This was how children should learn, Maria believed. They should be free to choose their activities, to start and stop as they liked. The desire to learn was natural in children, she felt. The teacher's role was to provide materials and show the children how to use them, but then the teacher should stand aside and let the learning happen. The children were really their own best teachers.

Finishing time _____   Reading time _____

Circle the best answer for each item. Do not look back at the passage.

1. This passage is about
   a. Maria's educational theories.
   b. teaching small children.
   c. using blocks for learning.
   d. the Children's House.

2. Maria wanted to improve
   a. the Italian universities.
   b. apartment buildings in Rome.
   c. the Italian schools.
   d. schools for poor children.

3. Maria was chosen as the director of the Children's House because she
   a. knew a lot about teaching children.
   b. was a professor and a doctor.
   c. liked working with small children.
   d. wanted to reform the educational system.

4. Maria's friends probably thought that working in a nursery school was
   a. suitable for a professor.
   b. suitable for a woman.
   c. unsuitable for a professor.
   d. unsuitable for a woman.

5. You can infer from this passage that Maria thought a nursery school should
   a. be very simple and bare.
   b. always have music.
   c. be comfortable and interesting.
   d. have only her teaching materials in it.

6. At first, the children were
   a. happy and excited.
   b. hungry and tired.
   c. interested and busy.
   d. unhappy and afraid.

7. You can infer from this passage that children in Italian nursery schools usually
   a. could do what they wanted.
   b. did not choose their acitvities.
   c. played with small animals.
   d. did not get rewards.

8. Maria believed that children naturally
   a. want to learn.
   b. don't want to study.
   c. like to play with blocks.
   d. are afraid of school.

9. The Montessori Method

As time went by, Maria continued to try out new ideas at the Children's House. In order for the children to be free in their learning, she felt they needed to become more independent. She had noticed that they liked to get out the toys and books by themselves. She encouraged them to do this all the time, and she taught them to put things away, too.

The eagerness of the children to do things themselves led Maria to teach them many everyday tasks. They learned how to wash, dress, and eat by themselves. Soon they were helping to prepare and serve the noon meal at school and were cleaning up the classroom. These "exercises in practical life" became an important part of Maria's teaching method.

In April of 1907, a second Children's House was opened, organized, and run like the first one. Here, too, the children started out unhappy and confused, but again, they soon changed. As news of the schools spread around Rome, visitors began to appear. They were all impressed. In those days, no one expected to see children so involved and happy, especially not children from poor families.

That first year, Maria did not try to teach the children to read or write. She thought, as most people did then, that children were not ready for reading or writing until they were at least six. However, the children wanted to learn, and their parents encouraged Maria to try. Many of the parents could not read or write themselves, and they saw how easily the children learned with Maria.

Thus, she began to experiment with writing. She cut pieces of paper and sandpaper into the shapes of large letters. The children felt the shapes, learned to copy them on paper, and practiced the sounds for each letter. Gradually, they learned to put the letters together and combine sounds. Then one day, some of the children were suddenly reading and writing whole words. Their excitement was extraordinary. They wanted to write all the time. They wrote everywhere—on the walls, the floor, and even on loaves of bread. For Christmas that year, two four-year-old children wrote a thank-you letter to the bankers who had started the schools.

By this time, the Children's Houses were well known all over Italy. In 1908, another was opened in Milan and two more in Rome. Maria could not direct all these schools herself so she began to train other teachers in her approach. Her theories and the experience of these years began to take a more definite shape, which she put into words in her book, *The Montessori Method*, published in 1909.

This small book had an enormous influence on teachers and schools, not just in Italy, but in many other countries as well. Not everyone was ready to agree with her, of course, and even today, some of her ideas are considered too radical for most schools. Other aspects of her teaching, however, have become standard practice in schools everywhere.

Circle the best answer for each item. Do not look back at the passage.

1. This passage is about
    a. what Maria thought about education in Italy.
    b. how Maria developed her ideas about teaching.
    c. how Maria started exercises in practical life.
    d. how Maria opened more Children's Houses.

2. Maria thought that children should
    a. be clean.
    b. get lots of exercise.
    c. learn to count.
    d. be independent.

3. The "exercises in practical life" taught children how to
    a. do daily tasks.
    b. brush their hair.
    c. read and write.
    d. play with blocks.

4. You can infer from this passage that Italian children
    a. were not usually very clean.
    b. were not usually happy and quiet in schools.
    c. were usually much happier at school.
    d. usually learned how to serve their meals.

5. People generally thought that children
    a. were ready to read and write in nursery school.
    b. could not learn to read and write in school.
    c. could not learn to read and write until age six.
    d. were ready to read and write at home.

6. To teach the children to read and write, Maria
    a. used colored blocks.
    b. sent the children to school.
    c. asked the mothers to help.
    d. used large letter shapes.

7. When the children started to read and write, they
    a. were confused.
    b. stopped talking.
    c. were very excited.
    d. wanted to eat bread.

8. Maria wrote a book
    a. to explain her teaching methods.
    b. to thank the bankers.
    c. about the children she had known.
    d. about how to teach reading and writing.

10. The Montessori Movement

Interest in the Montessori method grew in many parts of the world. By 1912, the Montessori method was officially part of the educational program in Italy and Switzerland, and it had been adopted by the school systems of London, Stockholm, and Johannesburg. There were Montessori schools in many European countries, as well as in the United States, India, China, Mexico, Japan, Australia, and Argentina.

For a few years, Maria continued to teach at the university and to work as a doctor. Then, in 1911, she decided to give up all other work so that she would have more time for the Montessori movement. She wished to train the teachers herself and to keep firm control of the many new Montessori Societies, as she did not want her materials and method to be used incorrectly.

In her work for the Montessori movement, Maria traveled constantly around Europe, giving lectures and training teachers. Her first trip to the United States in 1913 was an enormous success. In fact, in this period before World War I, Maria's ideas were extremely popular. Many articles and books appeared about her work, and educators were discussing her ideas everywhere. All kinds of people—teachers, politicians, priests, and princes—came to Rome to see Maria and observe her schools. To help her with all this work, Maria now had a group of followers, mostly young women who wanted to learn from her.

In 1912, Maria's mother died and for many years after that, Maria wore only black clothes. The death of her mother brought some changes in her life. Soon afterward, she took her son, Mario, back to live with her. She had visited him now and then during his childhood, but always as a mysterious stranger. One day when he was fifteen, Maria came to his school, and he guessed somehow that she was his mother. From then on, he stayed with her and used her name. He remained close to her for the rest of her life. When he married and had four children, she became a very loving and caring grandmother to them.

Another major change for Maria was brought about by the international situation. In 1916, she left Italy and went with Mario to live in Spain so he would not have to serve in the Italian army in World War I. Though she returned often to promote the Montessori method, she never went back to live in Italy. Her home remained in Spain until 1936, when she moved to Holland. Then in 1939, she traveled to India and remained trapped there for seven years during World War II. Afterward, she returned to Holland, where she died in 1952 at the age of eighty-two.

Though Maria continued to work for the Montessori movement until her death, interest in her method died down in her later life. She did not live to see how her ideas became popular once again in the 1960s.

Circle the best answer for each item. Do not look back at the passage.

1. This passage is about Maria's
   a. son, Mario.
   b. travels.
   c. later life.
   d. schools.

2. Italy and Switzerland
   a. used the Montessori method in their schools.
   b. sent many teachers to the United States.
   c. didn't use the Montessori method in their schools.
   d. invited Montessori to teach her method.

3. Maria gave up her academic and medical work so that
   a. her son could live with her.
   b. she could travel more often.
   c. she could spend all her time on the movement.
   d. her followers could spend more time with her.

4. Maria thought it was important
   a. for her followers to be women.
   b. to train Montessori teachers herself.
   c. to speak many languages.
   d. to teach her grandchildren herself.

5. You can infer from this passage that in 1913
   a. many Americans were enthusiastic about Maria's ideas.
   b. few Americans showed any interest in Maria's ideas.
   c. Maria was not very interested in American education.
   d. there were no Montessori Societies in the United States.

6. After her mother died, Maria
   a. didn't want to live in Italy.
   b. changed her name.
   c. brought her son home.
   d. went to the United States.

7. During his childhood, Mario
   a. never knew who his mother was.
   b. always knew Maria was his mother.
   c. didn't want to stay with his mother.
   d. wore only black clothes.

8. Maria had to move several times because of
   a. her health.
   b. her followers.
   c. several wars.
   d. her son.

UNIT 2   Africa Today

Time yourself as you read the following passages. Read each passage and answer the questions on the following page. Do not look back at the passage as you answer the questions.

1. Africa Today

Starting time _____

Newspaper and television reports around the world show Africa as a continent with many problems. They focus on the wars, the starving children, the terrible diseases, and the natural disasters. Other, more positive aspects of life in Africa are rarely shown.

There are, indeed, serious problems in many parts of Africa. The biggest problem facing Africans today is the continuing threat of wars. These wars are in part due to historic competition among tribes. However, in the past, the fighting was local and small scale. In recent years, it has become far more violent and destructive. This is partly because of the destructive power of modern weapons. It is also because the situation has changed dramatically.

Starting in the sixteenth century, European powers began to move into Africa. They took African people to sell as slaves in North and South America. They also took any valuable resources they could find, such as ivory, gold, or diamonds. In the nineteenth century, the European rulers divided up the continent into countries. They did not understand much about African tribal traditions, and so the borders of these countries did not match the traditional borders of tribal lands.

When the countries of Africa became independent in the twentieth century, there were often several different tribes in a country, and each tribe wanted to rule. The result was conflict and civil war. In many countries, the civil wars have been going on for decades as different groups fight for control of the government. Governing means having not only power, but also having access to wealth—and one of the few ways out of a life of poverty. In recent years, it has also meant having control over international aid and, therefore, access to food in times of starvation.

Many of the problems facing Africa today have been worsened by this fighting over control of the government. Countries that are at war have little time or resources to deal with poverty, hunger, or disease. They are unable to take any measures for a better future, and so many countries are becoming poorer and their problems are growing. For example, HIV, the virus that causes AIDS, has spread rapidly in Africa because of the lack of education and health care, as well as the lack of medical supplies. Other diseases, many preventable, have spread quickly for the same reasons.

In spite of these problems, however, many Africans are hopeful about their future. Ordinary people in many countries are joining together to change and improve their lives. Young and talented Africans are looking out to the rest of the world. They are experimenting with ways to use the Internet and other new technology to try to solve some of their problems. In the arts, and especially in music, many talented performers are showing the world what it means to be African. In this unit, the passages will focus on both the continuing problems facing Africa today and some of the interesting and positive developments there.

Finishing time _____   Reading time _____

Circle the best answer for each item. Do not look back at the passage.

1. This passage is about
    a. the diseases in Africa.
    b. independence in Africa.
    c. the situation in Africa today.
    d. newspaper reports about Africa.

2. According to this passage, the main factor preventing a solution to Africa's problems is
    a. disease.
    b. poverty.
    c. war.
    d. international aid.

3. Wars are more violent in the twenty-first century partly because
    a. modern weapons are more destructive.
    b. of the lack of education and health care.
    c. there has been an increase in natural disasters.
    d. valuable natural resources are lacking.

4. In the past, European powers
    a. fought over control of the government.
    b. tried to help the Africans economically.
    c. could not find any valuable resources in Africa.
    d. did not understand African traditions.

5. In many countries, different groups are fighting for control over the government so they can
    a. control the spread of the HIV virus.
    b. free their country from European rulers.
    c. change the borders of their country.
    d. become richer and control food supplies.

6. You can infer from this passage that international aid
    a. can help prevent fighting between groups.
    b. may sometimes be a cause of fighting.
    c. might not be helpful in preventing AIDS.
    d. usually has no effect on the fighting.

7. According to this passage, there is a close connection between
    a. access to wealth and level of education.
    b. international aid and the spread of disease.
    c. war and the spread of the HIV virus.
    d. African tribal traditions and poverty.

8. Many young people in Africa today are
    a. hopeful in spite of their problems.
    b. talented politicians and leaders.
    c. hoping to move to other countries.
    d. not interested in their traditions.

2. Nelson Mandela and Democracy in South Africa

Starting time _____

In the history of South Africa, Nelson Mandela is a key person and 1994 is a key year. Until then, a small minority of white people governed South Africa and blacks were forced to live separately from whites. In 1948, the white government had made the separation of races official with a policy called apartheid. Black South Africans were not allowed to live in the same area or go to the same schools or churches as white people. Blacks had to carry identification papers, and the government controlled their movement and their employment.

When the apartheid policy began, Nelson Mandela was thirty years old. He had completed law school, and together with his friend Oliver Tambo, he opened a law office—the first blacks to do so in their country. Mandela and Tambo disagreed with the policy of apartheid and they began working to try to change it. They became leaders of the African National Congress (ANC), a movement of blacks and whites for democratic political change.

The white government did not like the ideas of the ANC and soon it was banned (made illegal). However, Mandela and other members of the ANC continued to work against apartheid, leading large demonstrations and rallies. Mandela became the leader of the military wing of the ANC, and he traveled to Algeria for military training. Upon his return to South Africa in 1962, he was arrested and sent to prison.

While Mandela was in prison, other ANC leaders were arrested for fighting against the government. In June 1964, Mandela and the other leaders were all sent to South Africa's worst and most dangerous prison, on Robben Island. But still they managed to keep in contact with the antiapartheid movement and they did not give up hope. Mandela wrote his autobiography and sent it out of the prison with visitors, piece by piece.

Other members of the ANC told people around the world about Mandela and his struggle against apartheid. Many countries stopped doing business with South Africa. World leaders demanded that Mandela be released from prison. Finally, F.W. deKlerk, the white president of South Africa, decided to release him and allow the ANC to meet again. In February 1990, Nelson Mandela walked out of prison, a free man after twenty-eight years!

Mandela took over the leadership of the ANC once again and led talks with the white government for an end to apartheid. Many people feared that the white government would refuse to give up power and there would be a terrible war, a "blood bath." However, working together, Mandela and deKlerk were able to bring peaceful democratic change to their country. They were awarded the Nobel Peace Prize for this achievement.

The next year, 1994, the first multiracial elections were held, and Nelson Mandela was elected president. At the end of his term as president in 1999, new elections were held and another black man, Thabo Mbeki, was elected. After his election, President Mbeki remarked, "One democratically elected president was followed by another, the true test of democracy."

Finishing time _____   Reading time _____

Circle the best answer for each item. Do not look back at the passage.

1. This passage is about
   a. the policy of apartheid in South Africa.
   b. events in the history of South Africa.
   c. how black South Africans fought against apartheid.
   d. how Mandela brought democracy to South Africa.

2. Under the apartheid policy, black South Africans could not
   a. go to school or church.
   b. live where white people lived.
   c. carry identification papers.
   d. work for white people.

3. We can infer from this passage that
   a. many South African blacks supported the ANC.
   b. the ANC was not popular with South African blacks.
   c. other African countries were against the ANC.
   d. Mandela and Tambo disagreed with the ANC.

4. The white government of South Africa banned the ANC because it
   a. was a foreign organization.
   b. had no white members.
   c. wanted to change the government.
   d. wanted to make Mandela the president.

5. After Mandela returned from military training in Algeria, he
   a. was elected president.
   b. was arrested and sent to prison.
   c. began working to change apartheid.
   d. opened a law office with Oliver Tambo.

6. During his years in prison, Mandela
   a. wrote his autobiography.
   b. stopped working for the ANC.
   c. had no contact with the world.
   d. disagreed with Oliver Tambo.

7. Mandela was released from prison partly because of
   a. winning the Nobel Prize.
   b. the help of Thabo Mbeki.
   c. pressure from other countries.
   d. problems with his health.

8. Mandela's goal for South Africa was to have a
   a. government controlled by blacks.
   b. war against the government.
   c. military government.
   d. democratic government.

3. Food for Learning
Starting time _____

In Eritrea, a small country in northeast Africa, approximately 80 percent of the population is illiterate. That percentage is even higher for women. As in many developing countries, most Eritreans have traditional ideas about the role of women. They believe that women should stay home and take care of the family and should not try to get an education or look for a job.

These beliefs are one of the factors that prevent Eritrea and other developing countries from improving their economic situation. Experience in many countries has shown that educated women have fewer children and have more opportunities for improving their lives and the lives of their families. In Eritrea, in fact, there is great need for improvement. It is one of the poorest countries in the world, partly because of the dry climate and difficult farming conditions and partly because of thirty years of war with Ethiopia. For many Eritrean families, getting enough food is a daily problem.

To deal with these problems, the Eritrean government, together with the World Food Program, has a new program that offers food as a reward for learning. In primary schools, where there are many more boys than girls, all the children receive food packages to take home to their families. However, with the new program, the girls receive 50 percent more food than the boys. This way, parents are encouraged to send their daughters to school rather than keeping them at home.

Another government program that aims to educate women is Food for Training. Managed by the National Union of Eritrean Women, this program offers food rewards (also from the World Food Organization) to women and older girls who are willing to join the program. Because of the war with Ethiopia, many women are bringing up their families on their own. They often live in refugee camps, with no home or land of their own and no way to earn money. Most of these women are illiterate and have no skills they can use to find a job. They spend most of their day looking for food and preparing it for their families.

The Food for Training program helps the teenagers and women change their lives. If they agree to join the program, they receive a large package of food each month. In return, the women are required to attend free literacy classes for two hours every day. When Food for Training started with classes in two regions of Eritrea, 5,000 girls and women joined in the first two months. It is especially popular with teenage girls, age fourteen to sixteen, who have never had a chance to go to school before.

The organizers of Food for Training also plan to offer other kinds of courses for women, using the same system of food rewards. In these courses, they will teach women job skills and crafts such as basket weaving. These women will not only learn to read and write. They will become aware of what is going on in their country, and they will be able to have a voice in their future.

Finishing time _____   Reading time _____

Circle the best answer for each item. Do not look back at the passage.

1. This passage is about

    a. the educational system in Eritrea.
    b. new educational programs in Eritrea.
    c. the lack of food in northeast Africa.
    d. job skills training in Eritrea.

2. According to this passage, traditional ideas about women

    a. help improve the economy.
    b. make no difference to development.
    c. prevent economic development.
    d. are not common in Eritrea.

3. The Eritrean government is offering extra food to girls in school in order to

    a. encourage parents to keep girls at home.
    b. create more jobs for Eritrean teachers.
    c. change traditional attitudes about women.
    d. help girls get their housework done faster.

4. The war with Ethiopia

    a. made life more difficult for women.
    b. allowed women more freedom.
    c. offered opportunities to women.
    d. did not affect the lives of women.

5. We can infer from this passage that Eritrean women

    a. are not allowed to go to work.
    b. prefer a traditional style of life.
    c. are not interested in education.
    d. want to learn to read and write.

6. The new literacy programs are an example of

    a. the government of Eritrea working to keep its power.
    b. local and international organizations working together.
    c. the work of 5,000 women and teenage girls.
    d. the problems with international aid organizations.

7. The women who attend the literacy classes will have time to learn because they will

    a. not spend so much time looking for food.
    b. spend more time looking for food.
    c. not have to live on their own any longer.
    d. bring up their families on their own.

8. According to this passage, the literacy programs will

    a. help women become better citizens.
    b. teach women about international aid.
    c. allow women to spend more time at home.
    d. encourage women to leave their country.

4. The Internet in Africa

Starting time _____

When it comes to technology, Africa is far behind the rest of the world. For example, Africa has very few telephone lines compared with other areas. In fact, it has only about 2 percent of all the telephone lines in the world. In Africa, there are about 2.5 phone lines for every 100 Africans, while there are about 70 phone lines for every 100 Americans. There are also very few computers—only about 6 million on the entire African continent. As for the Internet, there are fewer Internet users in Africa than in the city of London alone.

The lack of telephones and computers in Africa may not seem like an important problem on a continent with many serious problems. However, more telephone lines and computers would allow more Africans to connect to the Internet. Through the Internet, Africans could have better access to information and better contacts with the rest of the world. In this way, they could end their dependence on others and begin to take control of their own development.

People in many African cities are already using the Internet. However, there are often problems with the quality and the speed of the satellite connections to the Internet. Cables can carry much more Internet data than satellites and can do it more quickly, so new cables are being put down on the ocean floor along the coast of Africa. One cable will go along the west coast, making connections from South Africa to eight other countries and finally ending in Spain. The other cable will circle all around Africa, connecting countries on the east and west coasts.

Though many people cannot afford to buy a home computer, they can go to "cybercafés" and pay for computer use by the hour. The cybercafés are especially popular with young people. They use the Internet to get in contact with people from other countries. One company that has opened many cybercafés is Africa Online, started by a young Kenyan who studied in the United States. Africa Online now has cybercafés in Kenya, Ghana, Ivory Coast, Namibia, Swaziland, Tanzania, Uganda, and Zimbabwe, and it is planning to open cafés in Egypt and other countries.

The Internet is also an important resource for students. School and college libraries often do not have many up-to-date books and students usually cannot afford to buy the books themselves. With the Internet, students can access libraries and databanks around the world. They can also sign up for and follow distance-learning courses at many universities in the developed countries.

As the connections for the Internet are made more direct and reliable, new opportunities will open up for jobs. The Internet will allow Africans to develop an information-based economy that can do business with the whole world. For example, even today an American health insurance company in Kentucky has hired computer operators in Ghana to do some of their correspondence work. With a direct Internet connection between Kentucky and Ghana, the real distance becomes unimportant.

Finishing time _____   Reading time _____

Circle the best answer for each item. Do not look back at the passage.

1. This passage is about
    a. the popularity of cybercafés.
    b. why the Internet is important.
    c. how the Internet can help Africans.
    d. building Internet cables in Africa.

2. According to this passage, few Africans use the Internet because
    a. there are few telephones and computers.
    b. they do not know how to use computers.
    c. the cybercafés in Africa are expensive.
    d. there are more serious problems to deal with.

3. Access to the Internet could
    a. prevent Africans from solving serious problems.
    b. make Africans more dependent on international aid.
    c. allow Africans to become more independent.
    d. create many problems for young Africans.

4. At present, in Africa
    a. people usually connect to the Internet by cable.
    b. few cybercafés have Internet connections.
    c. most people have Internet connections at home.
    d. people mainly connect to the Internet by satellite.

5. The new cables for Internet data will
    a. slow down Internet connections.
    b. improve telephone connections.
    c. speed up Internet connections.
    d. make computers cheaper.

6. In Africa, cybercafés are especially important for
    a. students.
    b. friends.
    c. teachers.
    d. workers.

7. An American insurance company
    a. is buying an African Internet company.
    b. hires Africans as computer operators.
    c. sells health insurance in Africa.
    d. plans to open a factory in Africa.

8. You can infer from this passage that
    a. many Africans study in the United States.
    b. few Africans are interested in the Internet.
    c. many Africans would like to use the Internet.
    d. many American companies hire Africans.

5. Pop Music in Africa

Starting time _____

Young musicians in African countries are creating a new kind of pop music. The tunes and the rhythms of their music combine African traditions with various forms of music popular today, such as hip-hop, rap, rock, jazz, or reggae. The result is music that may sound familiar to listeners anywhere in the world, but at the same time is distinctly African. It is different also in another way: Many of the songs are very serious and they deal with important social or political issues in Africa today.

Eric Wainaina is one of these African musicians. He grew up in Nairobi, Kenya, in a family of musicians. As a teenager, he listened to pop music from the United States, and later he moved to Boston to study at the Berklee College of Music. Now he has produced a CD in Kenya. Eric's most popular song, "Land of 'A Little Something,'" is about Kenya's problem of bribery, or paying others for illegal favors. He wants people to listen to his songs and think about how to make Kenya a better place to live.

Another musician who writes serious songs is Witness Mwaijaga from Tanzania. Her own experiences have helped her understand the suffering of many African women. At the age of fifteen she lost her home, but she was luckier than other homeless young people. She could make a living by writing songs and singing on the street. By the time she was eighteen years old, she had become a star. Her songs are written in rap or hip-hop style about the problems that she sees in Tanzania, especially AIDS and the lack of rights for women.

Baaba Maal, from Senegal, also feels that pop music must go beyond entertainment. He says that in Senegal, storytellers have always been important people. In the past, they were the ones who kept the history of their people alive. Baaba believes that songwriters now have a similar responsibility. They must write about the world around them and help people understand how it could be better. The words of his songs are important, in fact. They speak of peace and cooperation among Africans, as well as the rights of women, love for one's family, and saving the environment.

One of South Africa's most popular musicians is Brenda Fassie. She is sometimes compared to Madonna, the American pop star, because she likes to shock people in her shows. But she also likes to make people think. She became famous in the 1980s for her simple pop songs against apartheid. Now that apartheid has ended, her songs are about other issues in South African culture and life. To sing about these, she uses local African languages and a new pop style called *kwaito*.

In recent years, people outside of Africa have also begun to listen to these young musicians. Through music, the younger generation of Africans are connecting with the rest of the world and, at the same time, influencing the rest of the world.

Finishing time _____   Reading time _____

Circle the best answer for each item. Do not look back at the passage.

1. This passage is about how African pop music is

    a. usually about love and romance.
    b. more serious than most pop music.
    c. popular with young people in Africa.
    d. mostly written just for entertainment.

2. For people outside of Africa, African pop music is

    a. the same as other pop music.
    b. not usually very interesting.
    c. entirely strange to them.
    d. both familiar and different.

3. You can infer from this passage that most young African musicians want to

    a. copy American music.
    b. make a lot of money.
    c. help their countries.
    d. leave their countries.

4. The musicians mentioned in this passage all

    a. write about serious problems.
    b. studied in the United States.
    c. lost their homes at a young age.
    d. write songs in a new pop style.

5. Eric Wainaina

    a. prefers to sing in English.
    b. listened to traditional music.
    c. studied music in Boston.
    d. performs only in the United States.

6. Witness Mwaijaga writes about the problems of women partly because

    a. she has had a difficult life herself.
    b. there are many problems in Tanzania.
    c. she has had an easy life herself.
    d. there are no other women singers.

7. In Senegal, pop musicians are like the old storytellers because they sing about

    a. American jazz.
    b. the world around them.
    c. apartheid in South Africa.
    d. paying bribes.

8. In the 1980s, Brenda Fassie wrote songs

    a. about peace and love.
    b. copied from Madonna.
    c. in the *kwaito* style.
    d. against apartheid.

6. Transportation, Nigerian Style

Starting time _____

In Nigeria, villages and small towns often lack hospitals, markets, and government offices. That means Nigerians have to travel to the cities for these services. However, transportation can be a problem in Nigeria, as in many African countries. The public transportation system is limited and costly, the roads are poor, and few people own cars. But some people own motorcycles, and so with their motorcycles the Nigerians have invented a new kind of taxi.

While the name is different in various parts of Nigeria, the most common name for this new kind of motorcycle taxi is *okada*. The first okada riders were the owners of motorcycles who stopped on the country roads to give people a ride. Then the motorcycle owners realized that they could make money this way. They began to look for passengers and charge fares for the rides. Soon the okada system became a part of Nigerian life.

Though the okada has solved some transportation problems, it has created others. The biggest problem is that the government does not regulate the system. For instance, there are no rules about who can be an okada rider. The riders do not have to pass any special test or get a special license, so many of them are poorly educated and do not know the rules of the road.

Another problem is that the okada system is now big business in Nigeria. That means more people—mostly government workers and businessmen—are trying to get some of the profits. They buy motorcycles and rent them out at high prices to okada riders. The riders must then work hard in order to pay the rent and also earn a living for their families. That is why okada riders often drive fast and dangerously.

Yet another problem is the conflict that has developed between okada riders and bus drivers. Regular drivers of commuter buses often take a half day off and rent out their buses to "half-day" drivers. These half-day bus drivers, like the okada riders, must earn enough in fares to pay for renting the bus and earn a living. And like the okada riders, their income depends on the number of passengers they carry. Thus, they are in direct competition with the okada riders.

This competition has at times become a real battle, as both the okada riders and half-day bus drivers become more desperate. Okada riders and passengers have been injured and killed by buses at bus stops. There have been fights between bus drivers and okada riders, and the riders have set fire to several buses. Sometimes Nigerians have found that with all these problems, they have no transportation at all.

According to a local newspaper, many Nigerians are angry about this situation. They believe that the government should take control of the okada system and make sure that okada riders know how to drive safely. They also want the government to find a way to resolve the conflict between the okada riders and the bus drivers.

Finishing time _____   Reading time _____

Circle the best answer for each item. Do not look back at the passage.

1. This passage is about

   a. public transportation in Africa.
   b. conflict between buses and taxis.
   c. the okada system in Nigeria.
   d. traffic problems in Nigeria.

2. In Nigeria, *okada* is a common name for

   a. big business.
   b. motorcycle taxis.
   c. public transportation.
   d. commuter buses.

3. The okada system

   a. was started by the Nigerian government.
   b. began in the streets of Nigerian cities.
   c. was invented by a wealthy businessman.
   d. grew out of the need for transportation.

4. The Nigerian government

   a. has passed strict laws about the okadas.
   b. regulates the buses and the okada system.
   c. buys new motorcycles for okada riders.
   d. has no control over the okada system.

5. Okada riders

   a. all have a special license from the government.
   b. are often government workers or businessmen.
   c. can only use motorcycles that they own.
   d. often have to pay rent for their motorcycles.

6. We can infer from this passage that many Nigerians use okadas because they are

   a. less expensive than buses.
   b. less dangerous than buses.
   c. better regulated than buses.
   d. more profitable than buses.

7. Conflict developed between

   a. the government and okada riders.
   b. bus drivers and okada riders.
   c. okada riders and their passengers.
   d. businessmen and okada riders.

8. According to this passage, many Nigerians are

   a. happy with the transportation system.
   b. angry about the okada system.
   c. worried about the poor bus service.
   d. unhappy with the government.

7. From Nomad to Farmer

Starting time _____

For many African people, life has changed dramatically in recent years. This is especially true for the Tuareg people of north-central Africa. Historically, the Tuaregs led the life of nomads, people with no permanent home. They traveled across the Sahara Desert in caravans of camels, carrying goods between Arab Africa in the north and black Africa in the south.

The Tuaregs did not belong to either of these groups. They were a light-skinned Berber people, with a culture and language of their own. Europeans called them the "blue men" of the desert because they dressed all in blue, even their shoes. They were well known for their great skill in finding their way across the open desert, with only the stars to guide them. They were also known for their independent spirit. In fact, they loved the nomad way of life, which allowed them to come and go as they chose. National borders had no meaning for them in the desert. During the eighteenth and nineteenth centuries, Africa was divided up and ruled by various European countries, but this did not affect the Tuaregs, who continued to move freely.

In the mid-twentieth century, however, there were big changes in Africa. In many countries, black Africans began to break free of European rule and set up their own governments. As the new governments gained power, national borders became more important and it became more difficult for the Tuaregs to travel and trade. They fought against the changes, but eventually, national borders were closed, and the Tuaregs were forced to limit their travels.

At the same time, another big change had come to the area. People were beginning to use motor vehicles for travel across the desert. Cars and trucks were faster and more efficient than camels. Thus, the Tuareg caravans lost their important role in the desert. Then came the great drought of the 1970s and 1980s. With no rain, especially in 1984, large areas of grassland near the Sahara turned into desert. With no grass to eat, many animals died, including the Tuaregs' camels. Their old way of life was now definitely over.

The question was, how could the Tuaregs now make a living? They noticed that the people who lived near water holes could plant vegetable gardens and suffered less from the drought. Soon Tuaregs began to settle down near the old watering places in the desert. One of these was Timia, in central Niger. Until forty years ago, Timia was just a well in the middle of the desert where travelers stopped to rest. Now it has a population of about 6,000. Most of the people who live there were nomads in the past, but now they make a living from their fruit and vegetable gardens. They grow oranges, grapefruits, pomegranates, dates, and corn, which they send by truck to Agadez, a city about ninety-five miles away. Many miss their caravan days and some dream of teaching their children the old ways, but instead, they are teaching them to be farmers.

Finishing time _____   Reading time _____

Circle the best answer for each item. Do not look back at the passage.

1. This passage is about

    a. kinds of transportation in the Sahara Desert.
    b. how life has changed for the Tuareg people.
    c. the history of north-central Africa.
    d. how people grow vegetables in the desert.

2. The Tuaregs were famous for their

    a. beautiful clothes.
    b. fruits and vegetables.
    c. skill in the desert.
    d. strange language.

3. The Tuareg people loved the nomad way of life because it allowed them to

    a. have nice homes.
    b. trade with Arabs.
    c. move around freely.
    d. ride on camels.

4. In the twentieth century, many new African nations

    a. welcomed the Tuareg.
    b. closed their borders.
    c. traded with Arab countries.
    d. built roads across the desert.

5. People began to use cars and trucks to cross the desert because

    a. they were faster than camels.
    b. there was a terrible drought.
    c. national borders were more important.
    d. camels got lost in the desert.

6. The drought of the 1980s

    a. had no effect on the Tuaregs.
    b. helped new governments gain power.
    c. produced more grass for the animals.
    d. caused many camels to die.

7. The Tuaregs could no longer make a living as

    a. farmers.
    b. traders.
    c. soldiers.
    d. truck drivers.

8. We can infer from this passage that farming is possible in Timia because

    a. there is a well.
    b. people collect rainwater.
    c. many animals died.
    d. there is a city nearby.

8. The Exploding Lakes of Cameroon

Starting time _____

What comes to mind when you think of a lake? You probably imagine a pretty scene with blue water, birds, and fish. For the people in northwestern Cameroon, however, the image is very different. For them, lakes may mean terrible disasters. In 1984, poisonous gases exploded out of Lake Monoun and came down into the nearby villages, killing thirty-seven people. Two years later, Lake Nyos erupted. A cloud of gases rolled down the hills and into the valleys and killed 1,700 people.

Lake Nyos and Lake Monoun are crater lakes. They were formed when water collected in the craters of old volcanoes. The volcanoes under Lake Nyos and Lake Monoun are not active anymore. However, poisonous gases from the center of the earth continue to flow up through cracks in the bottom of the lake. This is normal in a crater lake. In most crater lakes, these gases are released often because the water "turns over" regularly. That is, the water from the bottom of the lake rises and mixes with the water at the top, allowing the gases to escape slowly.

However, in Lakes Nyos and Monoun, there is no regular turning over. No one knows the reason for this fact, but as a result, these lakes have more gases trapped at the bottom than other crater lakes. In fact, scientists who have studied Lakes Nyos and Monoun have found 16,000 times more gases. When a strong wind, cool weather, a storm, or a landslide causes the water to turn over suddenly, the gases escape in a violent explosion.

In the past, no one knew when the gases might explode, so there was no way for the villagers to escape disaster. Now a team of scientists from the United States, France, and Cameroon has found a way to reduce the gas pressure at the bottom of Lake Nyos. They stood a 672-foot plastic pipe in the middle of the lake, with one end of the pipe near the bottom and the other end in the air. Near the top of the pipe, the team put several holes that could be opened or closed by a computer. Now, when the gas pressure gets too high, the holes are opened and some of the gas-filled water shoots up through the pipe into the air like a fountain. With less pressure, a disastrous explosion is much less likely. However, the scientists are not sure that one pipe will be enough to prevent explosions. They hope to put in others soon and they plan to install a similar pipe and a computer system at Lake Monoun as well.

To protect people nearby until all of the pipes are in place, the scientists have installed early warning systems at both lakes. If the gas pressure rises to a dangerous level, computers will set off loud sirens and bright lights to warn the people in the villages. That way, they will have time to escape from the dangerous gases.

Finishing time _____   Reading time _____

Circle the best answer for each item. Do not look back at the passage.

1. This passage is about
   a. natural disasters in African countries.
   b. explosions caused by deadly gas.
   c. how scientists installed a pipe in Lake Nyos.
   d. gas explosions in two African lakes.

2. When the lakes in Cameroon explode,
   a. dangerous gases are released.
   b. water flows down from the hills.
   c. a dangerous wind is created.
   d. a crater is formed in the volcano.

3. Lake Monoun and Lake Nyos are
   a. like other crater lakes.
   b. not like other crater lakes.
   c. on top of active volcanoes.
   d. not on top of a volcano.

4. We can infer from this passage that
   a. other crater lakes do not explode.
   b. crater lakes almost always explode.
   c. the explosions are usually not harmful.
   d. Nyos and Monoun are typical crater lakes.

5. Lake Monoun and Lake Nyos explode because
   a. the gases rise to the top and mix with air.
   b. scientists have put in a computer system.
   c. people from the villages "turn over" the water.
   d. the gases are trapped at the bottom.

6. A team of scientists has
   a. removed all dangerous gases from the lakes.
   b. built a beautiful fountain near the lakes.
   c. put a pressure-releasing pipe in the lake.
   d. left the gases at the bottom of the lake.

7. When the gas pressure gets too high, the
   a. computer closes the holes.
   b. scientists leave the lake.
   c. holes in the pipe open.
   d. scientists put in a pipe.

8. The scientists
   a. are planning to install pipes in all crater lakes.
   b. have also installed warning systems at both lakes.
   c. do not know how to prevent the explosions.
   d. cannot install any warning systems at the lakes.

9. Does International Aid Do More Harm than Good?

Starting time _____

In parts of Africa, wars have been going on for many years. Everyday life in countries such as Sudan, Ethiopia, Eritrea, Somalia, and Zaire is constantly disrupted. Millions of people have lost their homes, schools, markets, and hospitals. In these conditions, food supplies disappear and people face starvation. During the past decade, international aid organizations have done their best to help prevent starvation by sending food to people in the war areas.

However, this is a short-term solution. Most aid workers agree that giving food to a warring country is only a temporary measure. It may save some people from immediate starvation, but it doesn't change the conditions that lead to starvation. The aid workers say that the first thing to do is to try to stop the fighting. The international community, including the United Nations, needs to help the warring groups find a way to make peace.

Some international aid organizations are thinking of changing the way they help people in warring countries. Workers say that food shipments can actually help keep a war going. Sudan is an example of a country that has received aid worth billions of dollars during its seventeen-year-long civil war. This aid has made very little difference in the lives of the Sudanese people, except in a negative way. Soldiers have stolen the food and local leaders have used it to control people. Food shipments have sometimes caused people to become dependent on aid. Some Sudanese farmers, for example, stopped planting crops after receiving food shipments.

Furthermore, the Sudanese government has used the shipments of food against other groups of Sudanese. It has allowed food to be distributed only in areas that support the government in the civil war. This means that some areas have not received any food at all. One such area is the Nuba Mountains. This large mountainous region in the south is isolated from the rest of Sudan. The people of Nuba generally do not support the central government of Sudan, since they have a very different history and culture. While the Sudanese government is Muslim, for example, the Nuba people are not. They also do not speak Arabic, as other Sudanese do; instead, they speak a language of their own.

Now, after pressure from international organizations, the Sudanese government has decided to change its policy and allow the Nuba people to receive international aid. However, the leaders of the Nuba people do not want shipments of food. What the people need, they say, is a very different kind of aid. Instead of food, they need material and equipment so that they can earn a living. That means aid such as farming equipment, weaving machines, or supplies for beekeepers. Above all, the Nuba people want to be able to produce what they need for their families. In this way, they can also serve as an example of how international aid can truly help people in the midst of war.

Finishing time _____   Reading time _____

Circle the best answer for each item. Do not look back at the passage.

1. This passage is about

    a. civil wars in African countries.
    b. international aid organizations.
    c. international aid in warring countries.
    d. food shipments to areas at war.

2. Because of the wars in many African countries,

    a. international aid organizations cannot send people food.
    b. many people do not have enough food.
    c. soldiers and local leaders face starvation.
    d. the people have extra supplies of food.

3. According to international aid workers, sending food to a warring country

    a. does not help people at all.
    b. helps only in the short term.
    c. helps make peace possible.
    d. allows leaders to distribute food better.

4. Food aid is often used by the government to

    a. control people.
    b. help people.
    c. pay workers.
    d. plant crops.

5. In Sudan, the government distributed food

    a. to all the hungry people.
    b. in the Nuba Mountains.
    c. only to some of the people.
    d. to areas that did not support it.

6. You can infer from this passage that what is happening in Sudan

    a. would not happen in other African countries.
    b. happens in other warring African countries.
    c. does not happen in other parts of the world.
    d. is the consequence of the food shipments.

7. The Sudanese government is going to

    a. send shipments of food to the Nuba people.
    b. allow the Nuba people to receive aid.
    c. start fighting the Nuba people.
    d. refuse all aid for the Nuba people.

8. The Nuba people are asking the aid organizations for

    a. new homes, schools, and markets.
    b. a new government in Sudan.
    c. large food shipments soon.
    d. equipment instead of food.

10. Africa's New Peace Park

Starting time _____

Wild animals do not know anything about nations and borders. They are interested in finding food and water, not in politics. However, because of the politics and history of Africa, many animals are in trouble. In the past, there were no borders between African countries, and the animals could travel freely. They moved from one place to another, according to the season or the weather. However, in the nineteenth and twentieth centuries, the continent was divided up into colonies and then into nations. Fences were put up along the borders, so the animals could no longer move about freely.

At the same time, animals were in trouble for other reasons. They were losing living space as the human population grew and people took over land for farming. Many Africans suffered from hunger, so they killed animals for food. Other animals were killed for their fur, tusks, or skin, and still others died in the many civil wars.

Some countries decided to protect their animals by creating national parks. Kruger National Park, created in South Africa in 1926, was one of the first. By the end of the twentieth century, it had become an important tourist attraction and a home for many kinds of animals. Among these, there were about 9,000 elephants, too many for the space in the park. It was not possible to let any elephants leave the park, however. They would be killed by hunters, or they might damage property or hurt people. South African park officials began to look for other solutions to the elephant problem.

As early as 1990, the governments of South Africa and Mozambique had begun talking about forming a new park together. In 1997, Zimbabwe agreed to add some of its land to the park. In fact, in both Mozambique and Zimbabwe the animals had suffered terribly in recent years. In Zimbabwe, severe droughts in the 1990s had killed many of the animals there. In Mozambique, a long civil war, and then severe floods, had led to the disappearance of many kinds of animals.

A new park would combine the Kruger National Park with parks in Mozambique and Zimbabwe. There would be no national border fences within the park, so that elephants and other animals from the crowded Kruger Park could move to areas of Mozambique and Zimbabwe. This new "transfrontier" park would cover 13,510 square miles (35,000 square kilometers). The idea of a transfrontier park interested several international agencies, which gave money and technical assistance to Mozambique to help build its part of the park.

In April 2001, the new park was opened, with new borders and a new name: The Great Limpopo Transfrontier Park. At the opening ceremony, former South African President Nelson Mandela called the park part of "Africa's success story." He said that "the peace park's initiative is an example of how to improve relations between nations." A border gate was opened between Kruger National Park and Mozambique, and seven elephants were allowed through. They were the first of 1,000 elephants that would be transferred to the world's greatest animal park.

Finishing time _____   Reading time _____

Circle the best answer for each item. Do not look back at the passage.

1. This passage is about

    a. how the Kruger National Park will save its elephants.
    b. how three African countries cooperated to make a new park.
    c. how many African animals have been killed for food, fur, and tusks.
    d. international cooperation in the developing countries.

2. African animals were in trouble in the twentieth century partly because of

    a. damage caused by too many elephants.
    b. the lack of national borders.
    c. the opening of the first national park.
    d. the increase in the human population.

3. Kruger National Park

    a. crossed three national borders.
    b. opened in the late-twentieth century.
    c. protected only elephants.
    d. was one of Africa's earliest parks.

4. At the end of the twentieth century,

    a. there were too many elephants in Kruger Park.
    b. the elephants were all dying at the park.
    c. elephants were killed by hunters inside the park.
    d. elephants could leave the park when they wanted.

5. In the 1990s in Mozambique and Zimbabwe,

    a. many animals died.
    b. animals were crowded together.
    c. tourists caused problems.
    d. there was a large animal park.

6. You can infer from this passage that the new peace park will be

    a. only in South Africa.
    b. too crowded.
    c. a tourist attraction.
    d. a problem for the animals.

7. International aid agencies helped Mozambique

    a. move its elephants.
    b. build part of the park.
    c. build fences on its borders.
    d. end a long civil war.

8. The Great Limpopo Transfrontier Park is

    a. like other African parks.
    b. open only to hunters.
    c. important for Africa.
    d. in northern Africa.

UNIT 3 Global Issues

Time yourself as you read the following passages. Read each passage and answer the questions on the following page. Do not look back at the passage as you answer the questions.

1. The Global Crisis

Starting time _____

This unit is about the planet earth. At the beginning of the twenty-first century, the earth is at a critical point in its history. People are changing it. They are polluting the air and water. They are cutting down forests and building houses, roads, and factories everywhere. As a result, global temperatures are rising and the climate is changing. Thousands of species of plants and animals are disappearing and the sea level is rising.

Life is becoming more difficult for many people, too. The destruction of the environment has affected people around the world in different ways. In the industrialized countries, it has negatively affected the quality of life and even caused illness. In other areas of the world, it has meant hunger, poverty, and even death. This is true in many of the developing countries where people were already poor. Due to environmental problems, these people are no longer able to make a living from the land. At the same time, the social, political, and economic problems that they face are growing.

All of these problems affect each other and can lead to disaster. In the year 2000, Hurricane Mitch in Central America was just such a disaster. It resulted in over 10,000 deaths, left millions of people without homes, and caused billions of dollars worth of damage. The real cause of so much destruction, however, was not the hurricane itself. The problem was partly population growth that meant people were more crowded together. It was partly international businesses, which took the best farmland in the valleys for their big plantations and forced people to move to the hillsides, which are often unsafe in storms. And finally, it was deforestation (the cutting down of trees) on the hillsides, which made the rain more destructive. Thus, human activity in many different forms caused a large part of the death and destruction.

Another kind of disaster is taking place in the southern oceans. In just the last decade, coral reefs have begun to die. Coral reefs are rock-like formations made by tiny animals. They are a vital part of the ocean ecology because they provide homes for thousands of kinds of water plants and fish. These reefs are very sensitive to changes in their environment and now, due to warmer ocean temperatures and pollution, large parts of the reefs are dying. Over half the coral reefs in the Indian Ocean are without life, and the same is true in the Caribbean Sea. Scientists predict that unless the situation changes suddenly, all these reefs will soon be gone. The loss of these reefs will have serious consequences for both the fishing and the tourist industries. Many people will be left without a way to make a living.

Around the world, individuals, businesses, and governments have neglected the environment. Now they need to act soon to try to resolve the many problems our planet is facing. In this unit, you will read about some of these problems, their causes, and some possible solutions.

Finishing time _____   Reading time _____

Circle the best answer for each item. Do not look back at the passage.

1. This passage is about
   a. pollution of the air and water.
   b. critical problems on the planet.
   c. the planet earth.
   d. disasters in Central America.

2. According to this passage, the earth is changing because of
   a. human activity.
   b. scientific predictions.
   c. pollution.
   d. its history.

3. We can infer from this passage that the global crisis is affecting people in developing countries
   a. less than in industrialized countries.
   b. only when they live in cities.
   c. more than in industrialized countries.
   d. and industrialized countries in the same way.

4. Hurricane Mitch
   a. killed fish in the southern oceans.
   b. resulted in population growth.
   c. did not cause much damage.
   d. killed thousands of people.

5. Hurricane Mitch caused so much destruction partly because
   a. lots of trees had been cut down.
   b. it had rained little that year.
   c. people in Central America were mostly farmers.
   d. fish were dying in the oceans.

6. Coral reefs are important to the ocean ecology because
   a. they help make the ocean temperatures warmer.
   b. they prevent pollution and overfishing.
   c. people often build their homes on them.
   d. many kinds of water plants and fish live on them.

7. In the Indian Ocean and the Caribbean Sea,
   a. all the coral reefs have already died.
   b. at least half of the reefs have died.
   c. there are few coral reefs.
   d. the coral reefs are all healthy.

8. If the coral reefs all die,
   a. many tourists will want to go see them.
   b. governments will build new ones.
   c. many people will be without food or jobs.
   d. storms will destroy the tourist industry.

2. The World Is Warming

Starting time _____

The evidence is clear. Wherever there is permanent ice—Greenland, Antarctica, the Alps, the Himalayas—that ice is melting. Anybody who has been to high mountains will have noticed this fact. Scientists agree that the cause for this melting is very simple: The earth's atmosphere is warming up.

The melting ice, in turn, is causing sea levels to rise as the extra water from the melting ice pours into the oceans. Already, sea levels have risen about 8 inches (20 cm) in recent years, and scientists believe they could rise at least another 20 inches (50 cm) by the year 2100. This could put many heavily populated coastal areas at risk. Coastal Florida, the Nile Delta, Bangladesh, and many other areas would end up under water.

Along with rising air temperatures, the ocean temperatures are also rising. This has brought changes in weather patterns, with more frequent and more severe storms. Rising ocean temperatures are also one of the factors in the death of coral reefs in the southern oceans. These reefs are the natural homes to 65 percent of the world's fish. When the reefs die, so do the fish.

The warmer air temperatures are also causing changes in the world's climate zones. In Europe, the southern countries along the Mediterranean are already becoming drier and more desert-like. On the other hand, countries in northern Europe, such as Germany and England, have experienced terrible floods from too much rain. Worldwide, agriculture will soon be negatively affected in many places. Life will become more difficult in the poorer countries of Asia and Africa, which already suffer from poor soil and lack of water. Millions of people could be forced to leave their homes and countries in search of food and a better life.

The climate changes are affecting wildlife as well. Scientists have noted that some animals have moved to new areas where temperatures are cooler. The monarch butterfly, for example, can now be found farther north in California than in the past. Other animals, such frogs and toads, are disappearing because they are unable to move to a new area or adapt to the changes.

Why are temperatures rising? Scientists no longer have any doubts about the cause. The burning of fossil fuels like coal and petroleum releases carbon dioxide (CO_2) into the atmosphere. CO_2 has always been a part of the atmosphere. However, over the past 150 years, the amount of CO_2 released into the atmosphere has increased enormously. At the same time, the forests that once absorbed CO_2 are being cut down. The result is a thick blanket of CO_2 that covers the earth, making it warmer.

There is only one way to slow down this warming of the earth and that is by reducing the amount of CO_2 released into the atmosphere. This can be done by replacing fossil fuels with new energy sources—such as wind power, solar power, or hydrogen fuel cells—that do not release CO_2 or other polluting chemicals.

Finishing time _____   Reading time _____

Circle the best answer for each item. Do not look back at the passage.

1. This passage is about
    a. pollution in the atmosphere.
    b. how climate changes affect wildlife.
    c. the warmer ocean temperatures.
    d. the rising temperatures on earth.

2. The ice in Antarctica is melting because
    a. sea levels are rising.
    b. the temperature of the atmosphere is warmer.
    c. more people are traveling to Antarctica.
    d. there are many high mountains on the continent.

3. By the year 2100, coastal Florida
    a. may have cooler water.
    b. will be heavily populated.
    c. will have coral reefs.
    d. could be under water.

4. The rising temperature of the ocean is
    a. killing many kinds of marine life.
    b. bringing better weather to tourist resorts.
    c. preventing storms from forming.
    d. helping many forms of marine life.

5. We can infer from this passage that climate change will result in
    a. more people moving from developing countries to industrialized countries.
    b. fewer people moving from developing countries to industrialized countries.
    c. more people becoming farmers in the developing countries.
    d. a better life for more people in the developing countries.

6. We can infer from this passage that the monarch butterfly
    a. prefers warmer temperatures.
    b. is not affected by climate change.
    c. does not like warmer temperatures.
    d. cannot adapt to climate change.

7. Scientists believe that the main cause of climate change is
    a. lack of CO_2 in the earth's atmosphere.
    b. an increase in the size of the earth's forests.
    c. the rising temperature of the oceans.
    d. the increase of CO_2 in the atmosphere.

8. The only way to slow down climate change is to
    a. increase the amount of CO_2 in the atmosphere.
    b. use nonpolluting kinds of fuel.
    c. burn more fossil fuels such as coal and petroleum.
    d. release other kinds of chemicals into the atmosphere.

3. Where Have All the Frogs Gone?

Starting time _____

In the 1980s, scientists around the world began to notice something strange: Frogs were disappearing. More recent research has shown that many kinds of amphibians are declining or have become extinct. Amphibians are animals, such as frogs, that live partly in water and partly on land, and they have been around for a long time—over 350 million years. They have survived three mass extinctions, including the extinction of the dinosaurs. Why are they dying out now?

Scientists are seriously concerned about this question. First of all, amphibians are an important source of scientific and medical knowledge. By studying amphibians, scientists have learned about new substances that could be very useful for treating human diseases. Further research could lead to many more discoveries, but that will be impossible if the amphibians disappear.

The most serious aspect of amphibian loss, however, goes beyond the amphibians themselves. Scientists are beginning to think about what amphibian decline means for the planet as a whole. If the earth is becoming unlivable for amphibians, is it also becoming unlivable for other kinds of animals and human beings as well?

Scientists now believe that amphibian decline is due to several environmental factors. One of these factors is the destruction of habitat, the natural area where an animal lives. Amphibians are very sensitive to changes in their habitat. If they cannot find the right conditions, they will not lay their eggs. These days, as wild areas are covered with houses, roads, farms, or factories, many kinds of amphibians are no longer laying eggs. For example, the arroyo toad of southern California will only lay its eggs on the sandy bottom of a slow-moving stream. There are very few streams left in southern California, and those streams are often muddy because of building projects. Not surprisingly, the arroyo toad is now in danger of extinction.

There are a number of other factors in amphibian decline. Pollution is one of them. In many industrial areas, air pollution has poisoned the rain, which then falls on ponds and kills the frogs and toads that live there. In farming areas, the heavy use of chemicals on crops has also killed off amphibians. Another factor is that air pollution has led to increased levels of ultraviolet (UV) light. This endangers amphibians, which seem to be especially sensitive to UV light. And finally, scientists have discovered a new disease that seems to be killing many species of amphibians in different parts of the world.

All these reasons for the disappearance of amphibians are also good reasons for more general concern. The destruction of land, the pollution of the air and the water, the changes in our atmosphere, the spread of diseases—these factors affect human beings, too. Amphibians are especially sensitive to environmental change. Perhaps they are like the canary bird that coal miners once used to take down into the mines to detect poisonous gases. When the canary became ill or died, the miners knew that dangerous gases were near and their own lives were in danger.

Finishing time _____   Reading time _____

Circle the best answer for each item. Do not look back at the passage.

1. This passage is about

    a. the study of amphibians.
    b. how pollution is killing amphibians.
    c. how the environment is affecting animals.
    d. how amphibians are disappearing.

2. We can infer from this passage that amphibians

    a. existed at the time of dinosaurs.
    b. are a very recent kind of animal.
    c. became extinct at the time of the dinosaurs.
    d. developed after the dinosaurs.

3. Losing amphibians means losing

    a. chemicals for factories.
    b. a chance to discover new medicines.
    c. scientists and doctors.
    d. knowledge about air and water pollution.

4. Amphibians lay their eggs

    a. in any stream they can find.
    b. only on sand.
    c. where there are buildings.
    d. only in the right conditions.

5. The arroyo toad is disappearing because

    a. it lives in ponds.
    b. there is a lot of air pollution.
    c. it is losing its habitat.
    d. a disease is killing its eggs.

6. Pollution, UV light, and disease are all

    a. caused by amphibians.
    b. reasons for the decline of amphibians.
    c. problems in southern California.
    d. caused by dinosaurs.

7. Amphibians are

    a. more sensitive to environmental change than most animals.
    b. less sensitive to environmental change than most animals.
    c. unaffected by environmental change.
    d. more sensitive to scientific experiments than most animals.

8. Scientists think that the decline of amphibians could

    a. cause a decline in other kinds of animals.
    b. be a good sign for human beings.
    c. cause environmental change.
    d. be a warning signal for human beings.

4. Farming the Wind

Starting time _____

Where will our electricity come from in the future? Scientists agree that people need to limit the use of fossil fuels like petroleum, gas, and coal. These fuels pollute the atmosphere with CO_2 and other chemicals, causing many environmental problems. Instead, people and governments will have to develop other kinds of energy that do not pollute, such as wind, solar, or hydrogen power. These kinds of energy are also renewable, which means there is no limit to the amount that can be produced.

One of the most promising of these sources is wind power. In recent years, the use of wind power has expanded rapidly, especially in North America and Europe. There are good reasons for this growth. First of all, wind power is clean. Using the wind to produce energy does not cause pollution or damage the environment. Furthermore, it is cheap. Recent technological improvements have made it one of the cheapest sources of energy today, and there are no hidden environmental or health costs that show up later.

There is nothing new about the idea of using wind power. The first machines to work by wind power were invented around 2,000 years ago in China. These machines, or windmills, appeared in the Mediterranean area in about A.D. 500 and then slowly spread to northern Europe. Unlike the old wooden and stone windmills, modern windmills are made of metal, with four steel blades that catch the wind. Tall and graceful, each one looks like a moving sculpture. These wind farms, usually built in groups of twenty or more, make a dramatic sight.

Wind farms are not completely problem free. In some places, birds have been killed by the blades of windmills. However, studies show that this only happens when the wind farms are built in areas where many birds fly through on their way north or south. Careful research before they are built can prevent this. Also, the latest windmill design, with slower-moving blades, is less dangerous for birds.

Another problem with wind farms can be the noise they make when there is a lot of wind. For this reason, large wind farms are usually built in areas with few people. There is a large wind farm in the province of Quebec, Canada, and another in a mountainous area of the western United States. Wind farms can also be built out to sea, like the ones off the coasts of Denmark and Germany or the one planned off the coast of Massachusetts in the United States.

Denmark and Germany are the countries with the highest percentage of electricity produced by wind power. In these countries, many small power companies and groups of farmers have built small wind farms that produce electricity for local use. These small wind farms have several advantages over large farms: They are inexpensive, they can be built to meet to local needs, and they are not noisy. These farms may help others to see how energy can be produced without harming the earth.

Finishing time _____   Reading time _____

Circle the best answer for each item. Do not look back at the passage.

1. This passage is about
    a. the cheapest sources of renewable energy.
    b. windmills around the world.
    c. the use of wind power to produce electricity.
    d. some problems with wind farms.

2. Unlike fossil fuels, wind power
    a. does not pollute the atmosphere.
    b. puts CO_2 into the atmosphere.
    c. is causing changes in the climate.
    d. has never been tried before.

3. We can infer from this passage that the use of fossil fuels
    a. has expanded rapidly in recent years.
    b. does not cause pollution or environmental damage.
    c. is less costly than the use of wind power.
    d. results in later environmental or health costs.

4. Modern windmills
    a. are really simple sculptures.
    b. do not have any blades to catch the wind.
    c. are made the same way as the old windmills.
    d. look very different from the old windmills.

5. Wind farms
    a. encourage technological improvement.
    b. produce electricity.
    c. help farms grow food.
    d. power factories that make steel.

6. Wind farms can kill
    a. people on planes.
    b. farmers at work.
    c. flying birds.
    d. small animals.

7. We can infer from this passage that large wind farms
    a. never make much noise.
    b. make more noise than small wind farms.
    c. frighten the birds with their noise.
    d. are not very noisy in the province of Quebec.

8. In Denmark and Germany, there are
    a. many small wind farms.
    b. few wind farms.
    c. many large wind farms.
    d. windmills on every farm.

5. Earth-Friendly Transportation Starting time _____

One hundred years ago, the invention of the automobile was viewed as a great step forward. Today autos are not always considered such wonderful machines. In fact, they are the cause of a number of social and environmental problems worldwide. The most serious of these is air pollution. In fact, burning gasoline and diesel fuel in motor vehicles releases many chemicals into the atmosphere, including large amounts of CO_2. Higher levels of CO_2 in the atmosphere have led to warmer weather and climate change around the world.

One way to limit the amount of CO_2 produced by cars and trucks is to encourage people to use motor vehicles less. In many places now, that will mean making major changes in transportation systems. In most parts of the United States, for example, the only way to get around is by car. It is often dangerous or impossible to travel on foot or by bicycle, and there may be few or no buses or trains. In some U.S. cities, public transportation does exist, but few people use it because it is often unattractive, inconvenient, and expensive.

The number of cars and trucks on the road can also be limited by charging drivers taxes and fees. For example, some countries, including Norway, Sweden, and New Zealand, require diesel truck drivers to pay for traveling on the roads. In a number of cities, including Singapore and some European cities, drivers of cars who wish to go downtown must pay a fee. These fees keep people from driving unnecessarily, and the money they bring in can be used for public transportation.

Pollution from motor vehicles can be further reduced by changing the engines of motor vehicles so they use different fuels. There are several nonpolluting fuels already available. One is natural gas. Several large cities in the Unites States are setting an example by replacing older buses and vans with vehicles that burn natural gas. Electricity is another important source of energy that pollutes less. Electric vehicles are becoming more efficient as the technology improves. In fact, the U.S. Postal Service has decided to use electric vehicles to deliver the mail. The "hybrid" car, already on the market in some countries, has an engine that runs on gasoline as well as an electric battery. Tests of the hybrid have shown that it burns about one-fourth the amount of gasoline used by an ordinary car.

Of all the new fuels, hydrogen is the "clean" fuel that scientists believe could be the fuel of the future. Hydrogen fuel cells create energy by combining hydrogen with oxygen. They do not release any pollution into the atmosphere—only water. A small amount of energy is required to produce the hydrogen, but this energy could be supplied by pollution-free solar or wind power. Though the first fuel cells, invented in the 1980s, were very large and quite expensive, the newest fuel cells are much smaller and less expensive. Hydrogen-powered vehicles could soon be sold at reasonable prices if governments and automobile manufacturers invest in the development of this nonpolluting technology.

Finishing time _____   Reading time _____

Circle the best answer for each item. Do not look back at the passage.

1. This passage is about
   a. ways to limit the CO_2 from motor vehicles.
   b. the amount of CO_2 produced by motor vehicles.
   c. a new kind of fuel for cars and trucks.
   d. different kinds of transportation around the world.

2. When gasoline and diesel fuel are burned, they
   a. don't release any chemicals.
   b. don't release any CO_2.
   c. release only water.
   d. release a lot of CO_2.

3. We can infer from this passage that most people in the United States
   a. take buses often.
   b. like to walk and bicycle.
   c. use cars a lot.
   d. travel a lot.

4. In Norway, Sweden, and New Zealand,
   a. drivers of cars have to pay for using the road.
   b. diesel truck drivers do not have to pay anything.
   c. diesel truck drivers pay for using the roads.
   d. bus drivers have to pay for using the roads.

5. We can infer from this passage that cars using "clean" fuel
   a. release only CO_2.
   b. do not release CO_2.
   c. do not get very dirty.
   d. are not convenient.

6. Several cities in the United States have begun buying buses that
   a. run on electricity.
   b. have old engines.
   c. burn diesel fuel.
   d. use natural gas.

7. A hybrid automobile
   a. uses gasoline and an electric battery.
   b. requires hydrogen and oxygen.
   c. is powered by solar or wind energy.
   d. does not pollute the atmosphere.

8. To create energy, hydrogen fuel cells require
   a. a small amount of water.
   b. carbon dioxide.
   c. a small amount of energy.
   d. hydrogen and oxygen.

6. A Thirsty Planet

Starting time _____

If you live in a city in North America or Europe, you have probably never thought much about water. Whenever you need some, you turn on the tap and there it is. Millions of people in other parts of the world are not so lucky. They have trouble getting enough clean water for their basic needs. This situation may soon become common all around the world, scientists believe. In fact, they say that the lack of clean water may be one of the biggest issues in the twenty-first century.

The reasons for this are clear. On the one hand, people are using more water than ever. Over the last fifty years, the population of the world has more than doubled. So has the demand for water—for home use, for farming, and for industry. On the other hand, supplies of clean water are disappearing. Many sources of surface water—such as rivers, lakes, and streams—are too polluted and unhealthy for use as drinking water. This has forced more and more people to drill wells so they can get water from underground.

There are enormous amounts of water deep underground in lakes called aquifers. Until recently, scientists believed this groundwater was safe from pollution. Then, in the 1980s, people in the United States began to find chemicals in their well water, and scientists took a closer look at what was happening. Weldon Spring, Missouri, for example, was the site of a bomb factory during World War II. The factory was destroyed after the war, but poisonous chemicals remained on the ground. Very slowly, these chemicals dripped down through the ground and into the aquifer. It took thirty-five years for the chemicals at Weldon Spring to reach the aquifer. Once they did, however, the water from that aquifer was no longer drinkable.

It probably never will be drinkable again. Groundwater is not renewed regularly by the rain, like lake or river water. Thus, if a harmful chemical gets into an aquifer, it will stay there for a very long time. Furthermore, it is nearly impossible to remove all the water in an aquifer and clean out the pollutants.

Industrial sites like Weldon Spring are one cause of groundwater pollution. There are thousands of such sites in the United States alone, and many others around the world. Groundwater pollution is also caused by modern farming methods, which require the use of large amounts of chemicals in the fields. And finally, yet another important cause of groundwater pollution is waste. That includes solid waste (garbage) thrown away in dumps and landfills, and also untreated human and animal waste.

The situation is indeed very serious. Fortunately, there are many aquifers and they are very large. Only a small number have been seriously damaged so far. But if the world does not want to go thirsty in the near future, further pollution must be prevented. Around the world, governments must make real changes in industry, agriculture, and waste disposal.

Finishing time _____   Reading time _____

Circle the best answer for each item. Do not look back at the passage.

1. This passage is about

   a. pollution problems.
   b. water supplies around the world.
   c. an industrial site in Missouri.
   d. groundwater pollution.

2. According to scientists,

   a. clean water is not necessary for millions of people.
   b. there will always be enough water for everyone.
   c. the water problem will soon be resolved.
   d. many more people may soon be without clean water.

3. One of the reasons why there is a water problem is because

   a. the population has grown.
   b. people wash their clothes more often.
   c. people in Europe don't turn off their water.
   d. the water is underground.

4. Another reason why there is a water problem is because

   a. lakes and streams are drying up.
   b. underground water is hard to get.
   c. surface water is too polluted to drink.
   d. people don't want to drill wells.

5. In Weldon Spring, people found

   a. many sources of surface water.
   b. chemicals in their well water.
   c. other aquifers underground.
   d. chemicals in the bomb factory.

6. If chemicals get into the groundwater,

   a. the water may never be good to drink.
   b. they can be taken out of the water.
   c. people can drink the water anyway.
   d. they soon wash away with the rain.

7. We can infer from this passage that industry, farming, and waste are

   a. the three main sources of groundwater pollution.
   b. only a small part of groundwater pollution.
   c. a problem only at sites of bomb factories.
   d. polluting all aquifers in the United States.

8. At present,

   a. none of the world's aquifers are polluted.
   b. most of the world's aquifers are polluted.
   c. most of the world's aquifers are still clean.
   d. none of the world's aquifers are clean.

7. All the Hungry People

Starting time _____

Throughout history, hunger has always been a problem. Wars and disasters have destroyed food supplies and caused starvation. Even in good times, there have always been some people who were not able to get enough food. However, there have never been as many poor and hungry people as there are today. According to a recent study, about 1.3 billion people live on less than $1 per day. About 1.1 billion people do not get enough to eat every day.

Hunger is a permanent condition for these people. It affects their health and shortens their lives. It affects the countries where the majority of the poor and hungry people live. When so many people go hungry, economic growth or political development is nearly impossible. Finally, hunger also affects the industrialized countries since millions of people move there from poorer countries, hoping to find a better situation.

Why are so many people poor and hungry? The single most important reason for this is population growth. From 2.5 billion in 1950, the world population grew to 6 billion in 2001. Food production also grew in that period, but not enough. In areas where population growth has slowed down, there are now fewer people suffering from hunger. This is the case in East Asia (especially China) and Latin America. In large areas of the world, however, the population is still growing rapidly. This is true of India, Bangladesh, Pakistan, and most African countries. In these countries, the number of people suffering from hunger has increased. Since the population is quite young, that means there are many hungry children. In India, for example, 53 percent of the children do not get enough to eat every day.

The solution to this problem may seem simple: produce more food. However, there are several factors that prevent an increase in food production. One of these is the dry climate in many of the poor countries. In the past, few people lived in dry areas because of the limited supply of water. Now more people are living there, but there is not enough water for everyone to grow enough food. Another factor preventing better food production is often the destruction of farmland. When too many people live in one area, the land suffers. Trees are cut down for firewood and plants are eaten by cattle, sheep, or goats. Soon the land is completely bare and unprotected. The good top soil blows away with the wind or washes away with the rain. The soil that is left is not good for growing food.

As a result of the many problems in the countryside, people move to the cities. However, the situation there is often even worse than in the country. Many cities in developing countries are growing so quickly that large areas have no public services, such as water or electricity. The living conditions are extremely crowded and unhealthy, and few jobs are available. As a consequence, families are not able to earn the money to buy food, and they continue to go hungry.

Finishing time _____   Reading time _____

Circle the best answer for each item. Do not look back at the passage.

1. This passage is about

    a. problems in developing countries.
    b. food production around the world.
    c. the worldwide problem of hunger.
    d. population growth around the world.

2. Compared to the past, today there are

    a. fewer people who suffer from hunger.
    b. more people who suffer from hunger.
    c. the same number of people who suffer from hunger.
    d. no people who suffer from hunger.

3. According to this passage, the main cause of so much hunger is

    a. population growth.
    b. the dry climate.
    c. economic development.
    d. the political situation.

4. During the last half of the twentieth century,

    a. food production didn't grow as quickly as the population.
    b. there was no growth in food production.
    c. the population grew at the same rate as food production.
    d. population and food production remained about the same.

5. We can infer from this passage that having fewer children

    a. makes no difference in a poor country.
    b. causes an increase in the food production.
    c. means fewer people go hungry.
    d. results in an increase in hunger.

6. Food production cannot increase in some poor countries because of

    a. slow population growth.
    b. the high percentage of children.
    c. the lack of water.
    d. poor health.

7. Another reason for poor food production is often

    a. lack of firewood.
    b. the destruction of farmland.
    c. cattle, sheep, and goats.
    d. lack of money and jobs.

8. According to this passage, people who move to the cities in developing countries

    a. have to work hard to earn money.
    b. usually find better living conditions.
    c. often decide to return to the countryside.
    d. often find terrible living conditions.

8. Why So Many Children?

In many of the developing countries in Africa and Asia, the population is growing fast. The reason for this is simple: Women in these countries have a high birth rate—from 3.0 to 7.0 children per woman. The majority of these women are poor, without the food or resources to care for their families. Why do they have many so children? Why don't they limit the size of their families? The answer may be that they often have no choice. There are several reasons for this.

One reason is economic. In a traditional agricultural economy, large families are helpful. Having more children means having more workers in the fields and someone to take care of the parents in old age. In an industrial economy, the situation is different. Many children do not help a family; instead, they are an expense. Thus, industrialization has generally brought down the birth rate. This was the case in Italy, which was industrialized quite recently and rapidly. In the early part of the twentieth century, Italy was a poor, largely agricultural country with a high birth rate. After World War II, Italy's economy was rapidly modernized and industrialized. By the end of the century, the birth rate had dropped to 1.3 children per woman, the world's lowest.

However, the economy is not the only important factor that influences birth rate. Saudi Arabia, for example, does not have an agriculture-based economy, and it has one of the highest per capita incomes in the world. Nevertheless, it also has a very high birth rate (7.0). Mexico and Indonesia, on the other hand, are poor countries, with largely agricultural economies, but they have recently reduced their population growth.

Clearly, other factors are involved. The most important of these is the condition of women. A high birth rate almost always goes together with lack of education and low status for women. This would explain the high birth rate of Saudi Arabia. There, the traditional culture gives women little education or independence and few possibilities outside the home. On the other hand, the improved condition of women in Mexico, Thailand, and Indonesia explains the decline in birth rates in these countries. Their governments have taken measures to provide more education and opportunities for women.

Another key factor in the birth rate is birth control. Women may want to limit their families but have no way to do so. In countries where governments have made birth control easily available and inexpensive, birth rates have gone down. This is the case in Singapore, Sri Lanka, and India, as well as in Indonesia, Thailand, Mexico, and Brazil. In these countries, women have also been provided with health care and help in planning their families.

These trends show that an effective program to reduce population growth does not have to depend on better economic conditions. It can be effective if it aims to help women and meet their needs. Only then, in fact, does it have any real chance of success.

Circle the best answer for each item. Do not look back at the passage.

1. This passage is about
   a. women in developing countries.
   b. economic influences on the birth rate.
   c. birth rates in developing countries.
   d. factors that influence birth rate.

2. In a traditional agricultural economy, a large family
   a. can be an advantage.
   b. may limit income.
   c. isn't necessary.
   d. is expensive.

3. When countries become industrialized,
   a. families often become larger.
   b. the birth rate generally goes down.
   c. women usually decide not have a family.
   d. the population generally grows rapidly.

4. According to this passage, Italy today is an example of an
   a. agricultural country with a high birth rate.
   b. agricultural country with a low birth rate.
   c. industrialized country with a low birth rate.
   d. industrialized country with a high birth rate.

5. Saudi Arabia is mentioned in the passage because it shows that
   a. the most important factor influencing birth rate is the economy.
   b. factors other than the economy influence birth rate.
   c. women who have a high income usually have few children.
   d. the birth rate depends on per capita income.

6. In Mexico, Thailand, and Indonesia, the government
   a. is not concerned about the status of women.
   b. has tried to industrialize the country rapidly.
   c. does not allow women to work outside the home.
   d. has tried to improve the condition of women.

7. We can infer from this passage that if women have a choice, they generally prefer
   a. to limit the size of their families.
   b. to work for the government.
   c. not to use any birth control.
   d. to have families with lots of children.

8. Governments are successful in slowing down population growth when
   a. women's opportunities are limited.
   b. they focus on the needs of women.
   c. the economic conditions of the country improve.
   d. they limit the availability of birth control.

9. Farming Today

When modern farming methods were introduced in the 1950s and 1960s, people believed they were the answer to world food shortages. Over the next few decades, food production did increase dramatically. However, the modern methods did not solve the problem of hunger—over a billion people still go hungry every day—and they created many other serious environmental problems.

According to modern methods, farmers plant only one crop in large quantities and use only the new "improved" seed types. These seeds require farmers to use lots of chemical fertilizers to make the seeds grow and chemical pesticides to kill harmful insects. They also require farmers to irrigate with lots of water. Farmers and scientists now realize that these methods may raise production immediately, but they have negative effects in the long term. For example, planting the same crop repeatedly and using lots of chemical fertilizers makes the soil unproductive. Also, the farming of very large, open fields results in the loss of valuable top soil.

There are often negative effects outside the farm as well. Farm irrigation uses up enormous quantities of water, causing water shortages in nearby cities and towns. The heavy use of fertilizers and pesticides leads to the pollution of groundwater, rivers, lakes, and even the ocean. It also leads to the development of superinsects that survive all pesticides.

For farmers in the developing countries, there are other kinds of problems. Often the only seeds available are the modern seed types. However, they may not be able to afford to buy the fertilizers and pesticides that these seeds require. There also may not be much water available or the farmers may not be able to pay for irrigation. Without chemicals and water, these seeds will never produce much, especially since poor farms are often located in dry areas. Thus, many farmers are not even able to feed their own families.

Fortunately, not all farms today fit this alarming picture. In both industrialized and developing countries, more and more farmers are turning to organic farming methods. No chemicals are used on an organic farm. Instead, the farmer takes advantage of the many ways that biology can help him. He can improve the productivity of the soil, for example, by planting several crops in a field at one time or by growing plants like peas and beans, which put nitrogen into the soil.

There are a number of reasons for the increase in organic farming. First, more consumers want fruit and vegetables that are free of chemicals. Second, people have begun to realize that there are many hidden costs connected with modern farming, such as the price of increased cancer risk from polluted groundwater. Furthermore, farmers are becoming aware of the benefits of organic farming. In Guatemala, for example, some farmers learned about organic farming from an international organization called World Neighbors. They experimented with ways to reduce erosion and increase productivity without using chemicals. In just a few years, the farm environment was healthier, and they were producing much more food.

Circle the best answer for each item. Do not look back at the passage.

1. This passage is about

   a. modern farming and organic farming.
   b. serious environmental problems.
   c. the effects of modern farming methods.
   d. the advantages of organic farming.

2. When farmers plant the new seed types, they

   a. do not need to irrigate their crops.
   b. usually plant many different crops.
   c. have to plant lots of seeds.
   d. need to use lots of chemicals.

3. Unproductive soil and erosion are

   a. the effects of climate change.
   b. the results of modern farming.
   c. due to scientific experiments.
   d. the necessary costs of farming.

4. Superinsects are developed from

   a. irrigating with lots of water.
   b. doing scientific experiments.
   c. the production of lots of food.
   d. the use of lots of pesticides.

5. We can infer from this passage that modern farming

   a. is less expensive than organic farming.
   b. does not require much money.
   c. requires farmers to spend money.
   d. makes lots of money for farmers.

6. To increase productivity, organic farmers need to

   a. understand some biology.
   b. use lots of chemicals.
   c. have help in economics.
   d. learn about technology.

7. Organic farming is becoming more popular because

   a. farmers are joining organizations.
   b. modern farming has hidden costs.
   c. it is connected with a higher risk of cancer.
   d. people like to try new ways of farming.

8. Farmers in Guatemala

   a. discovered the hidden costs of organic farming.
   b. raised their productivity by using chemicals.
   c. increased their productivity by organic farming.
   d. experimented with modern farming methods.

10. Greener Businesses

Business is often seen as the "bad guy" in environmental matters because people feel that businesses will do anything to make a profit. Unfortunately, this is too often the case. Many businesspeople, in fact, believe that they cannot make a profit and be kind to the environment at the same time. However, it does not necessarily have to be this way. Using common business strategies, companies have found ways to become environmentally friendly, or "green," and increase their profits at the same time.

One such strategy that businesses use is known as "product differentiation." This term means that a company advertises the fact that its product is different from other, similar products. A number of environmentally friendly companies have done this successfully. For example, in marketing their products, organic food companies emphasize the organic aspect. That is, they highlight the fact that no chemicals have been used to grow the food, and so it is better for consumers' health and for the environment. These days, many consumers are looking for products that have no negative health or environmental effects.

Another "green" business strategy that has been successful is waste reduction. Many companies have considered waste and pollution as a necessary part of the production process. They have done little to prevent either waste or pollution, unless there were laws that forced them to. However, other companies have realized that there are definite advantages to reducing waste and pollution. Less waste and less pollution means a more efficient production process. The 3M Company in the United States is a good example of this. In 1975, it started a program that rewarded employees for successful ideas about how to reduce waste and prevent pollution. This program has helped the company pollute much less and save more than a half a billion dollars.

Some companies have taken the idea of waste prevention even further and have become "zero-waste" companies. That means they produce no waste at all because everything from the production process is used or recycled. Asahi Breweries of Japan, for example, sends the waste from its beer production to farms to be used as animal feed. The plastic and cardboard pieces left over from packaging are all recycled, too.

Finally, companies can become "greener" by planning for a "greener" future. For example, two energy companies, Royal Dutch/Shell and British Petroleum, have started to invest in renewable energy sources, such as solar, wind, or hydrogen energy. Shell is also working with Daimler-Chrysler, an automobile company, and the government of Iceland on a special project to make Iceland the first country with a hydrogen-based economy. Other multinational companies have also realized that global warming and climate change could hurt their business, and they have decided to cut back on the amount of harmful gases that their factories produce. Of these, Dupont is one of the leaders. It aims by 2010 to reduce harmful gases by 65 percent from the 1990 amounts. It also plans to limit its energy use to 1990 levels and to use renewable sources of energy for 10 percent of all the energy it uses.

Circle the best answer for each item. Do not look back at the passage.

1. This passage is about

    a. business strategies for international companies today.
    b. how businesses can be both "green" and profitable.
    c. what businesses can do to become more profitable.
    d. why businesses are seen as the environmental bad guys.

2. Product differentiation means that the product is

    a. no different from other products.
    b. very profitable for the company.
    c. advertised as different from other products.
    d. good for your health and for the environment.

3. Companies that reduce waste and pollution

    a. save money.
    b. spend money.
    c. produce less.
    d. break laws.

4. The 3M Company rewarded employees for

    a. ideas that would increase its profits.
    b. helping prevent waste and pollution.
    c. successful strategies for marketing.
    d. improving product differentiation.

5. Asahi Breweries is an example of a company that

    a. uses animal feed to make beer.
    b. does not make any profit.
    c. has reduced waste and pollution.
    d. produces no waste at all.

6. Royal Dutch/Shell and British Petroleum are examples of companies that

    a. invest money in new buildings.
    b. do not look ahead into the future.
    c. want to lead new developments.
    d. produce a lot of waste and pollution.

7. We can infer from this passage that many companies

    a. are already "zero-waste" companies.
    b. are leading new developments.
    c. invest in renewable energy.
    d. look mostly at the present situation.

8. Iceland will be the first country to

    a. be free of hydrogen.
    b. have a new economy.
    c. use only hydrogen.
    d. have climate change.

Appendix 1

Record of Books Read

Title	Author	Date begun	Date finished	Number of pages

Appendix 2

Book Response Sheet

Title of Book: _____

Author: _____

Publisher: _____

Date Published: _____ Number of Pages: _____

Type of Book: _____ Fiction _____ Nonfiction

Native language: _____

Nationality: _____

Level of difficulty for you: _____ Easy _____ OK _____ Difficult

What did you like most about this book?

What did you like least about this book?

Appendix 3

Pleasure Reading Rate Finder

You can use your own book to learn to read faster. About once a week, check your pleasure reading rate. Just remember to time yourself when you read.

1. Find a page in your book that is full from top to bottom.

2. Count the number of words in three lines: _____ words

3. Divide that number by three to get the average number of words in one line: _____ words

4. Count the lines on one page: _____ lines

5. _____ × _____ = _____
       (number of lines)   (average words in one line)   (number of words on a page)

   Now that you know how many words there are on one page in your book, you can figure out your reading rate (words per minute).

6. Open your book and mark the page you are on.

   Before you start to read, write the starting time here: _____ min. _____ sec.

   When you stop reading, write the finishing time: _____ min. _____ sec.

7. How many minutes did you read? Finishing time minus starting time equals reading time: _____ min. _____ sec.

8. How many pages did you read? _____

9. How many words did you read? _____ words

   _____ × _____ = _____
       (number of pages)   (number of words on a page)   (number of words read)

10. To find your reading rate, divide the number of words by the number of minutes.

    _____ words ÷ _____ minutes = _____ words per minute.

Appendix 4

Pleasure Reading Progress Chart

Book Title _____

Author _____

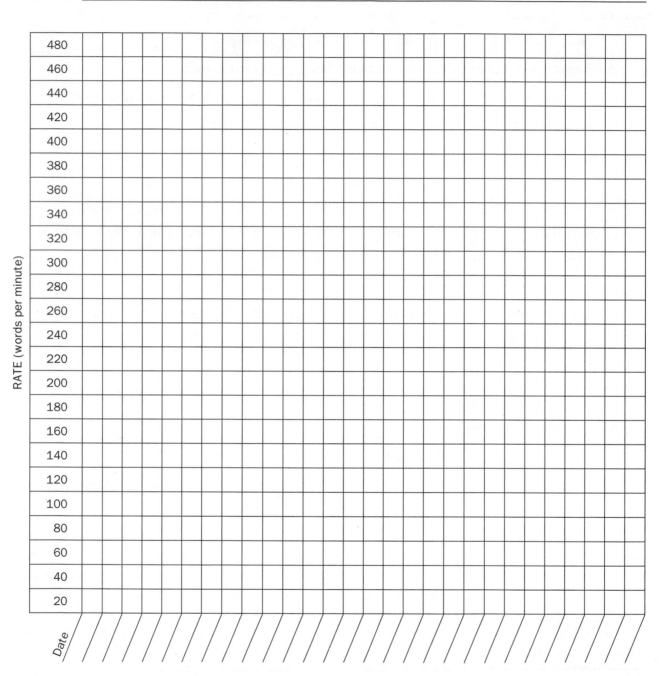

RATE (words per minute)

480
460
440
420
400
380
360
340
320
300
280
260
240
220
200
180
160
140
120
100
80
60
40
20

Date

Teacher's Guide

Introduction

In this Teacher's Guide, you will find general guidelines and specific suggestions for making the most effective use of *More Reading Power*. For a more complete explanation of the methodology and theory underlying our approach, see *A Short Course in Teaching Reading Skills* by Beatrice S. Mikulecky (Addison-Wesley, 1990).

The purpose of *More Reading Power* is to develop your students' awareness of the reading process so that they will be able to read in ways that are expected in school, college, or business. In order to allow the students to focus on the process of reading, the lexical and syntactical contents of the materials have been kept to a minimum (intermediate) level.

Many students have a conceptualization of reading that interferes with their reading in English. *More Reading Power* aims to help students acquire an accurate understanding of what it means to read in English. To accomplish this, the book addresses the reading process in a direct manner, and the various reading skills involved are presented as part of that process.

Student awareness of reading and thinking processes is further encouraged in many parts of the book by exercises that require them to work in pairs or small groups. In discussions with others, students need to formulate and articulate their ideas more precisely, and so they also acquire new ways of talking and thinking about a text. Students are also asked to write and then read each other's work so they can experience the connections between reading and writing.

A note about the Answer Key: In this second edition of *More Reading Power,* the Answer Key is supplied as a separate booklet. It is not included at the back of the student text book. While some teachers prefer to have the Answer Key separate from the text, others believe that students learn more effectively if they have access to the Answer Key to check

their own work. We encourage teachers to follow the latter approach, and suggestions regarding the use of the Answer Key are found throughout this Teacher's Guide. Teachers who prefer that their students not use the Answer Key can disregard these suggestions.

Using *More Reading Power* in Your Class

The role of the teacher in a reading class

The teacher is the most important element in a successful reading class. A good teacher can provide

- an anxiety-free environment in which students feel comfortable taking risks and trying new ways of reading.
- enough practice so the students can master new strategies.
- friendly pressure in the form of persuasion and timing.
- positive examples of how to approach a text.
- a model for the kind of thinking that good reading requires.
- an inspiring example of an enthusiastic reader.

Planning your reading classes

The materials in this book were designed to take approximately thirty-five hours of class time. This will vary according to the level of the students in your class and the amount of homework assigned. Classes and individual students also vary in the amount of time they need to complete different kinds of exercises in the book. Students should work at their own pace as often as possible.

A complete, semester-long **sample syllabus** is included at the end of the Teacher's Guide. Here are some additional suggestions for using *More Reading Power* in several different types of classes:

- **In an integrated skills class that meets for two to three hours per day, five days a week for one semester:** Use *More Reading Power* for a total of about 30–40 minutes, three times a week. There is a limited amount of class time to work on reading, so after teachers have introduced new units, many of the exercises can be assigned as homework.

Monday	Reading Faster, 15 minutes; Comprehension Skills, 20 minutes
Wednesday	Thinking Skills, 15 minutes Reading for Pleasure and Book Conferences, 20 minutes
Friday	Reading Faster, 15 minutes Comprehension Skills, 20 minutes

- **In an integrated skills class that meets for three hours per week for one semester:** Use *More Reading Power* for about one-third of the class time, for a total of about one hour a week. Again, there is a limited amount of class time to work on reading, so after teachers have introduced new units, many of the exercises can be assigned as homework. Divide class time approximately as follows:
  - Reading Faster, 20 minutes
  - Thinking Skills, 20 minutes
  - Comprehension Skills, 20 minutes

- **In a reading class that meets two hours per week for one semester:** Use the four parts of *More Reading Power* as well as the students' pleasure reading books in every class. Work for about 20–30 minutes on each part of the book.

- **In a reading lab:** As in the classroom, students should work regularly on all four parts of the book, dividing their time about equally among the four parts. It is essential

that students be given initial instruction in how to use each part of *More Reading Power* before they begin to work on their own.

Homework assignments for all types of classes can include

- Reading for Pleasure
- Thinking Skills
- Selected Comprehension Skills exercises.
  Keep in mind that the Comprehension Skills in Part 2 should be assigned for homework only after the students have practiced them in class.

Making the reading class exciting and effective

- Make reading **enjoyable for the students.** The reading class must always involve them fully and never be allowed to turn into "busy work."

- Make the students aware of the **purpose of their work.** This will increase their sense of involvement and allow them to become more active learners (increasing their metacognitive awareness).

- Always **focus on the thinking process** and not on the "right answers." The answer in any particular exercise matters far less than how the student arrives at it. Encourage students to take this same approach by frequently asking "Why?" or "How can you tell?" or "How do you know?" As the students are required repeatedly to articulate answers to these questions, they become more conscious of their own thinking processes.

- Ask the students to **work in pairs** whenever possible, especially on the Comprehension Skills exercises in Part 2. **Talking about the exercises** and explaining their reasoning can reinforce the students' awareness of process and purpose. It also facilitates language acquisition (when the conversation is in English).

- Emphasize the importance of trying to **guess the meaning of words** from the context. Students should be discouraged from depending on dictionaries during the reading class or while doing their reading homework.

- The Answer Key is intended to serve as more than just the repository of the "right answers." Students should **check their own answers** so they can work independently when appropriate. When their answers differ from the Answer Key, they should try to figure out how and why they may have made a mistake. However, they should also be encouraged to question the Answer Key and to defend their answers and their reasoning. Some of the exercises, in fact, have alternative answers.

- When students work individually (especially on Parts 3 and 4), allow them to **work at their own pace.** Speed should be encouraged, but each student must determine what that speed will be. Faster students should not have to wait for slower classmates, and slower readers should not be pressed too hard or they may become anxious and incapable of comprehending.

- **Testing Student Reading Skills:** Please see the *More Reading Power Test Booklet* for further exercises that can be used to test students on the skills presented in this book.

Specific Suggestions for Using *More Reading Power*

Part 1: Reading for pleasure

Many students have never learned to enjoy reading for pleasure (reading extensively) in English, though it is well known that it is necessary to read a lot in order to become a good reader. To get students reading, it is not enough for the teacher to just say to students, "Read a book." Students must first come to understand the importance of reading extensively, and then they must be encouraged to develop the habit of reading regularly for pleasure. *More Reading Power* provides several motivating features: a rationale for pleasure reading, guidelines for success, record-keeping, a list of carefully selected books, and suggestions for book conferences with the teacher.

Extensive Reading vs. Intensive Reading

Intensive reading is an activity in which students (usually in a class group, led by the teacher) carefully read and examine together a reading passage assigned by the teacher. Many traditional reading classes use this approach almost exclusively. Some teachers refer to this activity as "explication of the text."

Extensive Reading, on the other hand, is an activity in which students read a lot, and students all read different books—practically any books they want to read. What matters is that they are encouraged to read as much as possible.

While intensive reading can play an important role in developing an appreciation of the English language and selected English literature, it is only by reading extensively that students can develop their ability to read with fluency and understanding. Furthermore, extensive reading is essential for practicing and applying reading skills and for developing all areas of language skills. Research shows that vocabulary acquisition and writing ability, for example, are directly related to the quantity of reading that students engage in.

Student Selection of Books for Extensive Reading

Students are instructed to select books to read for pleasure on an individual basis. These books should be neither too easy nor too difficult. They should not be books that are required in other courses or that students have already read in translation. Most important, students should be encouraged to choose any book they want—fiction or nonfiction, representing literature or popular culture. What matters most is that the book is of interest to the individual student and that the student actually wants to read it.

In pleasure reading, complete books are recommended, not newspapers, magazines, or "readers," and not books that are made up of extracts of other books (such as *Reader's Digest Selections*) or collections of short stories by many different authors. There are several reasons for this. First of all, many students may never before have read a book in English that they chose for themselves. Thus the selection process will be a new experience for them, one that will help form a new literate identity.

Second, while magazines, newspapers, and book selections may provide reading practice, the goal of pleasure reading is for students to develop the habit of **sustained silent reading**, which is only possible with whole books. In addition, reading a whole book by a single author allows students to become comfortable with a writer's style and lexicon. This comfort is experienced as success, and actually allows students to read faster and faster as they proceed through their books.

Helping Students Select Books

One way to help your students select their books is to bring some of your own favorite books to the reading class and tell the students about them. These "book talks" serve two purposes. First, students find out about books that they might like to read. Second, students are provided with a model for how to talk about books, so that they will be able to talk about their own books and discuss them with others. When you present a book to the class, you should give a brief summary of the book's content, without too many details about the plot, and give your general reaction (Why did you like it or dislike it? Does it relate to your own experience?). Talk about various

aspects of the book: the characters, the setting, the mood, the author's intention, and so on. Discussion about books can be an effective motivating tool.

Students can also find books by participating in a class trip to a bookstore or library where they can browse and ask questions about books. Or, if the classroom has a library of suitable books, students can be guided to ones they might enjoy. They can also be encouraged to exchange books with classmates or with other students. Since students do not need to and, in fact, should not write notes or vocabulary in their pleasure reading books, there is no reason for them to buy the books (unless they want to be able to keep them afterward).

Motivating Students to Read for Pleasure

Students often tend to regard reading for pleasure as a less important element of the reading class. Since it is, in fact, a key to success in reading development, be sure to encourage your students to take it seriously.

- Require your students to bring their pleasure reading books to class and regularly devote some class time to pleasure reading.

- Assign reading for pleasure as homework and require your students to keep a record of how many pages they have read. Establish a requirement for the number of pages to be read per week or per semester.

- Check up on the students' pleasure reading by asking about the books they are reading or have read. This can take various forms:

  - Students can fill out a copy of Appendix 2: Book Response Sheet (page 252). Full written book reports are less useful, since they tend to diminish the student's enjoyment of the book.

  - Students can keep a reading journal in which they write regularly about their reactions to their book. They can write about characters they like or dislike, parts of the book that are particularly interesting or challenging, aspects of the setting or the style that have struck them, or larger issues that the book deals with (such as racism, war, the generation gap). To set an example, teachers can keep a reading journal of their own and read it aloud to students to give them a model for that kind of writing.

- Students can give an oral report to their classmates, with a brief description of the book and their opinion of it.

- Students can meet with you individually for a book conference. Book conferences are the surest way to evaluate student progress and promote pleasure reading. They can be the key to a successful extensive reading program. Not only do they provide you with feedback on the students' reading, but they also serve several other important purposes.

    Your questions about the book often represent a true "knowledge gap" between you and the student: The student knows more about the book than you do, and your questions are authentic, not "school questions." Your questions can serve as a model for the kinds of questions which a literate reader habitually asks him- or herself.

    The conference can also help the student acquire fluency in evaluative and elaborative language that will become the basis for good writing.

    Some teachers hold conferences during office hours or just before class. Other teachers hold book conferences with one student while the rest of the class is engaged in some other activity.

- Encourage your students to read faster during their pleasure reading. Students who read slowly often get bored or frustrated and may give up reading for pleasure. If they can read faster, however, they will enjoy their reading more. This will lead them to read more, which in turn will lead to better and faster reading, and so on. The first step in improving reading rate in pleasure reading is for students to find their reading rate in their pleasure reading books. Once students know their reading rate, teachers can help students improve by doing reading sprints (see page 184) and by asking students to time themselves regularly. Slower readers need to be encouraged to break their slow, word-by-word reading habits and to move their eyes more quickly down the page. They also may need to be reassured about comprehension. They do not need to understand every word or sentence. It is enough to be able to follow the story.

    Help students find their reading rate in their pleasure reading book by following the instructions in Appendix 3: Pleasure Reading Rate Finder (page 253). Be sure to read through this procedure carefully before you explain it to your students.

    Once students know how to calculate their reading rate, have them keep a record of it in Appendix 4: Pleasure Reading Progress Chart (page 254).

Part 2: Comprehension Skills

For many students, reading comprehension is a problem when they read in English, but since they can read in their own language, they tend to attribute their difficulties in comprehension to the English language, or they may feel that the fault lies in their own lack of ability. In fact, the problem usually lies in their approach to a text. With a better understanding of how information is presented in English texts and a greater awareness of the cognitive processes involved in reading, comprehension will almost certainly improve.

In Part 2 of *More Reading Power,* each new comprehension skill is introduced with a rationale and practiced in a series of exercises sequenced from simple to more difficult in order to build up the students' mastery of the skill. The skills include both "top-down" (concept-driven) and "bottom-up"(text-driven) modes of reasoning and comprehending.

Work on reading comprehension skills can be compared, in some respects, to weight-lifting. The weight-lifter learns how and why he or she must exercise certain muscle groups. Once the muscle group is targeted, the exercises proceed with gradually increasing weights. This is the same process that students should follow in reading comprehension lessons. As the "coach," you must be sure that the students understand how and why to do the exercises, and then stand by to provide advice, support, and increasing challenges.

You will find that you have the most success with these exercises if you do them yourself before you introduce them to the students. And before you assign the reading skills exercises, ask the students to read and discuss the Introduction to Comprehension at the beginning of Part 2.

How to Use the Comprehension Skills Units in the Classroom

1. Focus on one reading/thinking skill at a time.

2. With each skill, explain the purpose for doing the exercises and how the skill is important for effective reading.

3. Do an example or a sample exercise with the whole class. Model your thinking aloud as you do the exercise.

4. Put the students into pairs (whenever possible and appropriate) and assign one exercise for practice.

5. When the pairs have completed the exercise, discuss it with the whole class. Ask how the students arrived at their answers. Encourage friendly disagreement in the pairs and in the class as a whole. Ask, "What was your thinking as you decided on that answer?" Students are not necessarily "wrong" if they come up with an answer that is different from the Answer Key, as long as they can give a rationale for their choice.

6. In the same class and in the next few class meetings, assign additional exercises that focus on the same skill, increasing the complexity of the tasks. Make sure the students work together whenever it is feasible.

7. Assign an exercise to be done by individual students, either in class or as homework, so they can check their own ability and confidence in using the skill.

8. Assign further exercises as needed, based on your sense of the students' mastery of the skill.

While working on comprehension exercises, keep these two principles in mind:

- **Do not simply judge answers as right or wrong.** Instead, respond to students' answers with questions such as "Why?" or "How can you tell?" to encourage them to examine their reasoning processes.

- Whenever possible, **direct the students to work in pairs or small groups** since talking about the exercises helps develop awareness of thinking processes.

Unit 1: Previewing

1. Encourage students to guess as they work on these exercises. Often, they can remember more than they realize from their brief preview.

2. For Exercise 1, make a collection of books available to the students, preferably a mixture of textbooks, fiction, and nonfiction.

3. Remind students that they should preview everything they read, in all of their classes.

Unit 2: Scanning

1. Speed is essential in these exercises. To encourage speed, students may be timed, or they may do the exercises (in pairs) as a kind of race to see which pair can find all the answers first.

2. Do not spend time correcting or having students correct their answers, which are of very little importance to the exercise. You may want to spend a few minutes, on the other hand, discussing the cultural content of some of the scanning material, which may be unfamiliar.

3. Exercises 3 through 8 give students an opportunity to practice writing questions. Formulating questions for another student will help students learn to ask themselves questions as they read.

4. Continue to require the students to practice scanning after you have completed this unit by asking them to scan other materials. Continued practice is necessary for students to retain the skill.

5. Notice that though scanning and skimming are often taught as the same thing, they are really two very different skills. Scanning is a fairly simple skill that involves only a visual search for information on a page. Skimming, on the other hand, involves processing text for ideas, which requires far more complex thinking skills.

Unit 3: Skimming

1. Skimming is not (as it is sometimes thought) a simple matter of reading very fast; it is reading selectively. Only certain parts of the text are actually read when skimming.

2. These exercises must be timed in order to force students to work quickly through a text. Without the pressure of time, they will be tempted to read unnecessary parts and may be distracted from the purpose of the exercises.

3. As in the previous units, students should work in pairs to compare and explain their answers. Pair work helps students realize that there is no one right way to skim a text. What readers actually read while skimming depends on what they already know and on their interpretation of the text. In other words, it depends on what they are thinking, and, of course, no two people ever think exactly alike. Teachers should point this out to students and should allow for different responses to the exercises.

4. Students can be given additional skimming practice in the classroom by using several copies of a daily newspaper in English. The teacher may divide the class into small groups and give each group a newspaper. They should skim the newspaper for articles of interest and then discuss them.

5. Writing practice: A short research paper.
   Have students choose one of the texts from the exercises in this unit: "Eleanor Roosevelt," "Will the Net Replace Thinking?" or one of the book reviews. Students should read the passage(s) and then they should find two or more passages about the same topic (from books, encyclopedias, newspapers, the Internet, etc.). They should then skim the new articles to see if they include any additional information. When they have found enough new information, they should write a short paper about their topic, taking care to cite the sources of their ideas.

6. After you have used these exercises for training the students in skimming, the articles are excellent for use in intensive reading lessons, class discussions, and Internet research.

7. Be sure to have students apply the skill of skimming to other reading materials.

Unit 4: Vocabulary Knowledge for Effective Reading

1. In this unit, the emphasis is on helping your students to develop strategies that they can use whenever they encounter unknown vocabulary.

2. Exercises 1 through 7. The importance of trying to **guess word meaning** cannot be stressed too much. Students are often bound to their dictionaries. They need to learn that an English text usually gives multiple clues to meaning. They also need to realize that there are many advantages to guessing meaning, as pointed out in the introduction to this unit.

3. In Exercises 8 through 12, the emphasis is not on content words but on **function words**, the small words (such as pronouns and synonyms) that connect ideas in a passage. Research has shown that function words play a fundamental role in reading comprehension because these are the words that tie ideas together in a text. Thus, it is far more important for readers to understand how the function words work in sentences than to know all the content words in a sentence. Point this out to your students as a further argument for skipping over unknown content words.

4. Writing practice: Your students can gain further awareness of how function words operate in a text, and they can learn to control their use of function words by analyzing the function words in their own writing.

Use writing done for previous assignments or give your students a new assignment. Then ask your students, in pairs, to exchange papers and analyze the function words as they did in Exercises 11 and 12. If some of the referents are unclear, students should work in pairs to figure out how they might correct the problem.

Sometimes it is also helpful to take samples from several student papers for a class discussion of how referents can help or, if missing, confuse the reader.

Unit 5: Making Inferences

1. All reading is, of course, inferential by nature; the purpose of this chapter is to make students aware of what it means to infer and how it is an essential part of reading. In these exercises, an answer that is different from the one in the Answer Key is often possible. A "correct answer" is any answer that the student can support with evidence from the passage.

2. Writing practice: Some of the inference exercises have questions requiring short answers. Stress the importance of clear and complete sentences in answering those questions.

   In Exercises 6 through 8, the students are asked to tell what they think will happen next in the story or play. These questions can be the basis of additional writing assignments.

   After students have completed Exercise 10, ask them to write a review of a movie, play, or book for which readers would have to form their opinion based on inference. Then select some of the reviews to use in small groups or with the whole class. First, students should try to guess the writer's opinion about the movie, play, or book. Then they may discuss any differences of opinion on the subject.

After they have completed Exercise 11, students could do a writing assignment in which they explain which opinion they agree or disagree with.

Unit 6: Finding Topics

1. Since **discourse in English is usually topic-centered**, finding the topic is an important key to understanding a text. Thus, work on comprehension must begin by teaching your students what a topic is.

2. Encourage your students to work quickly in order to develop efficiency.

3. Working in pairs on these exercises, students will begin to internalize the key questions: What is this about? How do I know that?

4. Writing practice: Understanding and being able to work with topics is a fundamental skill in writing as well. Ask students to brainstorm some topics, and write them on the board. Then have each student select one of the topics and make a list of the details. This is the first step toward writing coherent paragraphs.

Unit 7: Discovering Topics of Paragraphs

1. Point out to your students that the topic of a paragraph is usually mentioned more than once in the paragraph. This is the writer's way of ensuring that the reader recognizes what the paragraph is about.

2. Alert students to the fact that the topic sentence of a paragraph is often the first sentence. In English—both oral and written—people expect to find out right away what something is about. With English language texts, readers expect to find the topic at the beginning, so they can orient their thinking. Thus, writers almost always provide the topic early on.

3. In a class that combines work on reading and writing, the introductory section of this unit can also be used to discuss the concepts of unity (the idea that a paragraph has a single topic) and coherence (the idea that all the sentences in the paragraph relate to that one topic). These terms can be introduced here and applied in later units as well.

4. Writing practice: Ask your students to write a unified paragraph, based on one of these topic sentences:
   - There is a lot to do in my hometown.
   - Shopping is an enjoyable pastime.
   - Electronic technology, such as television and VCRs and CD players, is constantly changing.
   - Everyone needs to know how to drive these days.

5. Internet practice: Students should choose a topic that they found interesting and find out more about that topic on the Internet.

Unit 8: Understanding Main Ideas

1. In this unit, students may have difficulty with the fact that the main idea is always a complete sentence that states both the topic and the idea(s) that the writer wishes to express about that topic. In other words, the main idea includes a topic and a comment. This might also be seen as a subject and a predicate. Students often mistakenly think that a topic by itself is the main idea.

2. Give students practice in producing a complete main idea sentence that accurately reflects the author's intended meaning by doing the following:
   a. Assign one of Exercises 2 through 6 as homework.
   b. In the next class, divide students into groups of three or four. Ask the students in each group to compare the main ideas they wrote individually.

They should then combine their efforts and write the best main ideas they can come up with.

   c. Have a representative of each group write that group's main ideas on the chalkboard.

   d. Ask the class to evaluate the main ideas and suggest possible improvements. This exercise offers an opportunity for a review of sentence definition and structure.

3. Writing practice: After your students have mastered writing main ideas, you can have them do the following exercise.

   a. Ask your students to write main idea statements about these three topics:
- Winter sports
- Getting married
- How colors can influence you

   b. Have the students work in pairs and check each other's work to make sure that they have written complete sentences.

   c. Ask students to choose one main idea statement and write a unified paragraph supporting the main idea statement.

   d. Tell the students to form small groups and compare paragraphs. Within the group, students can help each other improve the paragraphs.

   e. Collect the paragraphs and copy a few of them to use as a basis for discussion in the next class.

Unit 9: Identifying Patterns of Organization

1. Research has shown that readers comprehend and remember best those materials that are organizationally clear to them. However, many students are not familiar with the patterns of textual organization used in English and so have a more difficult time comprehending and remembering.

The explanation of why recognizing patterns can help comprehension is similar to the explanation given for the advantages to reading faster in the introduction to Part 4. In both cases, the same basic factors are at work: The brain does not work well with random pieces of information that must be stored in the memory as many separate items. The human brain works more efficiently with information that has a recognizable order. Thus, to allow the brain to work well while reading, the reader must constantly look for order in the text, by grouping words according to meaning and by following the patterns of discourse that writers normally use to express certain kinds of ideas in English.

2. In this unit, students will work with five of the most common patterns: listing, sequence, comparison/contrast, cause/effect, and problem/solution. There are other patterns of organization in English, of course, including spatial description, argument, and classification. You may wish to introduce one or more of these other patterns to your students, depending on their interests. Suitable examples may be found in books and magazines, and presented to your students in a set of exercises similar to those presented in this unit.

3. Note that in almost every exercise, students are asked not just to identify but also to write out the signal words and the details that are signaled. Although this may seem time-consuming and repetitious, it gives the students important practice that will help them gain confidence in their ability to recognize patterns and read for important points.

4. In an appropriate class context, you may want to point out to your students (and do additional work on) the connection

between the patterns presented here and the patterns used in outlining for note-taking or as preparation for writing.

5. Several of the exercises in this unit include some review of Units 7 and 8 (Discovering Topics of Paragraphs and Understanding Main Ideas).

6. In a writing/reading class, point out that the signal words for patterns can also be referred to as transitional words. They are the signposts that writers use to mark the shifts and turns in their thinking and that readers should use them to follow the writer from one idea to the next.

7. Writing practice: To give students further practice with patterns and with the use of signal words, find topics that fit clearly into each of the patterns and ask students to write paragraphs about each one, using at least three signal words per paragraph. Exercises 3, 7, 10, 15, and 18 offer writing practice in the five patterns.

Unit 10: Summarizing

1. Summarizing is usually viewed as a writing skill, but it is also a very useful reading skill, since it requires the reader to monitor comprehension. (Comprehension monitoring is a cognitive process that enhances comprehension.) In order to summarize, in fact, the reader must arrive at a thorough understanding of the main idea and the main points of a text.

2. Note that work on summarizing necessarily involves a review of the concepts of topics, main ideas, and patterns. Teachers should point this fact out to students.

3. Writing practice: Most of the exercises in this unit involve the students in actively writing summaries. In summarizing, they must try to condense and paraphrase the ideas in the text. These skills often do not come easily to students, but they are essential for many kinds of writing.

Part 3: Thinking Skills

Learning to read well in English means learning to think in English. However, many students have a habit of translating as they read and have great difficulty thinking in another language. The exercises in this part of the book are designed to help students make a transition from translating to thinking in English.

In order to complete the Thinking Skills exercises successfully, students will need to follow the way the ideas are presented in English. Correct completion could involve understanding English syntactic, semantic, and/or logical connections. The exercises gradually increase in length and complexity.

1. In order to ensure that students get the most out of this part of the book, be sure to go through the introduction very carefully with the whole class. In fact, you will come to a better understanding of the thinking process involved in these exercises if you actually work on at least ten of them before introducing this part of the book to your students.

2. Keeping track of progress is an important aspect of this part of the book. As described in the section called "Guidelines for Success" on page 162, students should always write the date in the margin when they finish working so that they know how they are progressing. This also makes it possible for you to monitor your students' work.

3. Students should complete these exercises at their own speed. However, they should be encouraged to work as quickly as possible. If they work slowly, they may continue to translate as they read, and they will not develop efficient reading habits.

4. Students may look back at the paragraph as they answer the questions, but they should not study it for long. Their first response is very often the correct one.

5. Some students may have trouble at first in following the logic of these exercises. If so, assign several exercises in class to pairs or small groups of students. They should discuss and decide on the answers and on the thinking processes involved. Afterward, those logical processes can be further clarified in a class discussion.

6. Students should not use dictionaries or ask anyone about word meanings while they are working on these exercises. They should be encouraged to use the context of the paragraph to guess the meaning on their own.

7. Many teachers assign the Thinking Skills for homework. This allows a natural way to include reading aloud in the class. Students often enjoy reading aloud the items they have done for homework, and the whole class can discuss any disagreements about the answers.

Part 4: Reading Faster

Learning to read faster must be a key part of any reading improvement program. There are two basic reasons for this. First, students in most academic settings are faced with an enormous quantity of reading in English. Many ESL/EFL students take three to four times longer than native-language students to complete reading assignments, which means that they have little time left to reflect on and assimilate what they have read.

The other reason for learning to read faster is that it leads to better comprehension. When reading faster, the eyes cannot focus on every word; they must focus on groups of words together. This makes it much easier for the brain to reconstruct meaning. Furthermore, since reading faster forces the reader to skip unknown or nonessential words, the brain can concentrate better on the general meaning of the text.

Be prepared to meet some resistance on the part of your students! Breaking them of the habit of word-by-word reading is not always easy. The habit may be of long standing and it may be connected with students' insecurities about understanding English. If this is the case, do not push too hard for immediate change, but try to build up students' confidence and willingness to take risks. Some students may be reluctant to read faster because of different attitudes toward reading in their native culture that lead them to feel that reading word by word is the only "real" way to read. With these students, you may need to spend extra time discussing the nature and variety of purposes of reading in English.

Why Read Faster?

1. It is important to have a thorough grasp of the rationale behind reading rate improvement so that you can explain it in terms the students will understand. For this reason, you should go through the students' introduction yourself first and, if necessary, consult other reference books for clarification.

2. Notice that the reasons given here for improved comprehension with faster reading are similar to those given in the rationale to Part 2, Unit 9: Identifying Patterns of Organization. Both explanations are based on a fundamental understanding of how the brain works in receiving and storing information; that is, that it works most efficiently when the information can be grouped into some kind of order. This is the basic reason for reading faster. When you read faster, your eyes sweep over larger pieces of text. That provides you with more data to use in grasping the author's meaning, which makes it easier to build up comprehension and to retain the information.

3. Along with a discussion of the rationale for reading faster, it is important for you

to discuss with your students the many different ways we read. Students may need to be reassured at this point that not all reading must be fast. There are times when slow reading is appropriate, as in reading poetry, complex technical material, instructions, or other material that is very dense with essential information. More often than not, students read slowly when they do not need to. They need to understand that learning to read faster will give them more flexibility.

How to Read Faster

1. Skip over unknown words.

You may be familiar with the use of cloze passages to determine reading ability or to teach grammar and vocabulary. The cloze passages here, however, serve a very different purpose: to convince students that they can understand the main points of a passage without reading every word. Furthermore, this kind of work with cloze passages encourages students to infer general meaning from partial information—a fundamental skill.

As always, students should know the rationale for these exercises before they begin. Do not ask students to fill in the blank spaces, because this would completely alter the purpose of the exercise in the students' eyes.

Stress the idea that unknown words can usually be ignored. Occasionally, it may be necessary to understand some words in order to comprehend the general meaning. In that case, the reader should continue reading and try to guess the meaning from the context. This skill is developed in Part 2, Unit 4.

If you wish to provide students with additional practice with cloze passages, choose a suitable text and blank out every seventh or fifth word (the more frequent

the blanks, the more difficult). The text should not contain difficult vocabulary or complex ideas that will be hard to grasp.

2. Do reading sprints regularly.

Be sure to study the procedure for reading sprints before using them with your students. Explain the procedure thoroughly to avoid confusion in the middle of the exercises. Students should use their pleasure reading books for doing the sprints. Later, they can do some more in the same book to measure gains in reading rate.

After the first session of sprints, students should be asked to repeat the sprints at regular intervals in class (once a week, once a month, etc., according to the frequency of class meetings) and at home.

Given the concentration required for doing these exercises, you should follow them with some relatively relaxing activity.

3. Check your students' reading habits.

Some of your students may have a habit of moving their lips or of following the text with their fingers while they are reading. If so, these students should be alerted, as they are often unaware of this habit, which slows them down as they read.

While working on Reading Faster passages, students should never write down meanings of words. This only reinforces the habit of translating and drastically slows down their reading. Students may need to be reassured that it is useful to write down new vocabulary, but not during faster reading sessions.

4. Do timed readings.

The example (page 185) introduces the students to the procedures they will follow for all the Reading Faster passages. They will have more success with the passages if they learn to **time themselves.** This allows them to work independently at their own pace.

Before reading any passage for timed reading, including the example, students should be instructed to **preview** before they read. If they have not yet started Unit 1: Previewing, in Part 2, you may need to introduce the concept of previewing.

Note that the **students should time themselves only while reading the passage**, not while answering the questions! Students should use the Answer Key to correct their own work after they complete each passage.

Timing Procedure for the Faster Reading Passages

1. When the class is ready to begin the example, the students should write the starting time on the line at the top of the passage. They should then start reading and read as quickly as possible with understanding. If there is a large clock visible in the classroom, the students can use it to note the time. If not, you can write the starting time on the chalkboard. Many students prefer to use their own watches, which often have timing devices on them.

2. As soon as they have finished reading, students should write the finishing time on the line at the end of the passage. If there is no clock, the students should signal when they finish and you can write the time on the chalkboard.

3. Students should then turn the page and circle the best answers to the questions (according to the text) without referring back to the passage.

4. After answering the questions, students can check their answers in the Answer Key. They should write down the number of correct answers. This is their comprehension score.

5. Students can then calculate their reading time by subtracting the starting time from the finishing time. Using this reading time, they can find their reading rate in the table on page 188.

The example usually raises some questions about timing procedures. Review the procedures again. Make sure that the timing procedures are clearly understood before you start your students on the first unit of Reading Faster. The reading rate for the example is the student's initial reading rate.

Reading Faster Passages

1. After students have gone through the introduction and before they start the Reading Faster passages, re-examine with your students their answers to the questionnaires in the introduction to the book. By now, students may have gained some insight into the reading process and have changed some of their views of what makes for good reading habits. In reviewing the questionnaires, students will, in effect, be reviewing some of the important aspects of reading covered so far.

2. Students are more likely to improve their reading rate if they set goals for themselves after they have established their initial rates. Many students find that they can double their rate by the end of a semester. A class discussion may help each student decide on a realistic goal. Students should then be reminded of that goal and pushed to try to achieve it.

3. Remind students regularly about previewing. Students may also need to be assured that previewing will not slow down their reading. The few seconds they

spend on previewing (it should only take a few seconds) will save them reading time afterward.

4. These timed reading passages should not be used for other purposes (discussion, comprehension skills, or grammar) during faster reading sessions. If students think that they may be held accountable to the teacher for what they are reading, they will not feel free to take risks and experiment with rate-building strategies. However, after all the students have completed a passage, it may be used in another context of the reading class. Many of the passages provide interesting material for general class discussion.

5. As they chart their progress in reading rate improvement, students may notice a drop in their rate when they start a new unit. This is a natural reaction to the change in subject matter and most likely the rate will increase again as they become more familiar with the new subject. They may also notice that there is a correlation between their interest in and knowledge about a subject and their reading rate and comprehension level. That is, the more interesting the passage and the more familiar the subject, the easier it is to read—and the better the reading rate and comprehension will be.

6. For a more complete explanation of the rationale and methodology for teaching faster reading and for additional practice materials for timed readings, see *A Short Course in Teaching Reading Skills,* by Beatrice S. Mikulecky (Addison-Wesley, 1990).

	Part 1 Reading for Pleasure	Part 2 Comprehension Skills	Part 3 Thinking Skills	Part 4 Reading Faster
Week 1	• Read book Introduction, pp. v–viii. • Read Teacher's Guide, pp. 255–259. • Introduce Part 1, pp. 1–14. • Help students set pleasure reading goals. • Help students choose a book. See the list of suggested books, pp. 9–14.	• Read Teacher's Guide, pp. 259–265. • Introduce Part 2, p. 16. • Introduce **Unit 1, Previewing**, p. 17. (see T.G. pp. 260–261) • Do Exercises 1 & 2, pp. 17–18. Remind the students to work very fast on previewing. • Discuss Guidelines, p. 19. • Do Exercise 3, pp. 20–21.		
HOMEWORK	Pleasure reading, 30 min./day.	Scanning should be done only in class.		
Week 2	• Check students' progress in their pleasure reading. Ask each student to tell the class the title of their book and how many pages they have read.	• Do Unit 1, Exercises 4 & 5, pp. 22–24. • Introduce **Unit 2: Scanning**, p. 25. (see T.G. p. 261) • Do Example and Exercises 1–4, pp. 25–33.	• Read Teacher's Guide, pp. 265–266. • Introduce Part 3, pp. 159–162. Work as a group on the examples. • Assign items 1–5, pp. 162–163. • Students should work alone and *without a dictionary*. Afterwards, ask volunteers to give their answers and explain their choices. Encourage discussion when answers vary.	
HOMEWORK	Pleasure reading, 30 min./day	Previewing and Scanning exercises should be done only in class.	Items 6–10, pp. 163–164	

	Part 1 Reading for Pleasure	Part 2 Comprehension Skills	Part 3 Thinking Skills	Part 4 Reading Faster
Week 3	• Check students' progress in their pleasure reading. • Explain book conferences and how students should sign up for a conference when they have finished a book.	• Do Unit 2, Exercises 5 & 6, pp. 34–37. • Introduce **Unit 3: Skimming.** p. 38. (see T.G. p. 261) • Be sure to emphasize the difference between skimming and scanning. All skimming exercises should be done in class, not at home. • Do Exercises 1 & 2, pp. 40–43.	• Check homework on items 6–10. • Ask volunteers to read these items aloud for oral reading practice. Encourage discussion when answers vary.	• Read Teacher's Guide, pp. 266–269. • Introduce Part 4, pp. 182–184. Stress the importance of timing. • Time students on the example, "The Iceman," pp. 185–186. • Teach students how to use the Progress Chart, p. 189. • Time students on Unit 1, passages 1 & 2, pp. 191–194. Check that they use the Progress Chart correctly.
HOMEWORK	Pleasure reading, 30 min./day.	Scanning and Skimming exercises should be done only in class.	Items 11–15, pp. 164–165	**No** Faster Reading at home.
Week 4	• Check students' progress in their pleasure reading.	• Do Unit 3, Exercises 3–6, pp. 44–52. • Introduce **Unit 4: Using Vocabulary Knowledge for Effective Reading**, p. 53. (see T.G. p. 262) • Do Exercises 1–3, & 5, pp. 54–58.	• Check homework on items 11–15. • Ask volunteers to read aloud for oral reading practice. Encourage discussion when answers vary.	• Time the students on passages 3–6, pp. 195–202. • Check that they are using the Progress Chart correctly. Give positive and encouraging feedback!
HOMEWORK	Pleasure reading, 30 min./day.	Unit 4, Exercises 4, 6, & 7	Items 16–20, pp. 165–166	**No** Faster Reading at home.
Week 5	• Check students' progress in their pleasure reading. • Begin to schedule book conferences.	• Unit 4: Introduce "Pronouns," p. 60, and "Synonyms," p. 62. • Do Exercises 8, 10, & 12, pp. 60–64. • Introduce **Unit 5: Making Inferences**, p. 65. (see T.G. p. 262–263)	• Check homework on items 16–20. • Ask volunteers to read aloud for oral reading practice. Discuss answers.	• Time the class on passages 7–10, pp. 203–210. • Check the students' individual Progress Charts. Give positive and encouraging feedback!

	Part 1 Reading for Pleasure	Part 2 Comprehension Skills	Part 3 Thinking Skills	Part 4 Reading Faster
		• Do Exercises 1 & 2, p. 67. • Do Exercises 5, 6 & 8, pp. 69–75.		
HOMEWORK	Pleasure reading, 30 min./day	Unit 4, Exercises 9 & 11; Unit 5, Exercises 3, 4, & 7	Items 21–25, pp. 166–167	**No** Faster Reading at home.
Week 6	• Check students' progress in their pleasure reading. • Hold book conferences.	• Do Unit 5, Exercises 9–11, pp. 76–78. • Introduce **Unit 6: Finding Topics**, p. 79. (see T.G. p. 263) • Stress the importance of knowing the topic of what you are reading. • Do Exercises 1, 3, 5, & 6, pp. 79–83.	• Check homework on items 21–15. • Continue with reading aloud and discussion. • Give Test 1 from *More Reading Power Test Booklet*	• Time students on Unit 2, passages 1–4, pp. 211–218. • Check students' progress. Give positive and encouraging feedback!
HOMEWORK	Pleasure reading, 30 min./day	Unit 5, Exercise 8; Unit 6, Exercises 2 & 4	Items 26–35, pp. 167–169	**No** Faster Reading at home
Week 7	• Check students' progress in their pleasure reading. • Hold book conferences.	• Introduce **Unit 7: Discovering Topics of Paragraphs**. p. 84 (see T.G. p. 263) • Discuss "What is a Paragraph?" p. 84. • Do Exercise 1, p. 85. • Discuss "The Importance of Knowing the Topic," p. 86. • Discuss "Recognizing the Topic of a Paragraph," p. 86. • Do Exercise 2, p. 87–88.	• Check homework on items 26–35. • Continue with reading aloud and discussion.	• Time students on passages 5–8, pp. 219–226. • Check students' progress. Give positive and encouraging feedback!
HOMEWORK	Pleasure reading, 30 min./day	Exercise 3	Items 36–45, pp. 169–172	**No** Faster Reading at home

	Part 1 Reading for Pleasure	Part 2 Comprehension Skills	Part 3 Thinking Skills	Part 4 Reading Faster
Week 8	• Check students' progress in their pleasure reading. • Hold book conferences.	• Discuss "Stating the Topic of a Paragraph," p. 89. • Do Unit 7, Exercise 4, p. 90. • Discuss "Topic Sentences," p. 92. • Do Unit 7, Exercise 6, pp. 92–93. • Introduce **Unit 8: Locating Main Ideas**, p. 96. (see T.G. pp. 263–264) • Discuss "Finding the Main Idea," p. 97. • Do Exercises 1 & 2, pp. 98–100.	• Check homework on items 36–45. • Continue with reading aloud and discussion.	• Time students on passages 9 & 10, pp. 227–230. • Check students' progress. Give positive and encouraging feedback!
HOMEWORK	Pleasure reading, 30 min./day	Unit 7, Exercises 5, 7, & 8; Unit 8, Exercise 3	Items 46–50, pp. 172–173	**No** Faster Reading at home
Week 9	• Check students' progress in their pleasure reading. • Hold book conferences.	• Do Unit 8, Exercises 4 & 5, pp. 102–104. • Introduce **Unit 9: Identifying Patterns of Organization.** p. 107 (see T.G. pp. 264–265) • Do the task on p. 107. • Explain pp. 108–109. • Introduce "Listing pattern," p. 109. • Do Example, p. 109. • Do Exercises 1 & 3, p. 110–112, and discuss.	• Check homework on items 46–50. • Continue with reading aloud and discussion. • Give Test 2 from *More Reading Power Test Booklet*	• Time students on Unit 3, passages 1–4, pp. 231–238. • Check students' progress. Give positive and encouraging feedback!
HOMEWORK	Pleasure reading, 30 min./day	Unit 8, Exercise 6; Unit 9, Exercise 2	Items 51–60, pp. 173–176	**No** Faster Reading at home
Week 10	• Check students' progress in their pleasure reading.	• Introduce "Sequence pattern," p. 112.	• Check homework on items 51–60.	• Time students on Unit 3, passages 5–8, pp. 239–246.

	Part 1 Reading for Pleasure	Part 2 Comprehension Skills	Part 3 Thinking Skills	Part 4 Reading Faster
	• Hold book conferences.	• Do Examples, pp. 112–113, and discuss. • Do Exercises 4 & 5, pp. 114–116. • Do Exercise 7, p. 117, and discuss. • Introduce "Comparison/ Contrast pattern," pp. 117–118. • Do Examples, pp. 118–119, and discuss. • Do Exercise 8, pp. 119–121. • Do Exercise 10, p. 122, and discuss.	• Continue with reading aloud and discussion	• Check students' progress. Give positive and encouraging feedback!
HOMEWORK	Pleasure reading, 30 min./day	Unit 9, Exercises 6 & 9	Items 61–70, pp. 176–179	**No** Faster Reading at home
Week 11	• Check students' progress in their pleasure reading. • Hold book conferences. • Tell students to prepare to talk to the class briefly (about 3 minutes) about one of their pleasure reading books. They should choose a book they liked and try to "sell" it to the class.	• Introduce "Cause-Effect pattern," p. 122. • Do Exercise 11, pp. 123–124, and discuss. • Introduce "Multiple causes and effects," p. 124. • Do Examples, p. 124, and discuss. • Do Exercise 12, p. 125, and discuss. • Do Exercise 15, p. 128. • Introduce "Problem/ Solution pattern," p. 128. • Discuss "Signal words and the problem/solution pattern," pp. 128–129. • Do Example, p. 129, and discuss. • Do Exercise 16, pp. 129–130.	• Check homework on items 61–70. • Continue with reading aloud and discussion.	• Time students on Unit 3, passages 9 & 10, pp. 247–250. • Discuss students' progress during the semester. Give positive and encouraging feedback!
HOMEWORK	• Pleasure reading, 30 min./day	Unit 9, Exercises 13, 14, & 17	Items 71–75, pp. 179–180	**No** Faster Reading at home

	Part 1 Reading for Pleasure	Part 2 Comprehension Skills	Part 3 Thinking Skills	Part 4 Reading Faster
Week 12	• Check students' progress in their pleasure reading. • Hold book conferences. • Start students' oral reports (about 2 or 3 per class).	• Do Exercise 18, p. 132. • Introduce "Recognizing patterns" p. 133, and discuss. • Do Exercises 19–21, pp. 133–137.	• Check homework on items 71–75. • Continue with reading aloud and discussion.	• Timed readings are complete. Use time in class to work on patterns of organization.
HOMEWORK	Pleasure reading, 30 min./day	Exercises 22 & 23		
Week 13	• Check students' progress in their pleasure reading. • Hold book conferences. • Schedule more oral reports.	• Introduce **Unit 10: Summarizing.** p. 141 (see T.G. p. 265) • Discuss "Summary Words", p. 141. • Do Exercise 1, pp. 142–143. • Discuss "Summarizing a Sentence," p. 143. • Do Exercise 2, pp. 144–145. • Discuss "Summarizing a Paragraph," p. 145. • Do Exercise 3, p. 146. • Discuss "Summarizing short passages," pp. 147–148. • Do Exercise 5, p. 148.	• Give Test 3 from *More Reading Power Test Booklet*	• Timed readings are completed. Use time in class to work on summarizing.
HOMEWORK		Exercises 4, 6, & 7		
Week 14	• Schedule more oral reports.	• Discuss "Summarizing Longer Passages," p. 151. • Do Exercises 8, 9, or 10, pp. 151–158.	• Discuss student progress in thinking in English.	
HOMEWORK		Remaining exercises		

Credits

Text Credits

Page 5, Copyright holder unknown. Every effort has been made to locate the copyright holder of this work. **Page 18,** From *A Brief History of Time* by Stephen W. Hawking, copyright © 1988, 1996 by Stephen W. Hawking. Used by permission of Bantam Books, a division of Random House, Inc. **Page 23,** Victoria Brittain and Larry Elliott, © The Guardian. **Page 35,** © 2002. The New York Times Company. Reprinted by Permission. **Page 37,** *Honolulu Advertiser,* Jan. 2, 1992. **Page 40,** "Broadcaster O'Brien Missing on N.H. Hike." *The Boston Globe,* Sept. 4, 2001. By Thomas C. Palmer, Jr., and Allen Lessels. Copyright 2001 by The Globe Newspaper Co. Reprinted by permission of The Globe Newspaper Co. via the Copyright Clearance Center. **Page 41,** "O'Brien Turns Up Safe, Sound, Thankful." *The Boston Globe,* Sept. 5, 2001. By Mac Daniel and Allen Lessels. Copyright 2001 by The Globe Newspaper Co. Reprinted by permission of The Globe Newspaper Co. via the Copyright Clearance Center. **Page 42,** © 2002, *The Washington Post.* Reprinted with permission. **Page 45,** "True-life 'Ice Bound' Tells Doctor's Story." *The Boston Globe,* Feb. 15, 2003. By Scott Bernard Nelson. Copyright 2001 by The Globe Newspaper Co. Reprinted by permission of The Globe Newspaper Co. via the Copyright Clearance Center. **Page 48,** Franklin and Eleanor Roosevelt Institute. **Page 52,** From the *Encyclopedia Americana,* 1993 Edition. Copyright 1993 by Grolier Educational. Reprinted with permission from the publisher. **Page 64,** Courtesy of Elizabeth A. Mikulecky. **Page 70,** *Red Carnations* by Glenn Hughes. Copyright © 1925 by Samuel French. Renewed 1953 by Samuel French. **Page 72,** *The Cactus Flower,* Copyright © 1966 by Abe Burrows, amended and renewed 1984. Reprinted by permission of William Morris Agency, Inc. on behalf of the Author. **Page 74,** "Til Death Do Us Part" is reprinted from *A Gram of Mars & Other Stories* by Becky Hagenston, published by Sarabande Books, Inc. © 1998 by Becky Hagenston. Reprinted by permission of Sarabande Books and the author. **Page 76,** Excerpt from "A Domestic Dilemma," from *The Ballad of the Sad Café and Collected Short Stories* by Carson McCullers. Copyright © 1951 by Carson McCullers, renewed 1979 by Flora V. Lasky, Executrix of the Estate of Carson McCullers. Reprinted by permission of Houghton Mifflin Co. All rights reserved. **Page 153,** "UCLA Researchers Identify Key Biobehavioral Pattern Used By Women To Manage Stress," UCLA press release on research by a research team led by psychologist Shelley E. Taylor, issued May 19, 2000. **Page 156,** Victoria Brittain and Larry Elliott, © The Guardian.

Photo Credits

Page 1, © Janis Christie/Getty Images. **Page 3,** © Corbis/Charles Gupton Photography. **Page 15,** © Royalty-Free/SuperStock, Inc. **Page 16,** © Corbis/John Henley Photography. **Page 20,** © Corbis/Marko Modic. **Page 23,** © Corbis SABA/Louise Gubb. **Page 48,** Franklin and Eleanor Roosevelt Institute and UN/DPI Photo. **Page 52,** Franklin D. Roosevelt Library. **Page 156,** © Corbis SABA/Louise Gubb. **Page 159,** © Steve Cole/Getty Images. **Page 181,** © Photodisc/Getty Images. **Page 190,** top: © Corbis/Hulton-Deutsch Collection, middle: © Eugene Fleurey/Dorling Kindersley Media Library, bottom: © Ralph Mercer/Getty Images.